Democracy by Force?

(A study of international military intervention in the civil war in Sierra Leone from 1991-2000)

by

Abass Bundu LL.B (ANU), LL.M, Ph.D (Cantab.)
Member of the Australian Bar; former Executive Secretary of the Economic Community of West African States (ECOWAS); former Foreign Minister of Sierra Leone; Consultant on Conflict Prevention, Management and Resolution.

Democracy by Force?: A study of international military intervention in the conflict in Sierra Leone from 1991-2000

Universal Publishers / uPUBLISH.com
USA • 2001
ISBN: 1-58112-698-0

www.upublish.com/books/bundu.htm

Cover design WEST AFRICA DOT NET INC.

Inquiries for speaking engagements should be addressed to The Foundation for Democracy and Development in Sierra Leone, 17 Dicey Avenue, Willesden, London NW2 6AR, England. Telephone: 44-208-452-2227; Fax: 44-208-452-7627; E-mail: abassbundu@hotmail.com".

DEDICATION

This book is dedicated to the memory of my brother, Alusine, who was brutally murdered in the rebel war in 1994, and to all other victims of the mindless cycle of hate and revenge which has ruined Sierra Leone from 1991 to date.

I dedicate it also, with eternal respect and adoration, to the memory of my late parents, Pa Santigie Kabonthor Bangura of Makomneh Village and Madam Isatu Kallay Bundu of Gbinti Town. They both hailed from Dibia Chiefdom, Port Loko District in Sierra Leone.

May their souls rest in perfect peace.

CONTENTS

CHAPTER 2
Intervention by Invitation

CHAPTER 3
The Role of Ecowas

CHAPTER 4
The Role of the United Nations

CHAPTER 8
The Domestic Fallout of the Rebellion

CHAPTER 9

GLOSSARY OF ACRONYMS

AFRC Armed Forces Revolutionary Council
APC All People's Congress Party
CDF Civil Defence Forces
DDR Disarmament, Demobilisation and
Reintegration Programme
ECOMOG Economic Community of West African
 States Ceasefire Monitoring Group
ECOWAS Economic Community of West African States
EU European Union
NIC National Interim Council
NPFL National Patriotic Front of Liberia
NRC National Reformation Council
OAUOrganisation of African Unity
PNP People's National Party
PPP People's Progressive Party
SLPIM Sierra Leone Progressive
 IndependenceMovement
SLPP Sierra Leone People's Party
RUF Revolutionary United Front
UN United Nations
UNAMSIL United Nations Mission in Sierra
 Leone
UNHCR United Nations High Commissioner for
 Refugees
UNOMIL United Nations Observer Mission in
 Liberia
UNOMSIL United Nations Observer Mission in
 Sierra Leone
UNPP United National People's Party

FOREWORD

The people of Sierra Leone will owe a heavy debt of gratitude to Dr. Abass Bundu, especially after the crisis, which they have lived through for more than nine years, will have been resolved. In nine chapters, with the thoroughness of a keen legal mind, he has written a carefully researched account of the important events about which most Sierra Leoneans have only vague memories or have only read accounts by journalists most of whom were biased, or have listened to second-hand news broadcast from local and overseas channels. Others, including students, who would like to know the true facts about events, have had little or no access to the information presented in this book.

Starting with the first assault which was made on democracy by a faulty interpretation not only of the provisions of the Constitution of 1961 'but also of the prevailing practice in Commonwealth countries when the Governor-General appointed the successor to the country's first post-colonial Prime Minister, Dr Bundu narrates the dangerous precedent set by the first military *coup d'état* in 1967, barely six years after Sierra Leone emerged as an independent country and joined the United Nations. He also describes other infringements against the democratic rights of citizens whom he describes elsewhere as the defenceless. These denials of democratic practice are the real source of a war that is unequaled in its savagery and senselessness in the memory of a country that is not acquainted with the legend of King Farma, the Conqueror, who, after a conquering match that took him to the shores of the Atlantic ocean, and wanting to show that he had no further use for his trusted bow and arrows, broke up the arrows and flung the bow across the sky where it remains forever to constantly remind all who see it that weapons of war should be forgotten and that all people should live in peace under a sky that is not made dark by the clouds of war.

Only a well-trained legal mind can describe as lucidly as Dr. Bundu has succeeded in doing. The importance of events, including rigged elections, arbitrary use of executive power, tribal nepotism, the intrusion of Ecowas into the internal affairs of one of its founding members, the flagrant abuse of fundamental human rights of individuals and groups, all of which have marred Sierra Leone's search for true democracy.

Dr Bundu has written not only as a lawyer but as one who has served not only his country as a member of parliament and as a cabinet minister, but also the West African region as the Executive Secretary of Ecowas. Because of this, many readers will wish that Dr. Bundu had described more fully the details about the struggle for political power between the Sierra Leone People's Party (SLPP) and the All Peoples Congress Party (APC), the underlying source of much that the country has suffered for more than thirty-five years, including the so-called "rebel" war declared by the Revolutionary United Front (RUF), into which Ecowas was drawn, and in which combatants on both sides and their allies and supporters have inflicted unspeakable barbaric and truly ghastly atrocities on innocent civilian men, women and children.

This book also offers many insights into the far from unbiased roles played by external actors in the Sierra Leone crisis, including Ecowas, the Organisation of African Unity (OAU), the United Nations Security Council and the diplomatic representatives of the United Kingdom and the United States of America. Other external factors references to which should kindle an interest for further exploration are the roles of the South African firm, Executive Outcomes, the British firm, Sandline International, and their ruthless mercenaries who first introduced the use of armed helicopters in Sierra Leone. Dr. Bundu will no doubt be encouraged before too long to write a sequel to this book.

I commend this book to all and sundry. More particularly, I recommend it to all the sons and daughters of Sierra Leone and their children, to the policy makers in the foreign ministries around the world, to the civil servants in the various international or regional organisations as well as to their NGO counterparts, to the international peacekeepers serving humanity around the world, and, finally, to all students of international law, international relations and politics. To all of them, this book should be essential reading if they are to improve their understanding of the unfortunate crisis in Sierra Leone.

John Karefa-Smart, M.D., M.P.
Washington, DC,
30 June 2000.

PREFACE

Sierra Leone has been at war with itself since March 1991. It urgently needs to be rescued from itself and from its warlords. Otherwise, its future is going to be shaped far less by what its people celebrate than by the painful experience of a war they would rather quietly forget. Blown to smithereens are the high standards of education, stability and prosperity that were once the envy of many a developing country. Today, most of the country lies in ruins, a mere shadow of its former self. The physical destruction of life and property aside, the citizens were made to see their next door neighbour as their worst enemy, routinely tearing each other apart and making the environment probably the worst place for children. In ways that are unprecedented in the history of the country, the conflict has fostered a culture of blame, not of accountability; of hate, not of harmony; and of dependency, not of self-esteem. A mosaic of thirteen different ethnic groups that once lived in harmony, interweaving with each other through marriage, has been rent apart, and it will take years to heal the wounds and mend the rifts. Was all this inevitable?

From the onset, there were only two ways of resolving the quagmire: either by military or political means. But for foreign military intervention, they were not necessarily mutually exclusive. The war proved unwinnable by neither side, and far from determining who is right, it has only determined who is left. The government could not subdue the rebels nor they the government. Yet, for many years, successive governments chose the military option. They ignored totally the warning of Sun Tzu, who, writing in the fourth century BC, said that "to win one hundred victories in one hundred battles is not the acme of skill. To subdue the enemy without fighting is the acme of skill."

Violence overtook negotiation and regime security human security, and all too frequently it was the beleaguered civilian population that was caught in the middle. In the process state structures came out unstuck and violence was seen as an end in itself, profiting only the belligerents. And it did not take long before truth, human rights and the nation's diamond fields came to be added to the list of casualties.

Away from the theatre where only guns talked, truth became the first casualty. A proverb in my native tongue says truth and lie always move together but it is always lie that takes flight in the end. Of course, no one believed the rebels but the government side was equally economical with the truth. The situation grew worse as successive regimes introduced more than a whiff of infantilism, turning rationality into a rare commodity. They prosecuted the war as if it were a contest between *personae*, never more so than during the tenure of the so-called democratically-elected government of President Ahmad Tejan Kabbah. Almost routinely, character assassination became the norm and its Radio Democracy, FM 98.1, donated by the British government, invented elaborate stories to defame and demonise almost anybody who disagreed with them. It spewed falsehoods *ad nauseam*, inciting its supporters to kill and maim and to malign and spread public hatred. Not even foreign emissaries, bringing tidings of peace, were spared from calumny.

Democratic opponents were dressed up in the garb of rebel collaborators. By engaging in such vitriol, cloaked with officialese, the government's calculation must have been that its propaganda would take root and multiply until it became commonplace, until it became parody and until it became popular jargon. Fortunately the majority of citizens displayed maturity in deciphering fact from fiction and most times they appeared bemused. Sadly, though, a few weaklings succumbed, wreaking untold havoc upon their neighbours.

Sycophancy and ethnicism also reigned. In fact, a construct developed that equated the quality of leadership as inversely proportional to the height of sycophancy. The higher the level of sycophancy the lower the quality of leadership and verse versa. The period after 1996 has been particularly noted for twinning sycophancy with poor leadership.

The British Broadcasting Corporation (BBC) became an unsuspecting accomplice, but it paid dearly for it. It broadcast on its popular Focus on Africa Programme an e-mail from an SLPP supporter in Freetown in which it was alleged that I was a "terrorist who, with others, was responsible for destabilising" Sierra Leone. In a libel suit I brought against the BBC in the High Court in England, it admitted that that allegation was "entirely false" and "totally unfounded" and broadcast a public apology on

June 28, 1999, as part of a final settlement. Outside of court, both the British government and *The Times* newspaper also tendered apologies, having mistakenly published a defamatory letter about me that President Tejan Kabbah had written to the British Prime Minister.

The second casualty was human security. The security of the defenceless civilian population was somehow disentangled from that of the government and given very low priority. Deliberately targeted by drug-maddened combatants, today it is impossible to identify an extended family in Sierra Leone that has not been a victim of some kind of human rights abuse. Naturally, each belligerent would like the whole world to believe that the other is more to blame. A more reasonable approach, however, is to treat each belligerent party as not free from chastisement.

The third casualty was human rights. Nobody expected anything but abuse from the rebels. But a great deal more respect was expected from those who claimed to be the government and a democratic one at that. Not only did they fail to prevent and punish abuses committed by their own forces and by militias and party vigilantes loyal to them, they themselves arbitrarily stuffed more than 4,000 people in a prison built to accommodate less than 500 inmates. Merely for voicing dissent, opponents were hounded down and burnt alive. Kabbah's restoration in February 1998 and its immediate aftermath will go down in the annals of Sierra Leone history for its orgy of oppression and vengeance and for its lynch-mob culture; in short, state terrorism. So prevalent was this that even now the country's justice system bears echoes of that period as known perpetrators of these heinous crimes continue to roam the streets of Freetown freely and with impunity.

The fourth casualty was the nation's diamonds. There was the belief, completely erroneous though, that the whole conflict was about control over the diamond fields. Simply because all belligerent parties had been helping themselves with the proceeds of illicit diamond mining and exchanging these for weapons does not make it the cause of the conflict. We must look elsewhere for that. Foreign mercenaries too became attracted, exchanging their services and weaponry for the precious stones.

If civilisation is about the values of truth and respect for human security and human dignity, the conflict has made Sierra Leone look like the relic of a vanished civilisation. It also contains vestiges of how *not* to respond to undemocratic regimes. Nowadays, such regimes are despised the world over but the international community is still much less certain about how to react to them when they come into being. This is not surprising, because there are as yet no settled international rules. The new challenge therefore is how to redesign the international political architecture to prevent undemocratic regimes from coming into existence. But we must start with incumbent governments first. They are the ones who must be prevented from retreating from respect for democracy and human rights. Where they fail to uphold these fundamental precepts, or threaten to undermine them, there should be a duty on the part of the international community to step in quickly as an independent and impartial arbiter before it is too late.

The conflict has also shown just how much the current leadership in Sierra Leone has lost its self-esteem. It has tended to depend almost entirely upon foreign solutions and the more it does this the more it loses autonomy. If this trend persists, the younger generation will naturally grow up with a penchant for distractibility. People understand well enough that the nation is embroiled in crisis, but there is nonetheless a seeming reluctance to come to terms with it. In the rural communities, there is an unending craving for a miracle. The idea of rising up to defend themselves against armed attacks did not occur to them until almost too late. By the same token, the city folks blamed the war on the rural folks and viewed it as if it were something happening in some foreign land. And this largely defined their attitude until the tragedy landed on their doorstep.

No translation of this diminished self-esteem is more demented than the unprovoked killings and mutilations of unarmed civilians; all eloquent testimonies of some kind of revenge-mania that gripped the nation. This is the mindset that has seriously poisoned the environment. Today Sierra Leone is viewed by many a professional, old and young alike, as the wrong country in which to live a decent life and raise children. Save for those with a bigger stake in the country or too poor to afford foreign travel, the people inside are relocating abroad while those outside are reluctant to return. Unless and until there is a sea change in attitude, radically reversing the consuming cultures of hate and revenge and of excessive dependence on foreign panaceas, the country's future will continue to be stalked by retrogressive forces.

This love of things new and foreign was vividly demonstrated in 1996. After the first ballot in the presidential election failed to produce a winner, the two front-runners went on to a run-off. They were people who, like James Jonah, then chief elections supervisor, had lived abroad the longest time and were therefore not too familiar in Sierra Leone, especially to the younger generation. Yet the enthusiasm that greeted the candidature of Dr John Karefa-Smart, whose party was barely six months old before the elections, was most extraordinary. Why did this happen? In the words of Larry Siedentop, a celebrated Oxford academic: "In a society where everyone is formally equal, there is a powerful urge to resist the claims to leadership of anyone who is local and familiar. There is a strong temptation to think it less humiliating to choose for leadership someone unknown over someone known. For surely such a person must be free of weaknesses, faults of character or intellect, which can be seen in those whom we know. That inclination or temptation to prefer strangers, to prefer someone unknown to someone known as a candidate for leadership, caters to a deep weakness in our nature. Yet it is both politically and morally dangerous to give in to this weakness in ourselves. It is dangerous politically because such an inclination is ultimately subversive of the dispersal of power. It is dangerous morally because it disguises, while at the same time reinforcing, a distrust of ourselves. It is as if in order to feel contempt for ourselves we have to become contemptible."[1]

All these factors influenced me in writing this book. The misconception, or dare I say benign neglect, of the international community was equally inspiring. Before 1997, there had been at least two successful military putsches, the first in 1967 and the second in 1992. But never before had the army made such a blind date with destiny than in May 1997. That year and 1991 will go down as the *anni horribiles* for Sierra Leoneans, particularly for those who, unable to escape the gun-fire, found themselves caught between three evils: rebel tyranny, indiscriminate bombings by the pro-government forces, and benign neglect, if not culpable irresponsibility, by the international community. This neglect is inexplicable save within the context of either a callous indifference or a negligible understanding of the conflict on the part of mandarins in Western capitals.

Two full years passed, with tens of thousands killed and whole towns and villages wasted, not to mention the sacking of Freetown in January 1999, before the West could see fit to step in and advise the parties to accept the compelling wisdom of a political settlement. Why did it take them so long? Whatever the reason, for me July 7, 1999, the date the Lome Peace Agreement was signed, marks both a watershed in the search for peace and a cut-off point for this book.

Gratitude is due to countless numbers of people. There are those who encouraged me to write and there are those who gave their precious time to read parts of the manuscript and make valuable suggestions. I can never thank all of them enough or by name. But a few persons at least deserve recognition: Ambassador Dauda Kamara, Dr A. K. Turay and Dr Steve Kanu for making valuable suggestions and Sheka Tarawallie and Tatafway Tumoe who helped with proof-reading. But, of course, I take full responsibility for the content. Another person I must mention is Lord Avebury, Vice-Chairman of the British Parliamentary Human Rights Group. He allowed me access to his correspondence with the British government on the Sierra Leone crisis, for which I owe him a big debt of gratitude. I should also like to mention the SLPP government under the leadership of President Ahmad Tejan Kabbah, which has shown clearly how *not* to govern a plural society at war with itself. It won neither the war nor the peace.

Predictable official reaction to this book could take many forms, particularly from a ruling élite which is yet to understand the most basic principles of human rights, more so from those people whose inflated egos might have been ruffled. Not least is possible intimidation from, among others, the police, who for years have bowed to the caprices of the ruling élite. The saving grace may now be that they are under the superintendence of a British bobby, for whom the protection of human rights is a prime duty. The civilised world is watching with keen interest.

What I have tried to do in this book is to put the highest possible premium on truth and justice and to show that they are always worth fighting for. The next stage of the struggle is to fight for democratic reconstruction and national reconciliation. This is why I particularly welcome the establishment of three bodies: the National Commission on Human Rights, the Commission on Truth and Reconciliation, and the Special Criminal Court for Sierra Leone. Provided they are able to assert true independence, credibility and impartiality, truth, liberty and justice could prevail and receive fresh affirmation in Sierra Leone. Without them peace is empty and reconciliation is everything but genuine.

Finally, I should like to record my appreciation and abiding affection for my wife, Khadija, my children and all members of my extended African family for their understanding and forbearance. Their experience in the hands of the combatants and Kabbah's government over the past four years has been nothing short of harrowing. For my sake they have endured physical and psychological abuse, bereavement, torture, intimidation and arbitrary imprisonment. Not once have they complained and this makes me feel extremely proud of all of them. Their support during the writing of this book also enabled me to survive the ordeal and emerge from it unvanquished.

ACB
London
31 October 2000

INTRODUCTION

The Sierra Leone crisis in perspective

In defining the perspectives of this study, I should begin by stating clearly what it is not. It is not an account of my personal experience nor is it one aimed at any particular *persona*. Nor is it a treatise on the political or constitutional evolution of Sierra Leone. Rather our central focus is on the internal armed conflict that has ruined a country, once the envy of the developing world. We shall also focus on how the search for a peaceful solution was utterly mismanaged. No analysis, however, can be complete without some insight, however cursory, into the political convulsions that have disfigured the country and their impact on its national values and aspirations.

Forty years of independence have produced a political tapestry that looks like a mosaic of chequered governance. No fewer than nine different leaders have been at the helm. Five attained the position through the ballot box, namely Sir Milton Margai (1957-64), Sir Albert Margai (continued Sir Milton's term from 1964-67), Siaka Stevens (1968-85), Major-General Joseph Saidu Momoh (1985-92) and Ahmad Tejan Kabbah (1996-2001). The rest, all military men, got there through the barrel of a gun.

At independence in 1961 Sierra Leone inherited from the United Kingdom a Westminster-style parliamentary democracy under the leadership of the Sierra Leone People's Party (SLPP). The early years were characterised by relative peace and stability. The blights of ethnicism and cronyism did not appear in any significant form until Albert Margai became Prime Minister in 1964. Those scourges got moulded into art form and became his administration's most pernicious legacy.

The success of the opposition All Peoples' Congress (APC) in the general elections of 1967 turned Sierra Leone into a beacon of democratic change in Africa in a way that no other country could claim to be. Regrettably, it was short-lived. The promise of a smooth transition of power suddenly turned into a nightmare. Siaka Stevens, the new Prime Minister, had barely taken the oath of office when he was overthrown in the nation's first ever *coup d'etat* on March 21, 1967. That putsch marked the beginning of the country's constitutional degeneracy from which, to this day, it is still to recover.

The APC ruled for 24 years. In that time it transformed the country into a republic and a one-party state. Undeservingly, however, the APC is often made the butt of those racking murk, thuggery and poor economic management of the country. By 1992 the economy was tumbling but prior to that time it is reasonable to credit the APC with substantial infrastructural development as well as with an extraordinarily good record of bonding its rich and tantalising ethnic diversity. Of course, it made mistakes along the way and some were serious. An example was opening up diamond mining to all and sundry, a policy that scuppered any ambitions it may have had of turning things around. The result of this openness was diamond smuggling, which quickly became a whole industry by itself, defying regulatory control and plummeting the public purse as never before. It was later to fuel the rebel war in the nineties. The reason for this is not hard to find. Diamond deposits are mostly alluvial and some lie only about six feet beneath the surface. So, all that is required are basic tools like a shovel, pick-axe and sifter. And the size of the gems also adds to the smuggler's appetite.

While the rebels of the Revolutionary United Front (RUF) were camping in the diamond fields and exchanging their winnings for arms, many people came to the conclusion that the whole conflict was about diamonds. But this is an exaggeration. From the start the RUF has never abandoned its ambition to seize political power; to help them in this pursuit, they turned to the country's diamond wealth.

During the time of the APC, the RUF was not able to cross the eastern province where they had started their insurrection in 1991. The first time hostilities spread outside that province was during the time of the National Provisional Ruling Council (NPRC). The NPRC had tried to justify its overthrow of the APC government on the grounds of the latter's ineffectiveness in defending the people against rebel aggression. So it made extravagant pledges of ending the war swiftly. In the end it failed however. The RUF not only forced a war economy on the country; they left an endless trail of unrecognizable shadows of once settled communities. Except for the Western Province in which the capital, Freetown, is located, the war rendered most parts of the country extremely perilous, forcing the rural population to migrate to district and provincial cities and townships. This was so up to the beginning of 1996, when a palace *coup* plunged NPRC junta into deeper disarray. In a sense, it was nothing short of a feat that power was transferred at all to an elected government.

Between the NPRC and the RUF they made sure that the elections were not free of intimidation and violence. Displaced voters became targets of brutalisation while others had their hands and feet crudely and savagely mutilated with machetes. Led by Foday Sankoh, an embittered ex-corporal of the Sierra Leone army, the motives of the RUF looked murky except for the pretext of ridding the country of corruption, misrule and one-party statism. Its insurrection had begun at the very time that the much-maligned APC government of President Joseph Saidu Momoh, who had succeeded Siaka Stevens in 1985, was laying the foundation for democratic elections under a new multiparty constitution. All that anyone opposed to his rule needed to do was to wait and take part in the then impending elections and vote him out of office. But instead the rebels and their backers chose violence. How they could reconcile that with their professed belief in democracy defies comprehension.

So, from March 1991 onwards, peace took leave of Sierra Leone. There are those who say that the RUF rebellion was a spill over from the NPFL in Liberia. They base themselves on Charles Taylor's banters with Robin White of the BBC during which he had threatened to teach Sierra Leone a lesson for permitting its territory to be used as Ecomog's staging base. However, the real reasons are different.

When the Liberian civil war broke out, Ecowas had asked the United States, basing itself on Liberia's claim of having some "special relationship" with that country, to help it find a speedy resolution to the crisis in Liberia in order to prevent it from spreading to other parts of West Africa. The Americans did help but not to the extent required. Their apparent dislike of the military leader in Liberia, Sergeant Samuel Kanyon Doe, had blinded them to the serious threat that the NPFL insurrection was posing to the security of the region. Within West Africa, however, the prevalent belief was that the Americans, with all their sophisticated intelligence-gathering capability, must have been aware of secret plans by certain revolutionaries to destabilise the region. They were the rebels' main backers. Yet the American attitude towards Ecomog remained lukewarm at best. Had it been more positive, things could have been different. What has amazed many people, however, is that, some ten years later, when it had become too late to take preventive action, the same Americans saw it fit to publicly and hypocritically acknowledge that rebel forces were indeed destabilising West Africa.

Peace partially returned to Sierra Leone in November 1996, when the Abidjan Peace Accord was signed. Unfortunately, it was short-lived as both sides openly undermined it. The RUF may have been tardy, perhaps even dishonest, in implementing their side of the bargain, but it cannot justify the government in surreptitiously planning the arrest and overthrow of its leader. Both actions were wrongful. From that moment on, the atmosphere got riven with distrust. The Abidjan Accord was superseded by another peace agreement signed in the Togolese capital, Lome, in July 1999. Unlike the 1996 Accord, the government found itself making a lot of concessions to the RUF under the 1999 Agreement. In return for momentary peace, the rebels received cabinet positions and Foday Sankoh was appointed as head of a new commission to oversee diamond mining, a position that carried the protocol rank of Vice-President.

Naturally, these concessions did not go down well with the citizenry. Poor at taking political flak, Kabbah was quick to find scapegoats. He blamed the British and American governments for pressuring him into signing the Lome Agreement. But both governments promptly issued disclaimers. "The United States did not pressure anybody to sign," State Department spokesman Philip Reeker protested at a press briefing in June 2000. Peter Hain, British Minister of State in the Foreign and Commonwealth Office (FCO), had called it a "myth" when he testified before the House of Commons Foreign Affairs Committee a month earlier. Then he added: "Together with the international community, we felt it necessary to support a very imperfect Lome Agreement..... because there was literally no alternative. At the risk of repetition, remember where we were. We were in a situation where the RUF had again attacked the elected government, attacked Freetown. The elected government had no army. President Kabbah had no alternative but to negotiate with Foday Sankoh in particular and the other rebels in general."

In truth, the Lome Agreement was the direct result of the government's inability to subdue the RUF on the battlefield. Having disbanded his own national army, Kabbah now had to rely on foreign forces and mercenaries while the war was growing incrementally horrendous. In those circumstances, he really had no choice but to negotiate and why he could not face up to it, is beyond comprehension.

Concurrently the country's economy was deteriorating so fast that the United Nations ranked it as the poorest of the poor, unable to meet even the most basic needs of its citizens. Even worse, the scourges of corruption and tribal nepotism, which had afflicted Albert Margai's SLPP government in the sixties, reared their ugly heads yet again, eroding whatever was left of national stability, the only difference being that this time they were shorn of all sophistry. With a mono-ethnic militia, the *kamajors*, at its beck and call, to whom it perceptibly accorded privileges over and above those enjoyed by the regular army, the country was being administered with two rival armies and so many were the skirmishes between them. Running two opposing armies should have been obvious to everybody that this simply would not work, and that sooner or later one of them would rebel. The storm finally imploded when 17 disgruntled soldiers seized power in a successful *coup* on May 25, 1997, forcing President Kabbah and his government to flee the country. Even before this, morale within the army had ebbed, leaving parts of the country, hitherto unaffected, to fall under rebel control. It did not take long before most of the countryside fell into rebel hands and became ungovernable.

The coupists then invited the RUF to join them and together they formed the Armed Forces Revolutionary Council (AFRC), with Major Johnny Paul Koroma as Chairman and Foday Sankoh as Vice-Chairman. Both the period of AFRC rule and the aftermath of Kabbah's violent restoration nine months later represent the darkest chapters in the nation's post-independence history. Ubiquitous scars of war, exemplified by pulverised towns and villages throughout the length and breadth of the country, silently convey a diminished sense of respect for human security. Human rights violations of the most bestial type were committed against innocent civilians. Today, mutilated civilians, young and old alike, are the living monuments of a war that has disfigured them as much as the ethos of the nation, casting a long shadow over its claim to any standard of modern civilisation. And cataclysmic scenes in towns and villages all over the country make war crimes appear too kind a term.

Kabbah's reaction was equally vengeful. He invited Nigeria's last military despot, General Sani Abacha, to intervene militarily. A military junta in Nigeria was claiming the right to displace another in Sierra Leone, all in the name of shoring up democracy. No paradox could have been greater. Ultimately, Abacha succeeded in reinstating Kabbah back to power, but won neither peace nor democracy. That was not all. An appalling mixture of rebel atrocities and mob justice gave full vent to anarchy everywhere, sucking the country deeper into a vortex that was to leave behind nothing but misery, destruction and a severely fractured society.

The government further responded by stifling its critics even more. By then it had become utterly frightened and ruthlessly intolerant of dissent, demanding uncritical acceptance of everything it did, no matter how misguided or wrong-headed. Even parliament was nobbled and so was the press. The perception that soon spread was that of a control-freak tendency at the heart of government, and one could even hear echoes that were reminiscent of the darkest days of the one-party system.

Intolerance turned into obsession, making even perfectly decent citizens froth at the mouth at the mention of the word "negotiation". "The rebels must be flushed" became their much-vaunted refrain. But beneath this bluster lurked fear, accompanied by the natural, defensive reaction of anger and revenge. The ruling élite was the first to lose control of its emotions, followed by its supporters, and both groups wallowed in pointing fingers at the innocent. As if this was not injury enough, they unleashed a vendetta that gave the word "collaborator" an offensive connotation. It became such a dim, thoughtless, parroted soundbite that its voguishness spoke more eloquently about the herd mentality of the ruling élite and its defect of character than it did about its imagined enemies. So-called collaborators became victims of murder, torture and degrading treatment. In many respects, Sierra Leone was beginning to look like a world turned upside down where words were given meanings that Humpty Dumpty wanted them to mean, nothing more nothing less.

Scapegoating political opponents was another pastime. It became a ruse for concealing the government's own shortcomings. It peaked after the reinstatement of Kabbah's government in February 1998. That government had returned from exile with a vengeance and became less constrained than in the past by the norms of liberal democracy and the rule of law. It is therefore not impossible that at some point it became overtaken by a kind of political triumphalism evidenced by a frenzied, consuming culture of hate. Political opponents became victims of gruesome revenge killings, arbitrary detention and trumped-up charges of treason and murder. Most treason suspects were convicted and sentenced to hang. How it happened that civil servants, merely serving their country in time of crisis, in keeping with hallowed, centuries-old traditions of the Civil Service, could be found guilty of treason or of aiding and abetting treason, defies reason. It also severely degraded the rule of law.

President Kabbah, Solomon Berewa, his Minister of Justice and Attorney General, and James Jonah, chief electoral commissioner turned Minister of Finance, were all voluntary accomplices of the illegal NPRC military junta, which was not without blood on its hands, for at least three years starting from 1992. Kabbah was Chairman of its Advisory Council and his Attorney General a member. They had willingly accepted those appointments probably believing they were serving a nation in crisis. None of them has been accused of treason or of aiding and abetting treason. The irony is thus inescapable that these same people, catapulted into office, did not hesitate to bring treason charges against persons who found themselves in exactly the same position they were barely two years before. If this is not political persecution, what is?

Mercifully, it did not take too long before the word "collaborator" lost its pejorative connotation. Foreign governments combined forces with the silent majority of citizens to point out the need for political dialogue. This was after the disbanded army, retaliating for Kabbah executing 24 of their colleagues, had marched into Freetown on January 6, 1999. They ran amok. Thousands of people died and thousands more of school children abducted, to say nothing about reducing large swaths of the city into rubble. Mercifully, however, political prisoners already in death row for treason were set free. After this, Kabbah's camp seemed to have lost its zeal for triumphalism though not its enthusiasm for slamming every dissenter as a villain of the piece.

From that time on, the government's writ ran but hardly outside the limits of Freetown. Beyond that point the rebels remained in control, amassing both wealth and munitions out of the diamond fields. Their threat to the nation's peace and security also remained largely undiminished. This massive loss of governmental control compelled the United Nations to act. First, it established the largest international peacekeeping force in recent times to help disarm the rebels and regain territorial control for the government. Second, it proscribed international trade in conflict diamonds, hoping that by denying the rebels the sinews of war it would degrade their fighting capacity. All this, however, came rather too late. If only the United Nations Security Council had acted sooner in 1997, by deploying the peace-keeping force envisaged under the Abidjan Peace Accord of 1996, the course of history might have been quite different.

The challenge now is how to pull the country back from its trauma, a task that demands extraordinary leadership as well as a spark of renewal. This is the central theme of this book. It attempts to address why a once placid and sophisticated nation came to be overtaken by a Dark Age of anarchy, characterised by mindless abuses of human rights? Why ethnicism so overwhelmed the nation as to rent it apart? How a senseless rebellion squandered the future of a nation by dehumanising and devouring its children, making them into combatants and victims of war? How a government totally failed in its duty to protect its citizens and how it failed also to link their security with its own? And how the international community, notwithstanding the injunctions of the United Nations Charter, relegated human security to the margins of an internal armed conflict?

But it is not about civil conflict solely. It is a study of the conventional and confused mindset of the United Nations. In particular, what is the constructive way forward? What lessons can the rest of Africa and the developing world at large learn from this tragedy? What lessons are there for the international community as a whole, and the United Nations in particular?

The book is organised into nine chapters.

Chapter One sketches an historical account of the opposites of democracy and political violence in Sierra Leone, particularly the malignant effect of military *coups d'état* and other forms of illegitimate intervention or manipulation in politics since independence. It traces this degenerative development from the first *coup* in 1967 through to the most recent – and possibly the last - *coup* of May 1997. It also shows how, contrary to conventional wisdom, treason did somehow prosper in Sierra Leone. For example, it has been shown, and by no less a person than Foday Sankoh himself, that his rebellion was driven less by love of democracy than by personal vendetta. In an interview with *New African* in November 1999, he confessed to harbouring a personal grudge for former President Momoh in particular. "Momoh is a traitor," he exclaimed. "He betrayed the army. The *coup* [Brigadier Bangura's *coup* of 1971] .... failed because of Momoh's treachery."[2]

For every such *coup*, the main victims have been freedom, democracy and human security. Democracy has been grievously harmed not only by the military but also by the beneficiaries of rogue elections. So much is this the case that the cynics are not alone in questioning whether democracy has any future in the hands of such rulers. Yet periodic democratic elections are unavoidably part and parcel of the process. As long as the likelihood exists in Africa that politics would continue to be marred by ethnic factors, then, until elections can be conducted reasonably fairly, public resentment and violence would remain inevitable responses. Hence the need to develop new mechanisms against rogue elections in Africa. Without these, no amount of external assistance and no degree of hope can make the difference between peace and conflict in post-electoral situations in Africa.

Chapter Two deals with military intervention by invitation in a conflict that is purely internal. Unlike Ecowas' interventions in Liberia and Guinea-Bissau, which were designated as "Ecomog" (Ecowas Cease-fire Monitoring Group), the Community, for good measure, withheld that designation from the "sub-regional forces" it authorised for Sierra Leone. The mandates of these two forces were quite different in terms of both operation and jurisdiction. The only common feature they had was that they were both *ad hoc* arrangements organised outside the framework of the Ecowas Treaty.

While, therefore, Nigeria alone is responsible for its military intervention in Sierra Leone, the same cannot be said for the

Ecomog operations in Liberia and Guinea-Bissau. The latter operations were eminently veritable undertakings by the organisation as a whole and have been generally accepted as Africa's first successful flagship in international peace-enforcement, peace-keeping, peace-making and peace-building.

Chapter Three examines the role of Ecowas, particularly the part played by its so-called "sub-regional forces". In many respects, they exceeded their mandate but the international community adopted the counterproductive strategy of see no evil, speak no evil, thus making itself an accessory to their transgressions. Indeed it provides a classical example of how *not* to delegate enforcement powers to a regional agency involved in an internal armed conflict.

Ecowas brokered three peace agreements – Abidjan in 1996, Conakry in 1997 and Lome in 1999. Each of them made some progress in the search for a peaceful solution but, as it also turned out, every step forward was a prelude to a step back. The reason was that none of them was founded on the principle of national consent. Strictly speaking, they were agreements between warring parties and the unarmed civilians had little or no say. Unsurprisingly, therefore, the clouds of glory, which each of them presaged, quickly evaporated in stalemate.

Chapter Four looks at the part played by the United Nations. Ostensibly the debate was about the protection of democracy, constitutional governance and human rights. And the organisation's proclaimed objective was to pressure the military junta into demitting office and making way for the restoration of constitutional order. Accordingly it delivered a robust pro-democracy message to the military junta. But it also left no doubt that its objective was to be achieved by peaceful means only. Notwithstanding, because of its new distaste for military regimes, the organisation seemed deliberately blind to the excesses of interventionist forces in Sierra Leone.

Questions that this begs are, first, whether the practice of the United Nations is consistent; and, secondly, whether its activism is not nowadays, especially after the end of the Cold War, defined by factors such as geography, race, natural endowment and national interest. The Orwellian thesis seems to still hold good, that while all nations are theoretically equal; in reality, some are more equal than others.

Chapter Five examines the role of domestic civil societies and demonstrates that internal civil disobedience, properly focused and managed, can combine well with the international policy of non-recognition to paralyse unconstitutional regimes, and possibly bring about their downfall without the need to fire a single shot.

Chapter Six examines what increasingly is being promoted as a new exception to the international prohibition against military intervention in internal affairs of states, namely forcible intervention in defence of democracy or human rights. The recent cases of Haiti, Republic of the Congo, Sierra Leone and East Timor are examined against the backdrop of international practice during the Cold War. They clearly confirm that there is as yet no general doctrine of democratic or humanitarian necessity. To suggest the contrary, just because there is growing international abhorence of undemocratic regimes which often abuse human rights, is to bend the law, which itself is wrong. What it does point to, however, is that international public opinion is crystallising in favour of developing rules of international law to respond to and match the new political dispensation. With the loosening of the iron grip of the Cold War, the consensus now is for greater international activism in support of democracy and human rights at state level, including possibly military action, but a new code of conduct, to be applied to all cases without discrimination, is required. Daunting as this challenge may be, the increasingly pluralistic post-Cold War world of today demands it. In time, it could develop into a bulwark against the growing phenomenon of social, religious, cultural and ethnic diversity transforming themselves into violent tendencies which, in turn, degenerate into internal armed conflicts and undermine the stability of fledgling democracies and thus international security.

Chapter Seven examines the extent to which international humanitarian law was respected by the belligerents in the internal armed conflict in Sierra Leone. As in all such conflicts, the first casualty was the truth. However inconclusive the identity of culprits may be for the purposes of accountability, the fact remains that no one can be in any doubt about the identity of the second casualty, human security. Yet, under successive peace accords, the warring parties shied away from creating an international criminal tribunal to bring to justice all alleged abusers of international humanitarian and human rights law. They settled instead for a poor substitute in the form of a Truth and Reconciliation Commission. Only when national and international pressure was brought to bear was agreement reached on the establishment of a quasi- international criminal tribunal the constitution of which might well fall short of satisfying all the essential requirements of independence, impartiality, credibility, effectiveness and conformity with international fair-trial standards.

Chapter Eight examines the government's own individual record of compliance with human rights obligations outside the theatre of combat if only as a yardstick for measuring democracy and tyranny. The focus here is particularly on the treason trials that followed Kabbah's restoration to power and the manner in which they were conducted. In many respects, the trials looked like a chrysalis of triumph and revenge was the driving force of justice in Sierra Leone. Also examined are cases of abuse of power, abuse of process, abuse of human rights, reprisals, declaration of public emergencies, effects of acts done by military juntas and the role of reconciliation in post-conflict reconstruction and peace-building. The proclivity of the constitutional government was to discount the interregnum totally, arguing, in some extraordinary way, that a vacuum did exist in Sierra Leone during that period. If this were to be accepted, then there are certainly not many countries around the world that have adopted this approach.

Chapter Nine looks at what should be done in plural societies to promote and guarantee domestic peace and stability, and, by extension, regional peace and security. If there is at least one object lesson that the internal conflict in Sierra Leone provides, it is that foreign military interventions in such conflicts seldom yield durable peace and security. On the other hand, peaceful autochthonous solutions, however protracted the negotiations might be, have generally proved more enduring. This is because while the former is generally viewed as imposed from outside with all attendant constraints, the latter enjoys the intrinsic merits of local ownership, public confidence and public trust.

Nor is there lasting relief in manipulative democracy. A new political architecture is therefore required from the international community, involving commitment, finance, expertise and technology, to deepen the roots of democracy and human rights in developing multiethnic societies so that they can grow into galvanising cultures. It must be an architecture that embraces both the culture of respect for human rights and of a reasonable balance between rights and responsibilities. This duty to respect human rights should be heavier on incumbent governments; in particular they must be able to guarantee real independence and impartiality to their electoral and justice systems in order to command public confidence.[3] This is vitally important, because, in less advanced plural societies with lower thresholds of self-control, elections can easily turn ugly, provoking ethnic or sectarian disputes which, in turn, rapidly degenerate into violence.

Progress dictates that primacy must now be given to the promotion and protection of representative government and respect for fundamental human rights in such societies, including, in particular, the international supervision of national elections and referenda. Perhaps the creation of a permanent mechanism for such electoral supervision at global, continental or regional level, is an innovation whose time has come and in which the international community needs to invest more seriously. If fairness is impossible because of volatile or corrupt conditions at the domestic level, the international community has more than a moral duty to step in and secure it. Justification for such intervention derives as much from international policy as from international preventive diplomacy. The only question is which of the following international actors should be entrusted with this most important task - the United Nations, the Commonwealth, the OAU or the regional agencies like Ecowas and SADC?

CHAPTER 1

Democracy and the Politics of Violence in Sierra Leone

Democracy prior to 1967

Sierra Leone gained independence from Britain on April 27, 1961 with a Westminster-style parliamentary democracy. The Queen was retained as head of state, represented by a governor-general. The first Prime Minister was Sir Milton Margai, a Mende by tribe and the first provincial man to qualify as a medical doctor. He died on April 28, 1964 and was succeeded by his half brother, Albert Margai.

In the pre-independence multi-party elections of 1951 and 1957, the Sierra Leone People's Party (SLPP), led by Sir Milton, predominated. Then it was hailed as pan-ethnic with membership drawn from across the ethnic and regional divides. However, it failed to build a grass-root base. Instead, like the erstwhile colonial administration, it relied almost entirely on the patronage of traditional rulers, the Paramount Chiefs, who became its rural backbone. This gave it an élitist outlook and to this day nothing much has changed. In the election of 1957, the SLPP won 25 out of the 39 ordinary seats in the House of Representatives.[4] Joined by 12 Paramount Chiefs, representing the 12 administrative districts into which the country had been divided, who by convention defer to the majority party in Parliament, and 8 victorious independent candidates, the SLPP's tally swelled to 45 seats in the 51-member House of the self-governing colony of Sierra Leone.

With Sir Milton's admirable qualities and leadership skills, only few could have been in any doubt about his ability to win the first post-independence election of 1962 with 28 seats. The surprise was the performance of the All Peoples Congress Party (APC). After only a year in existence, it won four out of six contested seats in the Freetown Municipal Elections in November 1961. It repeated this remarkable performance less than a year later in the General Elections of 1962, when it won 20 as against 28 seats for the incumbent SLPP government. It had contested 32 of the 62 seats and won 16. The Sierra Leone Progressive Independence Movement (SLPIM), led by Chief Tamba Mbriwa, won all four seats in Kono District and immediately allied itself with the APC, a natural alliance that has survived through the decades. All the 14 successful independent candidates and the 12 Paramount Chiefs pledged their allegiance to the SLPP to give it an absolute majority in Parliament.[5]

Siaka Stevens, along with 16 loyalists, had founded the Elections before Independence Movement on July 9, 1960. At a mass rally on October 17, it metamorphosed into a fully-fledged political party that came to be known as the All Peoples' Congress (APC).[6] Its platform was stridently proletarian and populist in contrast to the more conservative and élitist outlook of the SLPP.[7] The independence celebrations found most of its key members behind bars, having been detained under a state of emergency and charged with offences ranging from sedition, conspiracy, incitement to riotous behaviour. Far from weakening the party and dampening its courage, these politically motivated indictments bolstered its national image and standing as the general public came to view them as unwarranted harassment of the opposition.

(a) *The colonial legacy*

The axiom, prevalent in Europe in the eighteenth and nineteenth centuries, was that colonial territories could only be administered tyrannically. The settlers in America, however, were treated differently because, before 1787, they had had more than a century of experience in public discussion and government by consent. Because of this, local self-government received primordial value unlike the African colonies where it arrived too late and had only secondary significance. Thus, the pre-independence apprenticeship of African politicians in the art and craft of multi-party democracy was relatively short. In Sierra Leone, for example, in more than 150 years of British colonial rule,[8] the indigenous population participated in multi-party elections, with limited franchise, only twice, in 1951 and 1957. This was so, because the colonial administration did not need to establish political legitimacy and certainly did not encourage political pluralism until well into the terminal years of its rule. Nor did it establish the social and political organisation on the scale required for democracy to flourish. So the tuition the indigenous politicians received was neither in the theory nor in the practice of local self-government from which could have sprung self-reliance and the habit of association. Instead their tuition was in the theory and practice of authoritarianism, which had largely characterised colonial governance. Such, then, was the nature of the political inheritance of the new leaders at independence, along with a weak and wholly dependent civil society riven by patronage, human rights abuses and ethnic bias. As Adam Hochschild puts it, "the major legacy Europe left for Africa was not democracy as it is practised today in countries like England, France and Belgium, it was authoritarian rule and plunder."9

As independence drew near, the new political leaders had suddenly to unlearn, so to speak, this inheritance and imbibe at once a Westminster-style parliamentary democracy with all its integral concepts of human rights, institutionalised opposition, tolerance of dissent, public accountability, probity and transparency and a free press. This was to prove too much of a tall order. If only democracy had come sooner, it might have taken firmer root at independence with a certain amount of culture and experience to back it up and domesticate it. But this was not what happened. Parliamentary democracy was brought in during the late evening of colonial rule, and this largely explains why many of the early politicians either failed ruefully to understand the rules of the Westminster game or, if they did at all, they deliberately chose not to follow them. For many, politics was not a game but a battle, just like it had been in the days of old when colonialism flourished. Opposition was thus frowned upon by incumbent regimes as a demonstration of personal enmity, and unfortunately the politics of Sierra Leone has not much changed; it continues to be dogged by that mentality right up to the present.

But colonial authoritarianism was not the only legacy bequeathed to the African politician. As Roger Tangri has observed: "Even during the colonial period, most notably in territories such as the Gold Coast and Nigeria, politics was regarded by many as a commercial venture in its own right. Public office was viewed as facilitating private gain."10 William Foltz agrees. "In addition to satisfying individual or psychic needs," he said, "political office provided a school teacher or clerk with his only likely opportunity for personal financial advancement. A successful candidate for parliament would easily quintuple his salary and would have access to means for taking care of his extended family's needs and desires. Like most successful politicians anywhere, these men were truly hungry for office."11

Sierra Leone can easily be added to the list. Writing about his first experience as a minister in the mid-fifties, Siaka Stevens recalls in his autobiography as follows:

> "Most men in public positions the world over need money, but the need is far more acute for those who have only just left the bread-line. As far as an African is concerned, once he is elevated to a position of authority he is expected to support a horde of hangers-on, remote members of his family many of whom he never before knew existed. He must hand out largesse, educate not only his own children but those of family members, entertain more lavishly and more frequently than before and dress himself and his family in clothes befitting his status. It is all part and parcel of his new position. Money slips through his fingers like quicksilver and he can never have enough of it to satisfy his dependants. When it can be had so easily, when all that is required of him is his influence in tipping the scales in the award of a contract or manoeuvring some other proposition in favour of the donor, the temptation is enormous and it seems foolish to him to refuse such an offer. Fresh in his memory, too, is the hardship he suffered on the way up the ladder, the years of poverty and near starvation he endured and the longed-for education he could never afford, and perhaps also the stench and dampness of a prison cell. With plenty of money in the bank at least his own children would be spared such deprivation."12

The new political élite had seen how the colonial masters had acquired personal wealth, prestige and power for themselves and how lavishly they had lived their lives. They were just waiting in the wings to step right into their shoes, for a taste for luxury had led them into preoccupations with wealth and its perquisites – consumption, display and pleasure.

(b) *Post-colonial politics*

"Those who are conquered," wrote the philosopher Ibn Khaldun in the fourteenth century, "always want to imitate the conqueror in his main characteristics – in his clothing, his crafts, and in all his distinctive traits and customs". This was true of African leaders before and after independence. To this day, leadership positions in politics no less than in the public service continue to be highly valued, particularly so because of financial and other rewards of office-holding. The incumbents expect to earn big salaries, including such perks as free cars and free housing, domestic servants and so on. On top of this are the earnings possible mostly through the award of contracts or the grant of licences. So public office-holding is coveted as a major way by which leaders, politicians, public and civil servants alike, can escape from the poverty trap or from their otherwise marginal economic and social existence in an environment of declining opportunities and prospects. Little wonder that ruling parties everywhere often experience, albeit in varying degrees, internal convulsions as party stalwarts compete either to attain or to retain the limited number of coveted positions available.

Ruth First has described how Nigeria's First Republic "became an orgy of power being turned to profit."13 Sani Abacha plundered Nigeria "during his nearly five years in power before his abrupt death in June 1998 with such single-minded zeal that Western officials estimate that he may have had more than \$3 billion stashed away in overseas bank accounts, equivalent to what it took Mobutu of Zaire more than three decades to amass."14 In Ghana, Dr Kofi Busia admitted whilst he was Prime Minister that "there is not a single honest person in my cabinet."15 In Cote d'Ivoire, Cohen has shown how the "politico-administrative class has managed to obtain a disproportionate share of urban resources such as land, housing, education, jobs and social services."16 In the Central African Republic, apart from his huge personal wealth, Emperor Jean Bokassa's extravagant coronation in 1977 alone cost 12 million francs in a country where total revenues were not more than 14 million francs.

Politics in Africa has thus come to be seen as sleaze-ridden and undemocratic. The major difference with the developed world being that in Africa sleaze is perhaps more visible because of the depth and extent of poverty and deprivation. Sierra Leone is not different, except that the conflict has made it smell to high heaven. That conflict is not between ordinary folks as much as between and within the political élites. This partly explains why personal rivalry within the ruling élite as well as between rival political parties has grown fiercer and why the tendency to besmirch the character and reputation of the opposition has risen to unprecedented levels. So commonplace has it become that the ordinary man sometimes disarmingly dismisses it as "politics". Often the rivalry is fiercest amongst politicians for whom politics is the be-all and end-all.

The mindless rivalry in Sierra Leone may also be seen as the function of a decrepit economy. So long as the government dominates the dispensation of goods and services and the distribution of largesse, little is likely to change in the system of patronage. Incumbents see themselves as enjoying their turn at the expense of the opposition and the nation as a whole, sometimes even to the extent of officialising political victimisation. Clients reciprocate the benefits they receive from their patrons with tangible and intangible assets. These include strident demonstrations of allegiance and esteem, gathering of so-called intelligence but often scurrilous information about the patron's perceived political enemies and partisan support. Where ethnic rivalry is at stake, ethnic loyalty often resonates with the followership and the leadership in turn exploits it to further its own ends. It is this exploitation of ethnic differences to obtain otherwise unattainable goals that constitutes the most pernicious and unacceptable form of tribalism in African politics.

Unfortunately tribal demagoguery still infests the body politic in Sierra Leone; it peaked after February 1998, following the return of the government of President Kabbah and the demise of AFRC rule. Even though the RUF is not of northern origin, though led by a man with a northern name, Foday Sankoh, and even though the north suffered the worst carnage in the hands of the RUF, President Kabbah did not hesitate to blame northerners in 1996. If only to clear the air once and for all, and avoid future recriminations, it is vitally important that the true story of the origins of the RUF be told.

(c) *Split within the SLPP*

The death of Sir Milton in April 1964 led to a serious split in the SLPP over the issue of succession. The two leading contenders, Albert Margai and John Karefa-Smart, were both from the south. The former was a wily politician from Bonthe District while the latter, from Rotifunk in Moyamba District, was generally perceived as a principled technocrat committed to playing the political game solely by the rules. Perhaps because of this, he lost the party leadership to Margai. Against the protestation of 35 Members of Parliament, including three Ministers, the Governor-General appointed Albert Margai as Prime Minister. However, many believed that powerful Creole friends of Margai, in a position to advise the Governor-General, had twisted his arm into appointing him.

An unprecedented level of financial sleaze and cronyism marred Albert's rule. So also did tribalism as he slanted the SLPP towards the south and particularly his Mende kith and kin. This blatant tribalism, which had played a crucial factor in his succession, was to cost him the general election of 1967. And it also carried a particular poignancy to the events that immediately followed. As Siaka Stevens recalled:

"While stuffing his henchmen into the power-centres of politics, he was cramming every vacancy in the civil service and armed forces with fellow-tribesmen. Margai's retreat into a tribalism more divisive and a sectionalism more acute than any previously practised even by the SLPP, was the worst thing that had happened to Sierra Leone since independence. When we needed unity most, Margai set us at each other's throats. When we most needed to set tribalism aside, Margai exploited it with a frantic ruthlessness. When we were striving for equality, Margai made a cult of discrimination. There were two good reasons – good from his point of view – for this policy. By enlivening inter-tribal tensions he hoped to activate Mende sentiment in his own cause so that he could use it to keep power, however the election went."[17]

For precisely the same reason, the Creoles, whose support had been a key factor in Albert's succession, turned against him when the elections came. According to Cartwright:

"The Creoles, originally sympathetic, turned against him because of his apparent favouring of Mendes, his self-enrichment and his attempts to cut away legal safeguards they saw as necessary to protect their position. Northerners' initial suspicions of one Mende succeeding another were heightened by what they interpreted as 'tribal' biases in appointing Mendes to key civil service posts, building airports near Sir Albert's homes in Mendeland, and using northern chiefs against their people to keep the 'Mende' SLPP in power."18

Ethnicism and cronyism thus soiled Albert's record of leadership. That was not all. Step by step, Albert showed himself as a leader who was determined to strangulate multi-party democracy right from the start. This plan was laid bare by his enactment of the Public Order Act 1965,19 the Preventive Detention Act 1965 and the introduction of the 30-day absenteeism rule on 4 May 1965, to deprive Parliamentarians of their seats if absent for 30 sitting days. Not only were four APC Opposition Members of Parliament deprived of their seats under this rule while in prison on trumped-up charges, the party was prevented from holding legitimate political meetings in the rural areas where its rising popularity was proving unstoppable.

Karefa-Smart too suffered a similar fate. In fact it was popularly believed that that rule had been passed specifically for him. He was deprived of his parliamentary seat following his acceptance of a lectureship at Columbia University in New York. His teaching commitments had made it impracticable for him to attend all parliamentary sessions in Sierra Leone, so he quickly fell foul of the 30-day rule. He was to fall victim to this law for the second time 35 years later when the SLPP government, this time under Kabbah's leadership, used it again to deprive him of his parliamentary seat in July 2000. He was further denied the title and status of Parliamentary Minority Leader even though his party, the United National People's Party (UNPP), had won the second largest number of seats in parliament in the parliamentary election of 1996.

In 1965 Albert leaned heavily on the chiefs to stymie the growing popularity of the APC. As a party, the SLPP was nothing more than an aggregation of local chieftains in the provinces with a central control in Freetown that was less well organised. To quote Cartwright again: "From its beginnings, the SLPP had been entwined with the chiefs to a degree unsurpassed by any other governing party in Africa. With the advent of the popular franchise in 1957, the party had a chance to establish cadres of organisers independent of the chiefs, but Dr Margai showed no interest in such a move. Admittedly, there were difficulties; the growth first of the PNP and then of the APC required the SLPP to turn to the chiefs to suppress these opposition groups at the local level, and to develop party cadres would require either an 'ideological' appeal such as motivated the PDG [Parti Démocratique de Guinée] in Guinea, or material payoffs on a scale not readily obtained under British supervision."[20]

The rising popularity of the APC provoked a knee-jerk reaction. The SLPP's propaganda was that the APC was no respecter of chieftaincy and might even abolish it if it came to power. The chiefs were thus frightened into employing every strategy to frustrate APC political meetings and rallies. To help them further, Albert enacted the Public Order Act 1965. This obnoxious law, which unfortunately is still on the statute book, places severe restrictions on the right of the democratic opposition to hold public meetings in the provinces. Before such meetings can be convened, the convenor must first write to the paramount chief of the chiefdom concerned to give notice, in effect to seek permission. The chief is empowered to disallow such meetings or to impose such conditions as he considers necessary in the interests of defence, public order, public safety or public morality. Failure to comply with the chief's order is punishable with a fine or imprisonment.[21] As agents of the government and thus susceptible to intimidation, the chiefs felt compelled to deny permission to the opposition. Chiefs who disobeyed the government and granted permission to the opposition were deposed and banished, as was the case with Chief Koblo Pathbana of Marampa-Masimera Chiefdom and Chief Kande Luseni of Kamakwie, both from the north. They were deposed and banished to Pujehun District in the south.

The public outcry provoked by this law barely quietened when Margai provoked yet another. In December 1965, he introduced a Bill in Parliament to replace the Independence Constitution with a presidential form of government. This came in the wake of yet another parliamentary motion, calling for the introduction of a one-party system.[22] Apart from the intra-SLPP splits that these proposals provoked, a whirlwind of popular resentment quickly gathered. The country was soon divided along ethno-regional lines: the north supporting the stance of the opposition APC party, which opposed both measures, while the south and south-east sided overwhelmingly with the ruling SLPP government. Kono District in the east and Freetown, the capital, in the west, tilted the balance of public opinion in favour of the APC. Concurrently with these shifting loyalties came the announcement in January 1967 of an "uncovered" plot to overthrow the SLPP government allegedly by eight army officers suspected as unsympathetic to its political agenda.23 This was to damage the declining fortunes of the SLPP beyond reprieve. Albert Margai was clearing the deck for the elections, which were then only two months away. Detained without charge, these officers suffered arbitrary imprisonment. The military junta of the National Reformation Council (NRC) later released them.   Take note military tgts

Democracy after 1967

(a) *The first coup d'état 1967*

Such then was the atmosphere prior to the elections of March 17, 1967. The misrule of the SLPP government under Albert Margai turned into a huge political capital for the APC. Despite making "considerable efforts to rig the ...elections" for a variety of reasons he failed to do so effectively.24 The results declared by the Electoral Commission put the parties at 32 seats for the APC and 28 seats for the SLPP.25 Although four of the six former SLPP candidates, who had won as independents, were still being wooed, the SLPP counted them among its successful candidates. Accordingly, it greeted the Commission's declaration with derision and continued to assure the public that the result was 32 seats each. The four had in fact written to the Governor-General to reaffirm their independence so long as Margai insisted on remaining leader of the SLPP.

The announcement of the true election result was delayed, suppressed and then falsified on the authority of the chief of the army, Brigadier David Lansana. However, on March 21, the Governor-General appointed the Leader of the APC, Siaka Stevens, as Prime Minister and authorised him to form a government. Sierra Leone thus became the first country to effect a change of government through the ballot box in post-colonial Africa.26

41

No sooner this Opposition victory was declared than the military reversed it with a *coup*. Siaka Stevens was being sworn-in as Prime Minister when Lieutenant Samuel Hinga Norman, aide-de-camp to the Governor-General, on the instructions of Brigadier Lansana, arrested and detained him, the Governor-General and others. He then took control of the State House and the radio and television stations. The same day Lansana declared martial law and suppressed the announcement of the appointment of the new Prime Minister. The following day, he made a radio broadcast announcing a military take-over and repeating the orders he had given the previous day to institute martial law.27 The first ever *coup d'état* in Sierra Leone, unlawfully overthrowing a democratically-elected government, was complete, setting in train a constitutional degeneracy from which the benighted country is yet to fully recover. The *coup* not only uprooted the tender democratic plant the nation was trying to water, many believed it was the handiwork of a handful of ambitious politicians and civil servants who were afraid of losing their coveted positions if Stevens were allowed to take the reins of power.

Margai had also made tribal affiliation the primary qualification for recruitment into the officer corps of the army. By packing the army with his own tribesmen he had hoped to "guarantee SLPP control of the army well into the future".28 In 1967 the Mende proportion of the entire officer corps was estimated at approximately 52 per cent, well above the Mende proportion of the population as a whole. According to Thomas Cox: "On the most elementary level, a common ethnic and regional identity helped fashion an allegiance between army officers and civilian influentials once Mendes came to predominate in the upper echelons of both sectors. Client-patron ties between army small boys and civilian big men – facilitated by the close physical proximity of army barracks and ministerial quarters in Freetown – also helped mediate civil-military interaction and eventually allowed for the development of a kind of symbiotic relationship between the two élites. The army officers needed identification with prominent civilians to raise the former's status in the wider community and, indirectly, to further their military careers. The politicians required the assurance that in the event they could no longer hold the public trust, the army, guns drawn, would remain at their sides."29

Offering as justification for his *coup*, Lansana claimed that the Governor-General had erred in appointing Siaka Stevens as Prime Minister on March 21, before the election of the 12 Paramount Chiefs Members of Parliament had been concluded. But the Constitution contained no such provision and Lansana simply wanted to delay the process until a result emerged that was to his and the defeated Prime Minister's liking, forgetting that the election of chiefs was conducted on a non-partisan basis. The established constitutional convention was that neither the special seats for chiefs nor their allegiance had a bearing in the calculation of ordinary seats won by political parties. This was because by convention the chiefs were above party politics, or so it was conceived, and sat on the side of the majority party in Parliament.30 As confirmed by Cyril Foray: "From the precedents of 1957 and 1962 it had become a convention that chiefs must support the majority party in parliament, although as traditional rulers they were expected in theory to be non-partisan."31 It is therefore clear that the Governor-General's decision was unassailable in fact and in law. The real reason for Lansana's *coup* was that he "found himself obligated, by dint of his relationship with Sir Albert and the SLPP, to defend the ruling circle at any cost....."32 By their unwarranted action Lansana, Margai and the SLPP grievously harmed democracy when it most needed respect and the effect of that is still felt to this day.

(i) *The first counter-coup 1967*

In the midst of the confusion, political and social tensions rose irrepressibly. Lansana failed to gain the support of most of his subordinate officers, who suspected his motives as being less than altruistic. They therefore decided to get rid of him. But they, too, had no intention of handing over power immediately. On March 23, led by Major Charles Blake, the senior military officers relieved Brigadier Lansana of his command and proceeded to establish a military regime, styling themselves as the National Reformation Council (NRC), under the chairmanship of Lt.-Col. Andrew Juxon-Smith. Justifying their action the NRC said that the political atmosphere had become so emotionally charged that time was needed for cooling off. To that end, they set up several commissions of inquiry. One of them, headed by Mr Justice Dove-

Edwin, was empowered to investigate the numerous charges and counter-charges of electoral fraud. Two others, chaired by Justices Forster and Beoku-Betts, investigated allegations of corruption against former SLPP ministers and senior civil servants respectively. Over and above this, however, the NRC had their own agenda.

The Governor-General was relieved of his post and sent into exile in England where he remained until his death in 1969. Albert Margai and Siaka Stevens, both initially detained at the Pademba Road Prisons, were subsequently released and, after the crisis subsided, allowed to travel. Stevens and some of his key advisers sought refuge in Conakry, Guinea. Before that, he had spent some time in London briefing the British Government, Parliament and the media, because he said he had been "baffled" by the attitude of the British Government to the *coup* in Sierra Leone. In his autobiography, he recalls:

> "The question of Britain's attitude was more or less answered in the House of Lords when Lord Brockway asked Her Majesty's Government whether they would use their influence to secure consideration by the Commonwealth Secretariat of the Report of the Committee headed by Mr Justice Dove-Edwin into the circumstances of the last general election in Sierra Leone. In reply, Lord Shepherd, Minister of State for Foreign and Commonwealth Affairs, took the view that the matter was outside the Commonwealth's competence, as it was essential not to infringe the absolute inviolability of a member state's internal affairs. But he agreed to give consideration to the idea that the Commonwealth might establish a common institution, analogous to the European Commission, to which appeal could be made against abuses by member states..........I agree, and would not have it otherwise, that no Commonwealth member should interfere with the internal affairs of other member countries."

Stevens then added this somewhat prophetic comment:

> "However, it has sometimes struck me that this unqualified acceptance of one another is stretched to a point where military take-overs actually appear to be condoned. Certainly they are not discouraged. Not a word

of admonition was uttered, not a frown of disapproval creased the brows of the Commonwealth Prime Ministers when, for instance, those who illegally overthrew by force of arms the constitutionally-elected governments of Ghana and Nigeria, took their seats at the conference table and were received in audience by the Head of the Commonwealth."33

As will be seen in subsequent chapters, the policies of both the British Government and the Commonwealth have since radically changed. Far from adhering to the doctrine of inviolability of internal affairs of member states, they now outrightly condemn regimes which attain power by unconstitutional means.

(ii) *The second counter-coup 1968*

After a year in office, the NRC was, in turn, ousted in a bloodless *coup*. Staged by a group of non-commissioned soldiers on April 17, 1968, they constituted themselves as the Anti-Corruption Revolutionary Movement under Warrant Officer Class 1, Emadu Rogers. This Movement later changed its name to the National Interim Council (NIC). Within days, and guided by good professional advice from Alhaji M. L. Siddique, then Secretary to the Cabinet, justice was made to prevail. The NIC formally handed over power to Stevens, who was then sworn in as Prime Minister for the second time on April 26, 1968.

With this historical experience, Stevens was naturally sensitive to the divisions afflicting the country and the vital need for genuine reconciliation between the various ethnic groups vying for power. Accordingly, his first government in 1968 was a government of national unity. The cabinet consisted of 17 ministers, of whom three were paramount chiefs, one from each province. The remaining 14 ministers were drawn from the following parties: eight from the APC, four from the SLPP and two were independent parliamentarians.

Stevens ruled Sierra Leone for 17 years until his voluntary retirement in 1985, escaping many a *coup* plot. In that time he made momentous changes to the character of the Sierra Leone polity. It became a republic under an executive presidency in 1971 and a one-party state under APC rule in 1978; measures that he had rejected in opposition. Although Stevens' rule is often dubbed as autocratic, few can deny he had a streak of political genius that puts him in a class with no other leader in Sierra Leone. Joe Allie, the historian, is emphatic: "One of his [Siaka Stevens] greatest achievements was that he was largely able to unite the country. He was himself the symbol of this unity, for he never closely associated himself with any single group. He claimed to belong to various ethnic groups by birth, marriage or otherwise."34 From his government of national unity in 1968 through to his last, Stevens studiously cultivated the profile of a pan-ethnic cabinet that reflected the nation's rich cultural heritage without unduly sacrificing merit. This factor, more than any other, probably explains his staying power and became one of his greatest legacies to his party. Having drawn the heaviest support from the north, Stevens set about deliberately to win the south by identifying much more with it than he did with the north, having been born of a Mende mother in Moyamba in the south where his family had settled and where he himself had spent most of his adolescent life.

(b) *The second coup d'état 1992*

Before his retirement in 1985, Stevens handpicked the chief of the army, Major-General Joseph Saidu Momoh, as his successor. This immediately sidelined his Vice-President, Sorie Ibrahim Koroma, generally regarded as the heir apparent. Momoh was later endorsed in a plebiscite in which he was the sole candidate. Although there had been what seemed like a conspiracy of silence during the seven years' of experimentation with the one-party system, flowing from the discountenance of public debate and the muting of influential critics by way of lucrative job offers, the true temper of public opinion favoured a change. Also rampant allegations of sleaze and cronyism started slowly but steadily to erode the popularity of the APC.

Nevertheless, a buoyed popular mood did greet Momoh's succession. His proclamation of a "New Order" received enthusiastic support, heightening public expectation that the younger and more radical reformers would hold sway. Sadly this did not happen. In his first cabinet, Momoh retained the old guard for whom change was almost anathema. Nor did his second cabinet in 1988 stem the rising tide of public disquiet. On the contrary, his critics became more and more unafraid. They saw his appointments as ethnically unbalanced and disproportionately weighted in favour of his own Limba tribesmen and Mendes from the south by virtue of his wife being from that tribe. Square pegs were fitted into round holes in the name of national concord. With such sycophancy on the rise the quality of leadership inevitably dropped. Incrementally, public agitation for political plurality swelled, fuelled by a dismal economy, the pains of an IMF structural adjustment programme and a rebel insurrection that seemed interminable.

So, on the economic front, Momoh's "New Order" faltered. Unlike Stevens' era, he undertook no substantial national project during his seven-year rule. His forte was more in the constitutional arena. Nudged on by a vibrant parliament, Momoh presided over the re-introduction of a multi-party democratic constitution. This, of course, coincided with the whirlwind of democratic change then sweeping across Eastern Europe and other parts of Africa in the late eighties, but the credit for the smooth transition in Sierra Leone really belongs to Momoh. He was smart enough to recognise that, by August 1990, the days of the one-party system were numbered and that it was no longer rewarding to stand against the wind of change. As admitted by Momoh himself:

> "In early 1990, while addressing the people of Kono and Kailahun, I initiated the debate on returning the country to a multi-party democracy as long as that was the wish of the majority of the people. Without any form of pressure, I drew the nation's attention to the debate that was then raging in other parts of the world and to the collapse of Eastern Europe's single party dictatorships. After that statement, the debate became wide open and everyone has had the opportunity of freely participating in it. I want to express my great pleasure to all those who have shown objectivity and quality in their contribution to the debate on such an important issue."

He repeated this in 1991. Receiving the report of the Constitutional Review Commission he had appointed to review the Constitution, he said:

> "I am especially delighted to hear that you have recommended the establishment of a multi-party system. ... It has been my hope all along that we would move to a multi-party constitution. I have waited until this moment

47

to share my own views because I did not want to affect the work of the Commission. I am happy that the people have spoken out in favour of a multi-party democracy and that the Commission has put their thoughts into constitutional form."

These statements represent the high point of Momoh's commitment to political pluralism. He signed the new Constitution into law on September 24 and brought it into force a week later, on October 1, 1991, followed by the appointment of an interim administration to oversee the transition and preside over multi-party elections, then slated for the end of 1992. Thus, with consummate skill, Momoh guided the wind of change, avoiding the turbulence that had capsized many a democratic transition, and landing it gently on the platform of a multi-party democratic constitution that received both parliamentary and popular approbation with hardly rancour. With presidential and parliamentary elections pending, no fewer than eight political parties, including the SLPP, registered and were already campaigning when a group of subalterns in the army interrupted the process. They announced a *coup* on April 29 and immediately put paid to Momoh's *pax democratica*. It took nearly four years before Sierra Leoneans had another crack at democratic transition but in circumstances markedly different from those of 1991.

By the time of the *coup*, however, as a result of escalating insurgency in the countryside, growing numbers of people had become displaced internally while hundreds of thousands of others escaped to foreign lands as refugees. At the same time, unlimited redundancies were declared in the public sector, adding further insult to the injury of non-payment of salaries and wages. The economy tumbled. GDP dropped from 4.5% in 1990 to 2.8% in 1991 to minus in 1992, while the decay of public infrastructure worsened. In no time, Sierra Leone was ranked as the poorest of the world's poor nations.

While all this was happening, the eastern and southern districts, traditional strongholds of the SLPP, were rapidly falling under RUF control. Momoh's government was in a dilemma. To proceed with elections in those circumstances, as some APC stalwarts were urging, would most probably have produced an APC victory but Momoh could not have escaped the charge of taking undue advantage of the rebel war to make his party electable. No

48

elections could properly have been held in the rebel-infested districts in the eastern and southern districts. On the other hand, the idea of postponing the elections also drew criticisms from the opposition who argued that the government was unjustifiably using the war to prolong its rule. While this debate was going on, and the SLPP was being accused of complicity with the RUF rebels, the soldiers struck.

A military administration, styling itself the National Provisional Ruling Council (NPRC), came into being under Captain Valentine Strasser, who, at 27 years of age, became the youngest head of state in the world.35 President Momoh, with some of his Ministers, fled to Conakry, Guinea, where he sought refuge.

It is instructive to recall here that President Momoh had an especially warm personal relationship with the Nigerian military leader at the time, General Ibrahim Badamasi Babangida. They had been course-mates at military college in Nigeria. Largely because of this friendship, Babangida had sent a battalion of Nigerian soldiers to assist the Sierra Leone army in 1991. Momoh was therefore well placed to ask Babangida to intervene to reverse the *coup* had he been so minded. He did not. Instead he chose to endure the humiliation of his overthrow in silence, apparently out of consideration for the tragic consequences it would have had for the civilian population.

(c) *The RUF rebellion*

Before the *coup*, an insurgency had broken out in the forested districts of eastern Sierra Leone, near the border with Liberia. The rebel movement, calling itself the Revolutionary United Front (RUF), was led by a little known ex-corporal of the Sierra Leone army, Foday Saybanah Sankoh. At the beginning, the RUF consisted of Sierra Leonean recruits and some remnants of the abortive Ndorgbowusu uprising in Pujehun District in 1982, but the main body came from the National Patriotic Front of Liberia (NPFL) of Charles Taylor, now President of Liberia. Later on, as the rebellion spread through the eastern and southern districts, all SLPP strongholds, and as the people came to believe, rightly or wrongly, that it was SLPP-inspired and aimed at removing the APC from power, its demography changed. More and more people from those districts joined the ranks of the RUF. Murky as its political agenda may have been, its avowed aim was unambiguous – to overthrow the APC government and replace it with one of its own.

Because of the predominance of NPFL fighters in the early days, many erroneously believed that the RUF was a spillover from the NPFL insurgency in Liberia. This belief was fuelled by the fact that when Ecomog, the Ecowas peace-keeping force, used the Freetown harbour as its launching pad in August 1990, an angry Charles Taylor, in his many banters with Robin White of the BBC Focus on Africa programme, had vowed to wreak revenge on Sierra Leone. President Momoh's crimes were, first, he had refused to allow him to mount his insurgency from Sierra Leone; and, second, he had permitted Ecomog to use his country as a staging and supply base.

However, to see the RUF rebellion solely in this light is a gross oversimplification. The plain truth is that Taylor's personal attack on Momoh was mere propaganda, and it is an exaggeration for anyone to believe that that alone was the *casus bellum*. By agreement, Taylor had helped Sankoh in 1991. Sankoh had agreed to help Taylor in his rebellion in Liberia and in return Taylor had pledged to help Sankoh when his turn came to launch an insurgency against his own country. It is as simple as that. Even if Ecomog had been launched elsewhere instead of Sierra Leone, Sankoh's insurgency would still have taken place and Taylor would still have been bound to make good his pledge. The fact that the five Ecowas countries, initially contributing troops to Ecomog, were Nigeria, Ghana, Guinea, Sierra Leone and The Gambia was more than a mere coincidence. They all had dissidents fighting with Taylor in Liberia. For those leaders, the rationale for agreeing to participate in Ecomog was simple: it was better to stop their own rebels in their tracks in Liberia than to wait until they came up to their doorsteps. They knew that if they sat back and did nothing, they would be next in line after Liberia. They also knew that, from the refusal of the Americans to help despite a century-old relationship with Liberia, they could not rely on the West to come to their rescue. The post-Cold War realpolitik meant that African 'crises were now solely for African governments and their armies. These were some of the factors that

I took into consideration in designing the framework of Ecomog, as the then Executive Secretary of Ecowas.

The Sierra Leone army was small, about 3,694 soldiers in total, largely ceremonial and ill equipped to counter the insurgents. Armed with antiquated rifles, armoured cars that did not work, poor communications and no efficient ground transportation system to speak of, let alone air strike capability, they could hardly shoot, move and communicate. They proved to be less of a match for the RUF who were sporting brand new AK47s, RPGs, artillery batteries and good guerrilla experience in Liberia. Some parts of the country did come under rebel control by early 1992, but it is to the credit of the country's poorly equipped army that it was able to prevent them from overrunning the rest of the country. Guinea, Nigeria, United States, United Kingdom, Egypt and China, each of them sending some military assistance, aided them.

The causes of the rebellion fall outside the scope of this book, but it would be inappropriate to ignore them entirely. Suffice it, however, to say that at different times the rebels have advanced different claims for taking up arms. These include their dislike of the one-party system, their abhorrence of tribalism, corruption and political oppression, social and economic injustices resulting from the mismanagement of public resources, nepotism and patrimonialism of previous administrations, and Sankoh's personal grudge for Momoh. On the other hand, commentators like Robert Kaplan have proffered quixotic reasons for the breakdown of the social fabric which they attribute to population pressure and environmental collapse.36 And, lately, Western governments have added control over the diamond fields as a new dimension.

Thus, opinions vary, but those who dismiss the RUF as nothing more than rag-tag bandits or teenage dregs with no clear ideology or a rebel gang without a cause, make a great mistake.37 Even as late as June 1998, for instance, Ambassador Johnnie Carson, Principal Deputy Assistant Secretary of State for African Affairs, was characterising the RUF to the Foreign Relations Sub-Committee of the United States Congress in these terms:

"The RUF has no political support or identifiable constituency. This gang-like outfit has no clear leadership structure and even murkier political aims, save for greed and the sheer quest for power. It had refused repeated invitations to give up violence and join the political

51

process, knowing that it would not gain much voluntary support......The brutality authored by the RUF is political terror at its worst. It deserves the strongest condemnation from the international community and friends of Sierra Leone. The international community must act swiftly and with sufficient resources to help end these atrocities and alleviate the human suffering. The United States must play its part in this effort."[38]

Whatever view one takes of them, whether as bogus revolutionaries, plunderers or mere opportunists, it offers insufficient reasons why the conflict lasted as long as it did. Some other explanation must be found, and Paul Richards has offered one:

"The war in Sierra Leone drags on essentially because there are social factors feeding the conflict, and because the main rebel group feels it has not yet had a chance to get its political point of view across, and that it needs to do so to honour activists who died in its cause."[39]

Then he adds:

"Whereas it is true that the war in Sierra Leone is a terror war, and involves horrifying acts of brutality against defenceless civilians, this sad fact cannot in any way be taken to prove a reversion to some kind of essential African savagery. Terror is supposed to unsettle its victims. The confused accounts of terrorised victims of violence do not constitute evidence of the irrationality of violence. Rather they show the opposite – that the tactics have been fully effective in disorientating, traumatising and demoralising victims of violence. In short, they are devilishly well calculated.....In fact the war has a clear political context, and the belligerents have perfectly rational political aims, however difficult it may be to justify the levels of violence they employ in pursuit of these aims. The rebel leadership has a clear political vision of a reformed and accountable state. Failure to communicate that vision owes more to the poverty, incompetence, and sectarian isolation of the movement than to any inherent trend towards anarchy in today's devastated West African forests."

Be that as it may, there is also the astonishingly curious relationship between the RUF and the NPRC in 1992.40 It was like a group which, with foreknowledge of the *coup* and a deal in hand, was now waiting anxiously to answer a summons to be part of the new dispensation. For almost a month, the rebels held their fire but disappointingly no invitation came. They felt bitterly betrayed. With the fury of a lover's scorn, they resumed fighting. And no amount of importunity could get them to yield to another cease-fire. As admitted by Sankoh, in an interview with *New African* Magazine, "when Strasser overthrow Momoh, I was the first to send him a message, let's stop this war I said, let's come together, The answer I got from Strasser was jet bombers, artillery, mercenary attacks."41

This also explains why the RUF had totally ignored the unilateral cease-fire declared by the NPRC in November 1993. If indeed there had been a deal between the RUF and the NPRC prior to the *coup*, curiously the latter had reneged.

From that moment on, the agenda of the RUF changed. It was no longer to overthrow the APC government, a job already done for them by the NPRC but rather to overthrow by force any incumbent government in Sierra Leone. And in 1995 they came within twenty miles of achieving their aim but for the timely intervention of foreign mercenaries, first the Gurkhas followed by Executive Outcomes. But neither did these mercenaries win the war; they merely helped the NPRC to stem the advance of the RUF towards the capital of Freetown, the seat of government.

In 1995, the NPRC formed a political party, the National Unity Party (NUP), giving the impression of favouring the holding of elections and of their willingness to take part in them. While the civilian leaders of the NUP were in the field campaigning, the soldiers were busy in Freetown drumming support for their new strategy "peace before elections". The contradiction was clear. The political parties, which were for elections, joined forces with civil society to pile pressure on the NPRC junta culminating in two national consultative conferences held at the Bintumani Conference Centre in August 1995 and January 1996, respectively. The international community too stepped in, threatening sanctions if the elections did not take place.

Fearing the wrath of the international community, the NPRC succumbed. Elections were hurriedly organised, but more than half a million people, who had escaped rebel atrocities, were sheltering in neighbouring countries. They were disenfranchised. In very dubious circumstances, Ahmad Tejan Kabbah was declared winner. The proponents for elections had had no illusions about the risks involved. What had amazed them, however, was the scale of vote-rigging tolerated by the election supervisor, the Interim National Electoral Commission (INEC), and the international observers.

(d) *The Abidjan Peace Accord 1996 and its collapse*

Such was the backdrop to Kabbah's administration taking over the reins of power. In its first year in office, it was highly celebrated for signing a peace accord with the RUF in Abidjan on November 30, 1996, formally bringing the rebel war to an end. Commonly referred to as the Abidjan Peace Accord, it took effect upon signature and a special holiday was declared to mark the occasion. Kabbah received kudos from far and near. But they turned to gall when the Accord unravelled a few months later. Each party accused the other of *mala fides*. Fears of opposition from the United States Congress, which then was blocking payment of arrears of up to one billion dollars, ended hopes of the neutral United Nations peace-keeping force, envisaged under the Accord, being deployed. This was the death-knell of the Accord. It would have cost $47 million for eight months for 720 troops, 60 military observers and 276 civilian staff.

Sankoh went to Nigeria on March 2, 1997. General Abacha detained him for allegedly taking a pistol and a few bullets into the country.42 Accusing Sankoh of sending clandestine instructions to his fighters not to disarm, President Kabbah alarmed everybody by the swiftness with which he conferred recognition on the new RUF leadership. It was all done within 24 hours of the announcement by Phillip Palmer that he had replaced Sankoh as leader in a palace *coup* on March 15. While this was taking place in Freetown, sporadic fighting broke out not only between the RUF and the army but also between the *kamajor* militia and the army. This was provoked largely by the news of Sankoh's arrest in Nigeria. The mistrust this engendered was to make it almost impossible to revive negotiations between the warring parties for a long time.43 And, by the end of the first quarter of 1997, the Abidjan Peace Accord was all but dead.

Apart from attempting to end the war, the Accord had other objectives too. It sought to grant mutual recognition to the warring parties. The RUF was to recognise the legitimacy of President Kabbah's government in return for a blanket amnesty for past crimes and for being afforded the opportunity to transform itself into a registered political party. It also provided for the disarmament of all private militias and their re-integration into civil society under United Nations supervision; the repatriation of all foreign forces from the country; the down-sizing of the national army; national reconciliation; and the promotion and protection of human rights and socio-economic justice.

Apart from hostilities between the pro-government forces and the rebels, armed incidents increased wherever the *kamajor* militia and the army came into contact, resulting in heavy civilian casualties. Likewise the public highways everywhere became arenas of bloody clashes leading to disruptions of vehicular traffic and attacks on civilian passengers, reminiscent of past hostilities between the rebels and the national army.

Unlike the *tamaboros* and *kapras* in the north, who had been disbanded by the NPRC in 1993, the *kamajor* militia was left intact. When the SLPP came to power in 1996, it had anxieties about security, coupled with suspicions of disloyalty from certain elements in the army. This forced it to hang on to the *kamajors*, who virtually became the military wing of the SLPP party. Obviously the auguries did not look good. This development, exacerbated by public appointments to favoured acolytes from the south, revived old memories of the Albert Margai era of the sixties, the only difference being that he had not had the benefit of a *kamajor* militia at his beck and call.

As to be expected, the national army became nervous and envious and began to see the *kamajor* militia as a rival force. President Kabbah's speech at the Myohaung Day Parade in 1997 did not help matters either. He purported to clothe that militia with official status when he said: "Several countries maintain civil defence forces as auxiliary units to be called upon in time of need. Britain has its Territorial Army and the United States maintains the National Guard. These forces are not standing armies or rivals to the national armies of those countries. Their roles are no different than what is now intended to be assigned to the *kamajors*."44 Kabbah's barring the national army from performing security duties for the presidency was the last straw.

Nothing could have been more ominous of impending disaster. Not much time passed before the fighting spread all over the countryside. In one week alone, more than ten separate attacks were recorded on northern towns, leaving behind a gruesome pile of dismembered limbs and torsos; and, more than at any time before, the perpetrators adopted a ruinous scorched-earth policy. Scarcely a village or hamlet was spared of decimation.

Thus, even before May 1997, any pretence that the country was peaceful and stable was beginning to ring hollow. The government could only half govern, and the scene everywhere, except for the safe haven of Freetown, which had by then escaped the cruelty of the war, was one of chaos, unbridled lawlessness and complete breakdown of human security. Kabbah lost control of the country as well as the capacity to deal with myriads of security problems springing up everywhere, including parts of the country hitherto untouched by the war. Worse still, a succession of allegedly "uncovered" *coup* plots did little to restore public confidence. The country was thus steered towards the precipice and it was plain that, sooner or later, a crisis would result. The opportunity was thus created for anyone bent on derailing the country's fledgling democracy to do so.

Quite apart from this, according to the local press, the government was also waist-deep in muck, yet nothing was done to pick up the shovel. To stifle press freedom and repress democratic dissent, the government enacted the Media Practitioners Act 1997. Under this new law, the right to speak freely, an essential attribute of democracy, was all but smothered. Compounding the situation was drug-trafficking, nearly all from Nigeria. Discrimination was also brazen, as exemplified by the manner in which property, confiscated under NPRC decrees, was being returned to favoured party supporters while others were refused. All these merely added to the pile of mounting human rights abuses, gnawing ignominiously at the country's precarious stability. *The Economist* summed it up well: "[President Kabbah] was seen as weak and arrogant; unable to act decisively against corrupt vested interests, slow to get the economy under control and unwilling to make peace with the rebels. He also sidelined the army and relied on local self-defence militias, known as *kamajors*. That almost certainly helped bring on the *coup*."45

(e) *The third coup d'état 1997*

Few could therefore have been surprised when the military stepped in once more to interrupt civil governance of the country barely 14 months into Kabbah's administration. It staged a successful putsch on May 25, 1997.

The coupists formed a junta, the Armed Forces Ruling Council, and invited the RUF to join them. Together they constituted the Armed Forces Revolutionary Council (AFRC), with Major Johnny Paul Koroma, sprung from gaol, as Chairman and Foday Sankoh, then in detention in Nigeria, as Vice-Chairman. This immediately stymied the rebellion to the extent that fighting ceased between the national army and the rebels. The AFRC junta went on to suspend the 1991 Constitution, ban all political parties, political meetings and demonstrations, and usurp all legislative and executive powers.

Many reasons have been proffered for this overthrow but the failure to consolidate peace under the Abidjan Peace Accord, the rigging of the presidential election and the granting of extraordinary privileges to the *kamajor* militia over the national army stand out most prominently.

Kabbah's supporters sometimes allege that there was external complicity in the *coup* but there is no scintilla of evidence to support it. All foreign nationals, wanting to leave, were allowed to do so and some governments sent ships and aircraft. This was particularly true of the British, American and Lebanese governments. Not one complained of any mistreatment of its nationals. Nigeria, for its part, not wanting to be accused of lacking capacity to protect its own nationals, estimated at over 5,000, decided not to evacuate them.46

The immediate aftermath of the *coup* was exceedingly violent. Characterised by generalised looting, particularly of private property, and extreme cruelty, especially against women, fear and anxiety gripped the once placid capital of Freetown. All hell broke loose. Thousands of Freetown residents, including professionals, fled the country. This took a heavy toll on essential services in particular, resulting in the further deterioration of humanitarian conditions in the capital. Like President Momoh before him, President Kabbah decamped to Conakry where he sought sanctuary. But, unlike Momoh, he invited General Abacha of Nigeria to intervene militarily to restore his government back to power. This invitation alone was sufficient to undermine any claim that Kabbah was in effective control of the country.

(f) *The counter-coup 1998*

Abacha obliged. Intervening on June 2, 1997, his forces did not succeed in evicting the AFRC from the seat of power until February 12, 1998. After this, the Nigerian army virtually became an army of occupation until President Kabbah returned from exile a month later.

Before that, the opinion in certain quarters was that once the junta was dislodged from Freetown, that would spell the automatic collapse of the rebellion. It turned out to be most extravagant. Apart from proving stubborn fighters, the combined force of AFRC/RUF rebels staged one pitch battle after another against the Nigerians and the *kamajors* in many parts of the country. Occasionally, they even forced the pro-government forces to retreat and reinforce. Hundreds of former junta soldiers, who refused to join the rebels, were hurriedly retrained and reinducted into the fighting, much to the chagrin of the *kamajor* leaders, who wanted to see them retrenched. This was followed by severe press censorship.47 All these actions confirmed that while it may have been comparatively easy to subdue the junta in Freetown, pacifying the rest of the country was a different matter, to say nothing about the futility of the military option itself.

(g) *SLPP and the Army*

Having taken the baton of leadership from one military junta, only to become victim to another military *coup d'etat* in less than 14 months in office, one can reasonably understand President Kabbah's scepticism about the army's subservience to civil authority. But the problem was that his attitude did not always stop at scepticism. Much too often it degenerated into a kind of paranoia or hysteria. At no time was this more vividly dramatised than when he abruptly announced the disbanding of the entire army.

Apart from being an undisguised act of vengeance for his overthrow by the AFRC, it is not easy to decipher what else could have been behind this feat of temper against an army which the government must have known it needed as the country was still in the throes of war. However, walking down memory lane, one recalls that the SLPP party was the one that had instigated the *coups* of 1967 (Brigadier Lansana's *coup*) and 1992 (the NPRC *coup*) and both were against the APC government. Kabbah himself had supposedly played a significant behind-the-scene role as a way of paying back for his rapid promotion in the civil service by the SLPP government in the sixties, to say nothing about his marriage into a family with prominent connections with that party. Again throughout the NPRC junta rule from 1992 to 1996 he had played a larger than life role as Chairman of its Advisory Council which attempted to replace the 1991 Constitution even before it had been tested in practice. So the SLPP government of President Kabbah knew well enough what the army was capable and seemed to be in awe of its might. It therefore felt it could not govern unless the military was brought under its thumb by hook or by crook.

It also explains why Kabbah's government was anxious to pack the army with its own handpicked followers from the south and east of the country starting with its private *kamajor* militia. It further explains why the government remains resolute, despite many public protestations, to maintain that militia, using whatever guise it could find and using the analogy of the Territorial Army in Britain when necessary. So long as this attitude continues to lurk behind the intentions of the SLPP government, its relationship with the army, be it the former or the present, is likely to remain poor.

Much of the best safeguard against this threat to the quality of civil-military relations probably lies in asserting and strengthening civil authority and control over the military. Inter-personal relationships matter but they are not and should not be controlling as the national army is not a personal estate. It is better and certainly less prone to caprice to move towards building inter-institutional relations between civil authority and the military in Sierra Leone. But this might not be feasible and practicable until the army can be convinced, as well as the civilian population, that the crucial process by which civil authority is chosen is wholly independent and free of executive interference and corruption. To the army the best proof of this is when neither the security services nor any part thereof nor any private militia is deployed to carry out ballot rigging in any part of the country. In other words, government by consent must be by rules and procedures which not only provide for a level playing field for the players but the referee himself must be genuinely free of taint and manipulation. In this way a culture of respect for civil authority and control could develop and flourish among men and women under arms in Africa, and the civilian population would have the legal and moral right to demand no less.

(h) *Attempted overthrow of Kabbah in 1999*

At no time was that futility of revenge more clearly demonstrated than when rebels managed to penetrate the backbone of Nigerian defences in and around Freetown and stormed the city on January 6, 1999. Kabbah's government was dislodged from the seat of power for the second time in as many years.

His return to power in February 1998 appears to have been somewhat intoxicating. It induced a revenge fixation among his supporters. Crafted in ways that were pretentious about respecting the rule of law, the international community was hoodwinked into seeing no evil as the revenge culture overwhelmed the country. James Jonah, who had been very loud in condemning what he perceived was "genocide" on the part of the AFRC junta, was surprisingly squirmish when that same term was used to describe similar brutalities by pro-government forces against people of northern origin. For example, in Kenema District in the east, the *kamajors* reportedly carried out "a sinister plan to ... kill 'strangers', which in this case meant people from the north of the country, living in Kenema, which is predominantly Mende land. One school of thought suggests that some of the victims, including soldiers and ordinary citizens, such as petty traders, miners, and even the unemployed, were massacred in broad day light, while others were forcibly removed from their homes ... at the dead of night and taken to some undisclosed locations, where they were clobbered to death. What is worse.... in some cases, the acts of savage butchery were crowned by removing vital human organs for only-God-knows-what purposes."48

These pro-government vigilantes may have felt they were teaching their opponents a lesson; in fact, they were inflicting mortal wounds upon themselves. For when the rebels struck Freetown on that fateful day in January 1999, they too came with their hit list, just as the SLPP had done in February 1998. The scene everywhere was nothing short of apocalyptic as parts of eastern and central Freetown were reduced to rubble. Without trying to justify these acts of violence in any form, it is worth stating that painful though it was, what happened on that day confirmed the old adage that revenge does not pay.

But the attack on Freetown had not come suddenly. The government had had notice of it but decided to downplay it, assuring residents that the city was impregnable. Julius Spencer, Minister of Information, was so deft at painting silver linings around the blackest of clouds that his instinctive reaction to the most violent storm was to say it had cleared the air. He conveyed a confident message of victory that made most people become dismissive of any notion of power sharing.49 He even slammed as "disinformation" a statement by the United Nations Special Envoy that the northern half of the country had fallen to the rebels,50 and condemned the evacuation of British nationals as pandering to rebel tune to spread panic.51 But *West Africa* Magazine was not convinced. In its editorial of December 21, 1998, it opined: "In Sierra Leone, there has been no end in sight to the bloody conflict that is taking place in the country's interior. When President Clinton's Special Envoy, the Reverend Jesse Jackson, visited Freetown and called for negotiations with the rebels, some government ministers were said to be privately opposed to such a move. They believe that the RUF will be defeated militarily. But some think their real motive for opposing negotiations may have been founded on self-preservation. If the men in the bush were to be brought into the fold, so the argument goes, then some of those who are now in positions of power may have to make way for the newcomers. If so, a rethink by these politicians may well be in order."

Right up to the eve of the invasion, the citizens of Freetown were being lured into a false sense of security. "We have effectively thrown a security dragnet around the capital and residents need not have any fear," a Nigerian military officer boasted.52 When independent journalists like Winston Ojukutu-Macauley reported something different, they were swiftly thrown into jail. When the rebels finally struck, it not only dented Nigeria's image as a regional super-power, it shattered public confidence in its ability to defend the country. In the vain hope of vanquishing the rebels and redeeming its bruised military pride, something resembling a scorched-earth policy came close to characterising the Nigerian military's pursuits in eastern Freetown. Throughout those heady days, President Kabbah again lost autonomy, looking more like a titular head momentarily separated from his authority.

(i) *Cease-fire that never was*

After holding his silence for a week, Kabbah suddenly appeared at a press conference at the Lungi International Airport on January 7 and announced a cease-fire. Foday Sankoh had become a prisoner of General Maxwell Khobe, the Nigerian military officer whom Kabbah had appointed chief of the Sierra Leone armed forces. He took him out of Pademba Road Prison on December 23. Kabbah told the press that Sankoh had agreed to a cease-fire in return for his freedom.

But Sam "Maskita" Bockarie, RUF Field Commander, was not convinced. He insisted on Sankoh's release before agreeing to a cease-fire. On January 14, President Charles Taylor of Liberia announced that he had brokered a peace deal between the RUF and the Government. But Kabbah promptly dismissed him, saying Taylor was only concerned about protecting his mercenary fighters who had been trapped in the fighting in Freetown.

What this particular episode demonstrates, more than anything else, is that Kabbah still harboured hopes of gaining a military victory over the rebels. In fact, he was demanding military assistance from anybody who cared to listen, even from the United Nations and the Western Powers whom he accused of playing double standards in that they were fighting for democracy in Iraq but "doing nothing to defend democracy" in Sierra Leone. "If the world believes in democracy then it should come to our aid," he declared. For a man who had spent more than 20 years in the service of the world body, this outburst was most extraordinary. It showed he had learnt but little, for he ought to have been familiar with the ways of the United Nations and how it works, particularly the fact that by charter, by precedent and by principle, the organisation is bound to seek conflict resolution primarily by peaceful means.

It also shows that so long as Kabbah remained in that mood, the nightmare of the citizens of Freetown was not going to end. Kabbah's bravado came into the open during a visit by Nigeria's new Foreign Minister, Olisemeka, on January 25. He proclaimed: "Now there is only a military solution. We have to push the rebels far, far from Freetown."53 By this time Kabbah carried no risk: he was the only President in the whole world with no peace and no army he could call his own.

Earlier on, Julius Spencer had warned that because the Nigerian troops were having difficulty engaging the rebels, who were then mixing with civilians in the streets, anyone found in the streets would be considered a rebel and would be shot on sight. On the other hand, when the rebels captured the eastern and central parts of Freetown, they were forcing residents to come out and demonstrate for peace, threatening to burn down their houses. When the citizens yielded to rebel coercion, Nigerian jet bombers were despatched to drop bombs on them. About 30 people, mostly civilians, were killed in one such incident in central Freetown on January 7. In reply to Mark Doyle of the BBC, the Nigerian Commander said he would not hesitate to use any weapon to deal with any potential threat.54 Such was the dreadful dilemma of the hapless citizens of Freetown, caught between Charybdis and Scylla.

Thus the door to dialogue became shut and the voice of moderation marginalised each time the rebels gained the upper hand and the government was struggling to regain control of lost ground. It was no different on January 6, 1999. The Alliance for Peace and Democracy in Sierra Leone, a London-based group of Sierra Leoneans concerned about the terrible woes the conflict was inflicting, made an appeal to the warring parties. It called for a political solution around three main objectives: first, an immediate cease-fire accompanied by a comprehensive peace agreement; second, respect for the fundamental tenets of the Constitution in order to guarantee future stability; and, third, the holding of genuinely free and fair elections under international supervision. It also appealed to them to eschew violence and embrace political dialogue and inclusivism as underlined by both the Abidjan and Conakry Peace Plans.

The question of democratic legitimacy

Political power is, rightly, now bound up with the basic notion of legitimacy, which is founded solely on genuine democratic elections. But if elections are only as good as the conditions in which they are held, then few would disagree that the conditions in Sierra Leone in February and March 1996 were not exactly the most conducive for democratic elections. Most parts of the country were impenetrable due to the war, and more than half of the population was either displaced internally or sheltering abroad as refugees. In those circumstances, to describe the elections as lawful would be unexceptional but to say they were democratic is quite another matter. Yet it was this designation, parroted and dramatised by the government, that took centre-stage throughout the entire debate on the conflict after 1996.

Led by the United Kingdom and the Commonwealth, which respectively had bankrolled and monitored the elections of 1996, international condemnation of the *coup* was strong. It stemmed mainly from the belief that the elections had been democratic. In its editorial of January 15, 1999, *The Times* encapsulated the thinking in the West, when it wrote: "Sierra Leone now comes absolute bottom of various United Nations indices of global poverty. By any measure, it would seem to be a failed state. Complete breakdown, with the country divided between feuding warlords and no government able to exercise authority beyond the capital, would be a catastrophe – not just for Sierra Leoneans but for all West Africa......However grim the picture looks now, failure is not predestined..... President Kabbah has not so far proved a capable leader, but the symbolism of his democratic election is still important. It will be a costly and long struggle. But for the sake of all West Africa, Sierra Leone must not be allowed to fail."55

Is symbolic democracy enough? In the First World, where democracy is promoted as an international legal right, elections are either genuinely democratic or they are not. Voters may not like the victor or his party but will never resort to violence to remove him, because of the confidence they repose in the fairness of both the electoral process and its supervision. In the case of the Third World, however, there seems to be a tendency in the First World to tolerate election results even if they are not genuinely free and fair. Fairness in this context is seen as a thing of beauty, lying wholly in the eyes of the beholder. But why should the standard be different for the Third World if the principle of democracy is universal and indivisible? Why should a government be enthroned with democratic legitimacy if it is not one established by genuinely free and fair elections?

For Kofi Annan, it was democracy that was at stake in Sierra Leone. "The United Nations and the international community firmly uphold the principle that the will of the people shall be the basis of the authority of governments, and that governments, democratically elected, shall not be overthrown by force," he said. "The United Nations and the international community attach the greatest importance to a democratic order for Sierra Leone....The United Nations continues to stand ready to assist the people of Sierra Leone in their quest for a society grounded in democracy, the rule of law, respect for human rights, and the pursuit of peace and national reconciliation," he added.[56]

That statement underlines two things. First, the belief that President Kabbah had been democratically elected. Second, the desire by the Western Powers to emphasise their newly-acquired distaste for undemocratic regimes. The actual conditions surrounding the elections have received scant or no attention at all, as indeed also the protestations by the democratic opposition that the elections had begun with an identification of the winner followed by the adjustment of the voting figures to guarantee the result. In other words, what happened in 1996 was nothing short of manipulative democracy. Some foreign envoys in the country seemed to have been closely consulted. They did not raise any objection, perhaps because they believed it unwise to rock the boat when the country was trying to rid itself of a military junta. It is as simple as that.

In its publication *Comments on the Presidential Run-Off Election, March 15, 1996*, the main opposition party, the United National People's Party (UNPP), strongly challenged the fairness of the poll. It claimed that there had been substantial irregularities to vitiate the result, including multiple voting by registered voters and voting by unregistered persons including under-age children.

In the first presidential election of February 26, 1996, the average voter turnout for the whole country was 49.8 percent of registered vote. Voting took place in all electoral districts except Tonkolili, a stronghold of presidential contender, John Karefa-Smart, due to a contrived upsurge of rebel activity on the eve of the poll. Karefa-Smart therefore received only 22 per cent of the national poll as against 35.9 per cent for Kabbah. As no one obtained the statutory minimum of 55 per cent on the first ballot, the two leading contenders went forward to a run-off on March 15. On March 17, INEC announced Kabbah as winner, with 59 per cent of the vote, defeating Karefa-Smart with 41 per cent.

The UNPP argued that at least in four districts, traditional SLPP strongholds, the voter turnout was more than 100 per cent. After strong protestation by Karefa-Smart, the Chairman of INEC, Dr James Jonah, reluctantly admitted that there had indeed been serious irregularities. However, his remedy was to "penalise" Kabbah by reducing his vote by 70,000. This in effect adjusted the total vote in each of the affected districts to the statutory limit of 100 per cent of registered voters.

Jonah was apparently suffocated by the huge percentage of fraudulent vote. He thought by simply reducing Kabbah's vote to equal 100 per cent of registered voters that would take care of the problem. Legally speaking, it did not, because his action was not justified by the electoral law. Elections are contested and won on the basis of pre-established ground rules known to and accepted by all contenders in advance of the poll; they are not changed mid-stream at the whim of the election invigilator. Moreover, the identification of the rogue votes seemed selective and subjective and therefore neither fair nor accurate. How sure could anyone be that, of the 100 per cent votes that remained, they too were not tainted with fraud? At the end of the elections, Jonah was promptly rewarded, initially, as Ambassador to the United Nations and subsequently as Minister of Finance, making the stain of a rogue election look somewhat indelible. Indeed most people have viewed these appointments with a great deal of cynicism.

If INEC thought the irregularities were substantial enough to warrant reducing the winner's overall vote, the presumption must be that there indeed was a serious miscarriage of electoral justice.

Rectifying injustice in such a case, however, demanded more than expunging the rogue votes especially where one was not at all sure of the quantum of such votes. Two possibilities could have been considered. First, annulling the poll in the affected areas but this would have had the effect of penalising or disenfranchising genuine voters who may have had nothing to do with the fraud. A second and more rational approach would have been to invalidate the poll and conduct fresh elections in each affected district. Neither was done.

INEC's first computer printout on March 16 shows a poll in excess of 100 per cent for the following districts: Bonthe (155.2%), Kailahun (138.7%), Kenema (116.9%) and Pujehun (339.1%). Of these, the surplus vote cast for Kabbah was Bonthe (147.2%), Kailahun (136.8%), Kenema (109.8%) and Pujehun (327.9%). Had the poll been annulled in these four districts, the result from the rest of the country would have given Kabbah only 37 per cent as against 63 per cent for Karefa-Smart. The following day, a second computer print-out was published, adjusting the figures for the four districts as follows: Bo 99.6%, Bonthe 97.6%, Pujehun 97.2%, Kailahun 100%, Kenema 100%.[57] Not even countries with compulsory voting have been able to record this kind of turn-out.

The affected districts, undeniably strongholds of the SLPP, were the very districts which, again as reported by INEC, had borne the "the brunt of [the] war more than any other region in the country". And, continued the report, "[t]housands of villages with populations less than 1,500 persons had been completely obliterated and the inhabitants rendered hopeless. Most of these are living as internally displaced persons in the safe havens of major towns. A substantial proportion live in refugee situations in Guinea and Liberia."[58]

This physical situation notwithstanding, INEC claimed that voter registration had been completed in 30 out of 44 chiefdoms in the eastern province.[59] Moreover, on polling day, voter turn-out was recorded as 138.7 per cent for Kailahun and 116.9 per cent for Kenema, while for Kono district, the most populous of the three, it was only 48.1 percent.

Quite apart from this, when the voting figures for the southern and eastern districts are compared with those of other districts, which were then less severely affected by the rebel war and therefore better able to record higher voter turn-out, the result is extraordinary. For example, in the whole of the Western Area (including Freetown), which by then had only experienced marginal rebel incursion, voter turnout was only 55.7 percent of registered voters for Western Urban (Freetown) and 43.9 percent for Western Rural. In the North, Bombali District recorded 67.31 percent, while Kambia had only 47.3 percent, Port Loko 39.95 percent and Tonkolili 79.8 percent. The UNPP candidate won all these northern districts by very wide margins. Can this depressed turnout in the Western, Northern and Kono districts be attributable to voter apathy? If so, why was it peculiar to districts that had been comparatively less affected by the war? The war situation could hardly be blamed for the low voter turn-out in those areas since most of the population had, by the time of the poll, migrated to the urban centres, where they were able to vote without fear of intimidation. Some other explanation must therefore be found.

On top of all this, very close to the poll, a statement, attributed to the RUF, had appeared in the pro-SLPP press, threatening in no uncertain terms that unless the SLPP presidential candidate was returned winner, the country should not expect that the RUF would lay down its arms. It was even widely suspected to have helped in rigging the vote for the SLPP in the southern and eastern districts. This immediately raised speculations about the relationship between the RUF and the SLPP and they lingered until Foday Sankoh himself publicly confirmed that he had been a member of the SLPP.60

Finally, reference may be made to a statement contained in a position paper submitted by the AFRC delegation to the Abidjan meeting of the Ecowas Committee of Four on July 17, 1997. In that statement, the AFRC said that the 1996 elections had been "massively rigged and shamelessly manipulated." Prior to that, on July 1, in another statement, the AFRC junta had actually confessed to some of its own members rigging the vote for the SLPP candidate. It declared as follows:

> "A lot has been said and written about the 'democratic nature' of the Kabbah government. It is true that elections were held, but the time has come for the truth about those sham elections to be laid bare. It should be known, as we do trust that it will never recur, that elements of the Sierra Leone Army, on the instructions of the National

Provisional Ruling Council (NPRC) leadership, and with the tacit connivance of INEC, were instrumental in causing the elections to be won by the SLPP candidate, Alhaji Ahmad Tejan Kabbah, in parts of the southern and eastern provinces. The collaborators in this anti-democratic conspiracy were so over-zealous that their operation resulted in a totality of votes cast in those areas being far in excess of the total number of registered voters. When this was brought to the attention of the Chairman of INEC, Dr James Jonah, his disingenuous response was unilaterally to 'penalise' Tejan Kabbah by reducing the votes cast in the relevant areas to equal 100% of the registered electors. Thus has Sierra Leone been saddled with the 'undemocratic' Kabbah government. It is in the same light that the appointment of James Jonah as Sierra Leone's Ambassador and Permanent Representative to the United Nations is to be seen, as his reward for a fixing job well done. James Jonah's 'hysterical' ravings and ranting, following our intervention, must be seen in a similar light."61

Whatever view one takes of this confession, its evidential value is undeniable. It lies in the fact that it is a voluntary confession by the military itself that some of its own members had been guilty of vote rigging in favour of President Kabbah.

This alone is enough to cast a shadow over the fairness of the 1996 elections. So the less said about those elections as the foundation of legitimacy for the SLPP government the better. The only reason for the opposition not subjecting the INEC decision to judicial challenge was that, had it done so and succeeded, it would have meant holding fresh elections. The likelihood then was that the NPRC junta would have contrived every possible excuse, including the lash of financial penury, to delay holding fresh elctions. And the longer they delayed the longer they would have remained in office.

The 1996 irregularities also point to a dark cloud hovering over the next election if its supervision were to be left in hands other than those of an independent and impartial international arbiter. For the true test of the democratic process is not so much the organisation and conduct of the first election as whether that first election would be followed by others, consistent with democratic values and established electoral laws.

African electoral experience is replete with incidents of this sort. They all point to the fact that the real problem is not with the electorate but rather with incumbent political leadership. Their intolerance of dissent has made democratic transition an especially stressful exercise in many African countries. Sierra Leone is no exception. Almost every *coup d'état* in that country has had roots either in electoral fraud or in the unwillingness of the incumbent to accept defeat and give up power.

CHAPTER 2

Intervention by Invitation

Introduction

The first and second successful *coups d'état* of 1967 and 1992 respectively did not involve foreign military intervention and none was sought. Not so with the *coup* of 1997. From exile in Guinea, the overthrown "democratically-elected" President Kabbah invited the Nigerian autocrat, General Sani Abacha, to intervene militarily to reverse the *coup* that had toppled him. The two leaders capitalised on the strong wave of international condemnation of the *coup*, claimed a moral high ground and launched a military campaign in the name of fighting evil. They believed they could reverse the *coup* with a minimum of force, remembering how poorly the Sierra Leone army had been equipped, not to speak of its mangled morale. However, it turned out to be a gross underestimation. Even more surprising was the quiescence of the other Ecowas member states, which were much more concerned about Nigeria's deployment of military power in the region and about violations of the Ecowas Treaty than about anything else.

To the international community, the *coup* was unacceptable. The democratic legitimacy of President Kabbah's government was considered superior to the doctrine of effective control. So even though Kabbah had lost effective control of his country, this alone did not invalidate his invitation to General Abacha. It had also helped to suppress international criticism even though the intervention was being undertaken outside the framework of the United Nations Charter and by a military despot who was himself not free of international opprobrium.

The question remains nevertheless whether Abacha was justified to intervene militarily in a conflict that was purely internal? How different was it from that of Ecowas in Liberia in 1990? These are some of the key issues addressed in this chapter.

Foreign troops in Sierra Leone prior to May 25, 1997

Before Kabbah's invitation, it is significant to remember that a battalion of Nigerian troops was already in Sierra Leone. It had come there in 1991 at the invitation of President Momoh. Its mandate was limited to assisting the Sierra Leone army in its campaign against the RUF rebels, who, at that time, were being aided by the NPFL faction in Liberia. This assistance involved the manning of designated key points and key installations in and around Freetown initially - later extended to the provincial cities of Bo and Kenema - in order to relieve the Sierra Leone army of such duties and enable them to go to the frontline. As the then Ecowas Executive Secretary, I played a part in persuading the Nigerian leader, General Ibrahim Badamasi Babangida, that such assistance was both necessary and justified. I also had the rare privilege of twice briefing in camera the National Security Council of the Nigerian Military Government on the matter. Babangida had apparently encountered some resistance in the Council to Nigeria becoming involved in another foreign military adventure while the first one in Liberia was still unsettled. He therefore despatched General Abacha, then Minister of Defence and Chief of Defence Staff, to Freetown to make an on-the-spot assessment. I accompanied him on that mission. Abacha was persuaded and he so reported to the Council on his return to Nigeria. As a result, a battalion of Nigerian soldiers left for Sierra Leone.

Before this direct involvement, Nigeria's assistance had been limited to sending planeloads of arms and ammunition to President Momoh's government. Momoh visited Abuja after which he despatched Major Kellie Conteh in a desperate bid to obtain weapons from Nigeria.

As stated, the Nigerian troops were restricted to taking defensive roles only. They were specifically barred from taking part in military offensive save in self-defence or with the prior consent of their government. There was no formal defence pact and the arrangement was based entirely on the mutual friendship of the two leaders. Not until three years later, in mid-1994, was it formalised in a Memorandum of Understanding signed between General Abdulsalami Abubakar, then Chief of Defence Staff, representing the Nigerian Government, and Captain Komba Kambo, representing the NPRC junta. Under the Memorandum, the role of the Nigerian contingent was enlarged to include military training. For this, a small group of military trainers, under the command of Brigadier Zibri, was added to the contingent. They came to be known as the Nigerian Army Technical

Assistance Group (NATAG), similar to what Nigeria had done previously for the government of The Gambia.

Thus, the initial presence of Nigerian troops in Sierra Leone was as a result of the personal friendship between Babangida and Momoh. So when Momoh was toppled by the NPRC, he could easily have requested military intervention from his friend in Nigeria. He did not, apprehensive that such intervention might have resulted in unnecessary loss of civilian life and property. Thus, even against his own best interest, Momoh clearly displayed a depth of concern for human security.

Both by design and by operation, the Nigerian army in Sierra Leone (NATAG) was not part of Ecomog though under the ultimate command of its Field Commander. Ecomog was a multilateral peace-keeping contingent established in 1990 solely for the Liberian conflict. On the other hand, NATAG was in Sierra Leone purely on a bilateral basis. The fact that it was put under the command of the Ecomog Field Commander did not make them one. It was purely fortuitous that the Field Commander was Nigerian and was also the most senior Nigerian military officer in the vicinity. So the Nigerian forces in Sierra Leone should not be confused with Ecomog in Liberia. Different regimes had governed their operations. For example, whereas Ecomog in Liberia was accountable to Ecowas through the Executive Secretary the Nigerian troops in Sierra Leone were not.

This separateness was subsequently confirmed by the Status of Forces Agreement (SOFA) between Nigeria and Sierra Leone signed on March 7, 1997. SOFA makes it clear that the preoccupation of the signatories was with the defence of Sierra Leone against external aggression and not with the internal armed conflict in the country. Article 2 reads: "The Government of the Federal Republic of Nigeria shall make available the military and security assistance of the Nigerian Forces Assistance Group (NIFAG) for the sustenance of the sovereignty and territorial integrity of the Republic of Sierra Leone". At the time SOFA was signed, fresh hostilities had just broken out between the Sierra Leone army and the RUF in breach of the cease-fire under the Abidjan Peace Accord. There was thus ample justification, if one were needed, for including unambiguous clauses in SOFA to permit Nigerian forces in Sierra Leone to take part in military operations against the RUF quite apart from their right to self-defence. But no such provision was made. On the contrary, Article 21 of the SOFA specifically barred the Nigerian army from deploying in "any offensive role except in defence of its localities".

This arrangement stands in stark contrast to that for the Guinean troops in Sierra Leone, who had been there long before the Nigerians arrived. Their mandate, which flowed from a mutual defence pact between the two countries signed by President Ahmed Sekou Touré and President Siaka Stevens in the 1970s, obliged them to assist the Sierra Leone military in offensive operations against the RUF.

The invitation to intervene

Abacha was chairman of Ecowas when Kabbah sent his invitation. According to James Jonah, then Sierra Leone's Ambassador to the United Nations, Abacha and Kabbah were the best of friends just as Momoh and Babangida had been. But, unlike Momoh, Kabbah's "democratically-elected" government joined cause with a dictator to etch in blood its so-called "sovereign right" to kill its own people in the name of restoring democracy. On June 2, 1997, Abacha's army fired its first salvo at the city of Freetown.

True to Abacha's penchant for unilateralism, there had been neither consultation with other Ecowas leaders nor any vestige of evidence of an Ecowas decision in favour of military intervention. Some countries clearly broke ranks. For while the Nigerian Foreign Minister was proclaiming a right to intervene, President Rawlings of Ghana dispatched a ministerial delegation to Freetown. He even cancelled his own plans to attend the OAU summit in Harare in order to devote his personal effort to the search for peace. Kwamena Ahwoi, Ghana's Foreign Minister, after recalling the Ecomog experience in Liberia, explained his country's stance. "Ghana's approach would be to stress more on a negotiated political settlement which upholds respect for the democratic choice of the people of Sierra Leone," he said.62 Radio Ghana, in its report on the June 2 military intervention, characterised it as "the Nigerian operation". Victor Gbeho, then Deputy Minister of Foreign Affairs, led the Ghanaian delegation to Freetown on June 19. On arrival, he declared that "the best way to resolve the crisis is by diplomatic means to reach a negotiated settlement rather than by fighting". At the end of the visit, the AFRC Chairman assured the Ghanaian delegation of their intention to demit power within six months after setting up a comprehensive programme of disarmament and demobilisation.

Differing perceptions about the crisis in Sierra Leone thus surfaced within Ecowas. Abacha, like a Roman Emperor, believed solely in his military might, while Rawlings relied on a political solution. It also explains why Abacha had cared little about the need for regional consensus. Given these differences, it is not surprising that an editorial in *The New York Times* characterised the operation thus: "The first Nigerian military moves in Sierra Leone went badly. After Nigerian naval forces bombarded the capital city, Freetown, local troops attacked and overran Nigerian positions. Nigeria has since sent in reinforcements and new fighting seems imminent unless Ghana's efforts to work out a negotiated solution quickly succeed."[63] According to the newspaper, the intervention had been aimed mainly at establishing Nigeria as the dominant regional power and regional policeman. In a similar editorial, *The Times* of London commented: "In Sierra Leone, the armed forces of Nigeria, one of Africa's most appalling military regimes, are now fighting to put down an armed *coup* in the name of democracy."[64] Thus, the international press had no doubt about the nature and character of the intervention.

The position of foreign governments outside the region was not different. Tony Lloyd, British Minister of State in the FCO, acknowledged on March 2, 1999, that: "When General Abacha was the military dictator in Nigeria – doing things that we could not or would not want to work alongside – there was no question of us supporting Nigerian military intervention in Sierra Leone. That ought to have been unthinkable. I make no apology for that."[65]

Ecowas leaders, who should have met almost immediately following the *coup*, did not in fact meet until August 29, three months after the first Nigerian bombardment. The conclusion, therefore, is inescapable that the Nigerian military intervention in Sierra Leone had not been based on any Ecowas decision. Nor was it carried out under its aegis. Rather the weight of evidence strongly suggests that Nigeria *qua* Nigeria had carried out the military operation unilaterally and precipitately. This is the crux of the problem and it also marks a significant point of departure with the Ecowas military action in Liberia in 1990.

If further confirmatory evidence were required for this, none can be stronger than the admission by President Kabbah himself, following his reinstatement. He said he was "grateful to Nigeria for helping us. It is a fact, an undeniable fact, that Nigeria as Nigeria has played a very important part in democracy and peace and security......"[66]

That admission contrasts with his ambivalence on the very day the Nigerian intervention took place. On May 30, 1997, tension had arisen as a result of the public disclosure by the Parliamentary Minority Leader, John Karefa-Smart, then in Freetown, that the Nigerian military was planning to attack the city in an operation code-named "Operation Wild Chase" on June 2. The attack did take place, resulting in scores of civilian casualties.[67] But, because it failed to topple the junta, President Kabbah, who was already in Conakry, tried to deny the Nigerian bombardment and to dismiss as untrue Karefa-Smart's public warnings. Karefa-Smart had been invited by both the junta and the Nigerians to mediate. He tried hard but his efforts came to nought when the Nigerian Commander, believing in the awesome might of his forces, threatened to use force if the junta did not surrender by 4:00 a.m. on June 2. The Nigerians became angry at Karefa-Smart, whom they blamed for disclosing their secret plans to bomb the city, thereby destroying their chances of a "surprise surgical strike".

With respect, this criticism is unfounded. First, Karefa-Smart had learned about "Operation Wild Chase" from the Sierra Leone junta. This obviously means that whatever the Nigerians were planning, it was no longer going to be a "surprise." Second, when the attack came, not a single military target was hit. In fact, the bombs, which had come from the direction of the Atlantic Ocean, had fallen on residential areas along the seafront. So there was nothing "surgical" about the strike. Thirdly, far be it from any intention to help the junta, the citizens of Freetown for having warned them in advance complimented Karefa-Smart. Ironically, after blaming Karefa-Smart for the failure of their operation, it was he they turned to for help when some 300 of their soldiers were taken prisoner by the junta. He interceded and secured their release, reminding the junta of its obligations under the Geneva Red Cross Conventions.[68]

Characterisation of the intervention force

The absence of Ecowas consultation notwithstanding, Abacha and Kabbah remained resolute in their characterisation of the Nigerian intervention force in Sierra Leone as "Ecomog". This was done in order to clothe it with some international or regional legitimacy. The question is whether this was not a mischaracterisation.

Ecomog had been established in 1990 specifically for the Liberian crisis.69 It consisted of military contingents drawn initially from five Ecowas member states,70 later expanded to eleven.71 It was placed under the command of a Force Commander provided by Ghana and afterwards under a succession of Field Commanders provided by Nigeria, all of whom were accountable to Ecowas through the Executive Secretary. Ecomog's mandate was to rescue and protect Ecowas citizens, to monitor and verify a cease-fire to be agreed between the belligerent parties, and to restore law and order so as to create conditions for genuine democratic elections in Liberia. Its territorial remit was Liberia where it was to remain until elections were held and an elected government installed. The operation was financed initially out of the resources of an Ecowas Special Emergency Fund. When the Fund got exhausted, each troop-contributing country was asked to take over its troops' financial and logistical responsibilities.

Thus, the remit of Ecomog was country-specific; it was not a general mandate to apply force whenever or wherever in West Africa. Nor could that mandate be altered except by the collective decision of the Ecowas leaders. Although eleven Ecowas countries were actively involved in Ecomog at the time of the *coup* in Sierra Leone, only Nigeria sent troops to take part in the June 2 attack and subsequent offensives. No other Ecowas troops participated.72 This remained the position until 1999.

Thus, prior to the Ecowas summit of August 29, 1997, there were no *Ecowas* or *Ecomog* forces in Sierra Leone. Nor were the forces there carrying out any Ecowas mandate. The Nigerian troops in Sierra Leone were there as Nigerian troops, purely on a bilateral basis. They were authorised neither by Ecowas nor by the United Nations. Nigeria alone, therefore, must bear full responsibility for the operations of its troops in Sierra Leone during that period.

Both as a citizen of Sierra Leone and the Executive Secretary of Ecowas responsible for the creation of Ecomog, I felt duty-bound to clarify the confusion that had arisen. I did so in a radio interview I gave to the BBC Focus on Africa Programme on June 2. I started by saying clearly that I was opposed to the *coup* that ousted President Kabbah from office. However, I was also strongly opposed to Nigeria's military intervention as contrary to the Ecowas Treaty. I suggested that instead of fighting, the citizens of Sierra Leone should see it as a challenge and a duty to resolve their internal crisis by peaceful means. They had done so before in the context of the Bintumani conferences and they could do it again if given a chance. Kabbah's government-in-exile did not agree with me and immediately branded me as a "rebel collaborator".

Under the Ecowas Protocol on Mutual Assistance in Defence 1981, military intervention is specifically barred in conflicts that are purely internal. Whatever right of intervention may have existed under general or customary international law, it is severely qualified by this Protocol, which established a particular rule of treaty law as between the parties thereto. And this particular treaty law overrides any general right of intervention that Ecowas and its member states may claim under general international law.

Collective Ecowas involvement came only after the Ecowas summit of August 29, 1997. However, in light of the treaty provision aforesaid, that involvement cannot be anything but political. This is so, because, legally speaking, the right or freedom of the collective Ecowas community cannot be greater than that of its individual member states. Secondly, even if this view is wrong, that is not the end of the matter. The Ecowas decision to intervene militarily is also up against the provisions of Article 53 of the United Nations Charter, which demand that there should be prior Security Council authorisation before any military intervention can be valid. No such authorisation was given until five weeks after the Ecowas summit, when the Council adopted resolution 1132 on October 8.

Be that as it may, Ecowas decided to establish a "sub-regional force" in August 1997 and authorised it "to employ all necessary means" to impose an embargo on Sierra Leone. Apart from Nigeria, the only other country with troops in Sierra Leone was

Guinea, but as already opined, those troops were operating under a different legal regime. Moreover, it is instructive to note that unlike the military operations in Liberia in 1990 and in Guinea-Bissau in 1998, both of which were accorded the designation of "Ecomog", that designation was withheld from the "sub-regional forces" in Sierra Leone. Furthermore, the sub-regional forces in Sierra Leone had no other command and control than that set up by the Nigerians. Indeed, the whole idea of a "sub-regional force" had been predicated upon contributions of troops by as many Ecowas countries as possible, but this did not happen until much later, in 1999, when the Nigerians were joined by a token of Ghanaian soldiers and a battalion of Malian troops.[73] Even so, the accolade "Ecomog" was still withheld from them.

The unilateral nature of the initial Nigerian action was subsequently confirmed by an explosive meeting of Ecowas Foreign Ministers in Lome on December 17, 1997. Many delegations had openly criticised Nigeria's military intervention in Sierra Leone. They protested that "Nigeria had sent thousands of troops into Sierra Leone and had imposed a total blockade months before Ecowas and the United Nations had approved limited sanctions." Furthermore, that although Ecowas had been unanimous in its condemnation of the Sierra Leone *coup* and was determined to see the deposed President restored to power, nevertheless it had "never advocated the use of force to achieve that end."[74] This chiding of Nigeria is all the more remarkable because Ecowas members were well known for adhering to a convention of not scolding each other in public. So the frankness of the criticisms is significant. It probably also explains why, in spite of numerous appeals, no other Ecowas state saw fit to send troops to the "sub-regional force", particularly when they were needed most to enhance operational effectiveness. As admitted by James Jonah in a press briefing on February 17, 1998: "Of all governments, Nigeria is the only one which was prepared not only to put its treasury but also its blood in the service of Sierra Leone."[75]

The unilateralism of the Nigerian military has been further confirmed by the practice of the United Nations. After referring to foreign military action in Sierra Leone for a long time as "Ecomog," the Secretary-General, Kofi Annan, surprisingly addressed a letter dated August 13, 1999 neither to the Ecowas

Chairman (President Eyadema of Togo) nor to its Executive Secretary. Instead it was addressed to the new President of Nigeria, Olusegun Obasanjo. This missive had dealt with the question of cooperation between the sub-regional forces and UN peacekeepers in Sierra Leone, pursuant to the Lome Peace Agreement of July 7, 1999. In other words, the letter was addressed to the leader of the country whose troops they actually were.[76] President Obasanjo replied on August 19.

The appointment of Colonel Maxwell Khobe, Nigerian Task Force Commander, as head of the Sierra Leone defence forces on April 16, 1998 provides further evidence for not treating the Nigerian troops in Sierra Leone as Ecomog.[77] If Khobe had been an Ecowas or Ecomog officer, it would have been impossible for him to accept that appointment without running foul of Article 20 of the Revised Treaty of Ecowas 1993. That Article stipulates that an officer of the Community, in the performance of his duties, owes his loyalty entirely and is accountable only to the Community. In this regard, he is barred from seeking or accepting instructions from any government and is prohibited from undertaking any activity that is incompatible with his status as an international civil servant. Likewise, all member states are required to respect the international character of the staff of the Community and must not seek to influence them in the performance of their duties. If Khobe was truly a servant of the Community, then his appointment by Kabbah was a clear breach of the Ecowas Treaty. The truth is that he was not and had remained throughout as a military officer of Nigeria under the command of his Commander-in-Chief, the Nigerian head of state. Therefore there was no breach of the Ecowas Treaty.

The mandate of the sub-regional forces

The only mandate the sub-regional force had from Ecowas was to enforce an embargo on Sierra Leone. After the Ecowas Summit of August 29, 1997, the Ecomog Commander, Major-General Victor Malu, was heard breathing fire and brimstone. He said that "Ecomog needed the mandate and now that we have got it, the world would see the difference."[78] On another occasion, he added: "We have not been enforcing an embargo up to now because it was not official. We know very well how to impose a blockade, and anyone who doubts our will or ability should look at the ports in Liberia which we blocked with sunken ships".[79] These are implicit admissions by the Commander himself that his forces had operated in Sierra Leone without an Ecowas mandate prior to August 29. Nor did he have any authority to use force generally in Sierra Leone or anywhere else.

Neither did the United Nations give any such mandate under resolution 1132 (1997). On October 22, Sir John Weston, British Ambassador to the United Nations, expressing dismay at Nigeria's aerial bombings in Sierra Leone, questioned the authority Nigeria had to undertake such action. He even threatened to raise the matter in the Security Council, adding that several other delegations were similarly concerned about the bombings, which killed and injured scores of civilians and caused thousands to flee the capital.[80]

Monie Captan, Liberian Foreign Minister, was no less critical: "Liberia does not support the bombing in Sierra Leone by Ecomog and will not encourage the use of its land to attack the junta in Sierra Leone. Our position is very clear. We will support the UN resolution and the decision taken by Ecowas. The decision of Ecowas is that no use of force is authorised in Sierra Leone whatsoever, and we support that decision."[81] This was immediately followed by a closure of Liberia's borders with Sierra Leone.

Now the proper definition of the mandate of the sub-regional force in Sierra Leone is important as it could have a bearing on the future of regional security in West Africa. This is because the concept underpinning the creation of Ecomog remains valid, with unlimited potentialities in Africa and beyond. Though limited in objectives, its accomplishments, particularly in restoring Liberia to durable peace and stability through elections in July 1997, have been widely acclaimed. Those elections brought eight years of internecine conflict to an end. Abacha's unilateral military adventure in Sierra Leone, on the other hand, being a complete aberration, must never be allowed to contaminate Ecowas' worthy achievements. It is therefore important to distinguish the two military operations. Ecomog only started operating in Sierra Leone after the Lome Peace Accord was signed on July 7, 1999.

The kamajor affair

Private militias have been prominent in the Sierra Leone tragedy. The most active is the *kamajor* militia, a Mende word meaning traditional hunter. The *kamajors*, drawn entirely from one ethnic group dominant in southern and eastern Sierra Leone, were brought into organised formation after the NPRC *coup* in 1992. Since then they have fought alongside the army against the RUF. When the SLPP came to power in 1996 they fought against the army, perceived as pro-APC, as well as against the RUF. And when the army seized power from the SLPP in 1997 and formed the AFRC junta, they allied themselves with the Nigerian army and fought against both the AFRC junta and the RUF. Its true origin as an organised fighting force is as obscure as its frequently changing allegiances.

Conceptualising the *kamajor* militia as a sort of *leveé en masse* by the civilian population determined to defend their towns and villages against advancing rebels may be valid. However, this concept breaks down every time they turn their guns on the army. In any event, both the Abidjan Peace Accord of 1996 and the Lome Peace Agreement of 1999 demand that all civil defence forces should be disarmed and demobilised. Whereas the NPRC had disbanded the *tamaboros* and *kapras* (also meaning hunter) in the north long before the Abidjan Accord was even conceived, this was not extended to the *kamajors*. They were allowed to continue and progressively their activities began to attract official insignia, leading many an observer to think that their sponsors might have been harbouring something more than the agenda of a *leveé en masse*.

Protected by their chief promoter and leader, Samuel Hinga Norman, Deputy Defence Minister in the Kabbah government, the *kamajor* militias have survived notwithstanding protestations from the military. They began to see themselves as strong enough to challenge even the army and many times they did. Little, if anything, was done to restrain them.

Also before the *coup*, the policy of the Kabbah government was aimed at downsizing the national army from an estimated 14,000 to about 3,000 soldiers. To implement this policy the plan then was first to absorb the *kamajors* into the national army in order to neutralise the threat that suspected pro-APC military elements were posing. Had this been implemented, it would have had the effect of unknotting the delicate ethnic balance that the military had come to symbolise in years past and of drawing resentment and disaffection from other ethnic groups in the country.

Reliance upon the *kamajor* militia continued well after the *coup*. For instance, a contingent estimated at over 3,000 *kamajors* began a push towards Bo, the second largest city in Sierra Leone, in late August 1997 from positions along the Liberian border, and was reported to have already overrun some villages along the main highway linking Bo to south-eastern Sierra Leone. People, who ordinarily carried only hunting rifles made by local blacksmiths, were now sporting a huge arsenal of modern weapons, including armoured cars, rocket-propelled grenades, bombs, and brand new assault rifles. Foreign sources were accused of supplying these weapons,[82] and many fingers pointed at the Nigerian army as the main supplier.[83] It also reportedly received the lion share of the weapons supplied by Sandline International contrary to the arms embargo under resolution 1132 of the UN Security Council.

Most worrisome is the obscure agenda of the *kamajors*. When so little was, and is still, known about them, public caution is natural and understandable. However, one thing at least is clear. It is a very dangerous thing for a state to maintain two or more rival armies; it is even worse when one army is public and the other is private. It is worse still when one of them is ethnically based. To give the *kamajors* a less than tribal outlook, the SLPP dubbed them the title of civil defence force They have publicly pledged loyalty to the SLPP in return for financial support and equipment. This, in turn, has had the effect of heightening concern and provoking other ethnic groups, like the Temnes and Konos, to set up their own private militias and to request official training and logistics for them. All this was happening at a time when history and common sense dictated the urgent need for a comprehensive programme of disarmament of all combatants and private militias in the country.

The Nigerian military may be forgiven if, at the beginning, it was not too familiar with the ethnic bias of the *kamajor* militia when it decided to arm them. Its main motive then was that it needed an ally and did not much care where it came from. However, it learnt its lessons fast. By January 1998, it had itself become sceptical about the true motives of its erstwhile ally. First, it accused them of being more interested in mining diamonds for self-enrichment than in fighting the rebels.84 Secondly, to the discomfiture of the government, the *kamajors* all too frequently put themselves beyond the pale of military discipline, forcing the Nigerians to express misgivings about their suitability for the new national army. They preferred instead the disbanded soldiers whom they described as better trained, more experienced and already battle-tested.85 The failure of the *kamajor* leadership to arm-twist the Nigerians often led to skirmishes between them.

Nigeria's unilateral embargo on Sierra Leone

Before the *coup*, Sierra Leone had already been placed at the very bottom of the United Nations list of poor countries in the whole world. There were also warnings of an impending food crisis that was growing worse by the day. The food deficit forecast was put at more than 80,000 tons, which could only be met by food aid. By the beginning of July 1997, food prices had soared on account of shortages, and starvation was gripping various parts of the country. Red Cross officials recorded 15 deaths by starvation in the townships of Mapaki and Mabonto in the north, 68 in four chiefdoms of Moyamba District in the south while residents of Bo were reported to have resorted to eating sapling stems.

It was not different in the health sector, whose alarm signals were becoming very audible. ICRC described the situation as rapidly deteriorating and likely to grow worse with the onset of the rainy season. Already, there had been sharp increases in the number of cases of malaria, Lassa fever, dysentery and respiratory infections. "The people cannot afford any more to buy medicine because there is only little cash flow in the country [with the banks closed]. And, on the other side, the stock of medicine available in the country is getting scarce. So we have started to operate different clinics and health centres in Freetown," the ICRC delegate had warned. Similarly, the health authorities in Makeni reported that in just two days more than 320 children had died in the northern province alone from cholera and typhoid fever and that hundreds more were in a critical condition.86

Thus, by mid-July 1997, Sierra Leone was already trapped not only by war but also by famine and disease, which were growing at a most alarming rate. The signals were all too evident that the situation could spiral out of control. Notwithstanding, the Nigerian intervention force did not hesitate to impose a unilateral blockade on the country.

The precise date when this blockade started is unclear, but by July 12, just days before the first diplomatic engagement between Ecowas and the AFRC junta, it was said to be already in force. Apart from air and sea, the blockade was extended to the highway linking Freetown with the rest of the country, preventing even local foodstuff and produce from entering the city. In a rare demonstration of remorse for the widespread suffering that this blockade caused, Colonel Maxwell Khobe, Nigerian Task Force Commander in Sierra Leone, ordered the opening of the Orugu Bridge at Jui, just outside Freetown. His was just before the peace talks between Ecowas and the AFRC junta at Abidjan in July 1997. However, he warned that: "If the talks ...fail..... and Ecomog is given the mandate by Ecowas to forcefully remove the coup-makers from power, Ecomog will invade Freetown and bomb the city to remove them."[87]

On July 31, following the collapse of the talks in Abidjan, Tom Ikimi, Nigeria's Foreign Minister, gave notice of toughening the blockade. "We will do nothing that will hurt the ordinary citizens of Sierra Leone, but products like petroleum products, food, and arms and ammunition would be restricted completely." Turning food into a weapon of war, he added: "The effect of an embargo on food .... on the civilian population is unfortunate, but those who seized power in Sierra Leone have to be taught a lesson".[88]

On August 4 also came the announcement that the Nigerian leader had ordered a full-scale embargo on Sierra Leone.[89] Before that, he had merely warned business interests in Sierra Leone to withdraw, adding that with the successful conclusion of the Liberian peace process, his junta now had plenty of time to devote to the crisis in Sierra Leone.[90] Following this presidential decree, the Nigerian Commander, on August 6, warned all states to observe his country's "economic blockade against the junta in Sierra Leone" and international shipping and airlines to keep out of Sierra Leone's territorial waters and airspace. "Any action in contravention of this warning," the statement went on "is at the peril of the ship or aircraft concerned. Ecomog reserves the right to mete out appropriate reprisals if this warning is violated."[91]

The AFRC junta in Freetown protested angrily. They challenged the Nigerian embargo as "illegal" in that no organisation with proper competence had authorised it. They concluded their protest with a call for a negotiated settlement, adding: "As a member of the international community, we have stressed that the best method to help Sierra Leone in the crisis is to allow or create a forum for peaceful negotiation and diplomacy."92

It did not take long before the Nigerian blockade was put to the test. A Russian ship, MV Ivanov, laden with nearly 7,000 tons of rice was the first cargo boat to evade the embargo and dock at Freetown on July 31. It was greeted by cheering crowds of starving civilians at the quay.93 A Ukrainian ship, MV Kapitan, also took food into Freetown. The captain of the ship had reportedly warned the Nigerians not to interfere with his ship. "In the event that we are attacked while delivering food and other essential supplies to Sierra Leone, we will prove to the Nigerians what military might we also have. Ukraine has one of the largest naval fleets in the world and Nigerians know the might of Ukraine where the most deadly military weapons are made," he said.94 A Hong Kong-owned ship, flying the Panamanian flag, also evaded the blockade and reached Freetown with a cargo of marine fuel oil for electricity generation. Another Hong Kong-registered tanker, MV Jian She 31, reportedly carried 55,000 tons of gasoline and 2,000 tons of gas oil on August 10. By then, the fuel shortage in Freetown had grown so acute that petrol was selling at three times the pre-coup price. Food shortages had also worsened, due partly to the unauthorised blockade and partly to the lack of fuel to transport supplies from the rural areas.

The Nigerians were well aware that their blockade was unauthorised. So they greeted with great enthusiasm the Ecowas decision to impose an embargo on Sierra Leone on August 29, 1997. However, they erroneously believed that that Ecowas decision alone was sufficient to give them legal authority. While the Field Commander in Liberia was declaring his new mandate as sufficient to bring down the junta, his Task Force Commander in Sierra Leone was promising the strictest policing of the country's territorial waters that would ensure that even canoes did not dodge the blockade.95 Accordingly, the tempo of naval surveillance increased. On September 4, the Nigerians fired on two container vessels to prevent them from berthing in Freetown. Some of the shells missed and fell on a residential suburb in Freetown. The following day a Greek-Cypriot ship carrying rice, MV Proteus, docked in Freetown after she had been fired at. Three days later, Nigerian Alpha jet fighters bombed a Ukrainian cargo ship, MV Seaway, as she offloaded cargo at the quay. A local shipping company official said that both vessels were carrying rice.96

Thus seen, contrary to international law and practice, the Nigerians declined to exempt humanitarian supplies from their so-called blockade, inflicting untold suffering on the civilian population. They insisted that all humanitarian supplies bound for Sierra Leone must first go through Liberia or Guinea for inspection and dismissed as "immaterial" international concerns about the delay this would cause. The result was a significant rise in infant morbidity and mortality due to malnutrition.97 One might wonder what the international reaction would have been if horrifying images of starving and dying children had been flashed on prime time television in the West?

While the Nigerian blockade was in operation, marine insurance premiums inevitably shot up. The London-based seafarers union, the International Transport Workers Federation, condemned the Nigerian blockade and British insurers added Sierra Leone to their black list. This immediately subjected ships going into Sierra Leonean waters to additional war risk premiums. Moreover, the Lloyds Underwriters' Association and the Institute of London Underwriters issued a general notice of cancellation, effective from midnight on September 12, 1997, affecting most insurance coverage, which could now only be obtained upon payment of very high premiums.98

Even after the adoption of limited sanctions by the United Nations on October 8, the Nigerians continued to use their Alpha jet fighters to fire at ships allegedly attempting to run the blockade. A statement by Ecomog Headquarters in Monrovia threatened to attack two vessels, MV Sky and MV Mercury, if they failed to leave Freetown by a given deadline. "The ships ...currently discharging in Sierra Leonean waters … will be neutralised by Ecomog military aircraft if they fail to leave," the statement had warned. They accused the vessels of delivering arms and oil products to the junta and claimed the right under the UN mandate to strike at them within the territorial waters of Sierra Leone.99

All this shows how much power the Nigerian forces had arrogated to themselves, power that resolution 1132 (1997) of the Security Council did not give them. That resolution had merely authorised Ecowas, in conformity with applicable international standards, to halt inward-bound maritime shipping in order to inspect and verify their cargoes and destinations. It certainly did not authorise the random bombing of maritime shipping.

It is impossible to assume that this misapplication of the United Nations embargo by the Nigerians was merely the result of ignorance. On the contrary, a statement by Ecomog Headquarters on December 10, 1997, reveals just how much they knew what they were doing. A Chinese tanker, the Haigon You-301, with her crew of 17 persons, had been intercepted and arrested. The ship, which had been accused of violating the United Nations embargo by attempting to supply fuel to fishing trawlers within Sierra Leone's territorial waters, was escorted to the port of Monrovia for interrogation and search.[100] This clearly shows that the Nigerians were well aware of the limitations on their power and that they were capable of enforcing the embargo correctly if they wanted to.

CHAPTER 3

The Role of Ecowas

The OAU mandate to Ecowas

The *coup* in Sierra Leone coincided with the holding of the OAU's annual summit in Harare, Zimbabwe. Nigeria was represented there in full force, augmented by a delegation from the exiled government of President Kabbah, which was allowed to take Sierra Leone's seat. The case these two delegations presented went unchallenged as they campaigned vigorously for the use of force. Kofi Annan backed them. He strongly exhorted African leaders not to accept as *fait accompli*, *coups* which topple elected governments sometimes for sectional interests and sometimes simply for their own. Nonetheless, the OAU did not sanction the application of force in Sierra Leone.

Nor was the mood outside of the OAU favourable to military intervention, especially one led by General Abacha's military junta. The United States, for example, while deploring the *coup* for overturning an elected government, did not conceal its opposition to the use of force. Nicholas Burns, State Department Spokesman, stated: "We have not taken a position of direct support for the Nigerians. But we do support the objective that the rebels cannot win. They cannot succeed in overturning a democratically-elected government and installing in its place a bunch of military officers who do not know how to run a country."101 Britain's position was similar. Baroness Symons, Parliamentary Under-Secretary of State in the FCO, even after the sacking of the junta, stated: "Her Majesty's Government welcome the fact that the rule of the military junta in Freetown has been brought to an end, but we do not endorse the Ecomog action. It was important that in all these circumstances regional organisations act within their mandate from the Security Council."102 Her counterpart in the House of Commons, Tony Lloyd, Minister of State in the FCO, buttressed this when he said that: "while we welcome the fact that the rule of the military junta had been brought to an end, we were unable wholeheartedly to endorse the Ecomog action. We believe that any use of force should be based in international law."103

On June 4, the OAU adopted a resolution on Sierra Leone. It condemned the *coup* and called for the immediate restoration of constitutional order. It also called on all African countries and the rest of the international community to withhold recognition from the junta, and especially appealed to the leaders of Ecowas "to assist the people of Sierra Leone to restore constitutional order to their country."104 The OAU also underlined "the imperative need to implement the Abidjan Peace Agreement" which, it said, "continued to serve as a viable framework for peace, stability and reconciliation in Sierra Leone."

This decision was without precedent. The OAU had never fashioned out any rules for judging the legality or otherwise of regimes in Africa which come into existence unconstitutionally. The key question therefore is on what principle was the OAU decision based? Can it stand in the face of the exclusionary principle of non-intervention in internal affairs embodied in Article 3(2) of its Charter?

These questions are all the more important when viewed against the failure of the organisation to act in a parallel situation in Congo (Brazzaville) in October 1997. The constitutional government of President Pascal Lissouba had been violently overthrown by his adversary, former President Denis Sassou Nguesso, backed by foreign forces from neighbouring countries. There could be no clearer case for OAU condemnation. Like Sierra Leone, an elected constitutional government was overthrown by violent means resulting in a massive outflow of refugees, yet the OAU did not condemn it. Even worse than Sierra Leone, the overthrow was carried out with the help of foreign forces, contrary to the Charter of the OAU. Still there was no condemnation.105

Be that as it may, there was acknowledgment by the OAU that the responsibility for returning Sierra Leone to constitutional order was first and foremost one for the people of Sierra Leone. Secondly that in performing this duty they were entitled to seek assistance from Ecowas and the wider international community. Put another way, the OAU was laying down the substratum on which any solution to the crisis must be based, namely the will of the people of Sierra Leone. Any such solution must have three elements: genuine popular support, consistency with the goals of the OAU and the UN, and effectiveness.

Did Ecowas carry out this mandate? Did it recognise the fundamental rights of the people of Sierra Leone? What role was given to the Abidjan Peace Accord?

Execution of mandate

Outside the North Atlantic Treaty Organisation (NATO), no regional organisation is better known in peacekeeping than Ecowas. This new image began with its involvement in the Liberian crisis in 1990, bolstered further during the Guinea-Bissau crisis in 1999. In both cases, the regional leaders met, deliberated and decided to set up a regional military force designated as Ecomog under the auspices of Ecowas. When it came to the Sierra Leone crisis in 1997, however, the designation "Ecomog" was deliberately withheld until 1999.

By 1992 Ecowas' contribution to the search for solutions to regional conflicts had received praise from Boutros Boutros-Ghali, UN Secretary-General, who described the cooperation between it and the United Nations as one of the finest on record. Since then, the organisation has earned further kudos from different quarters, including from NATO leaders during their own campaign in Kosovo. Today, imperfect as some aspects of Ecomog may have been, the overwhelming opinion is that its success transcends West Africa; it has come to be accepted as Africa's flagship in peace-making, peace-keeping and peace-enforcement.

1. *The Ecowas Foreign Ministers*

  (a) *The Conakry Meeting of June 26*

The Ecowas Foreign Ministers first discussed the Sierra Leone tragedy in 1991, essentially as part of their deliberations on the Liberian conflict. At that time, partly because successive governments in Sierra Leone wanted the conflict kept within the bounds of domestic criminal law, but mainly because the organisation was already over-stretched in Liberia, its assistance to Sierra Leone was minimal. The best it could do then was to encourage member states, able and willing to do so, to give bilateral military assistance to Sierra Leone. Guinea and Nigeria came to the rescue but even at that their assistance was comparatively small.

The *coup* of May 1997, however, did make the situation graver. Yet, it took almost three months before the Ecowas heads of state were called to a meeting on August 28. The question is why was an extra-ordinary meeting of heads of state not convened immediately? If a meeting of all of them was impracticable, why was a meeting of the Standing Mediation Committee, established in May 1990, not convened? The absence of an early meeting was surely not in keeping with the decision of the heads of state taken at their extraordinary summit in Mali in November 1990, to the effect that whenever the use or threat of force is contemplated a meeting of the Authority should be convened. When, on June 2, the Nigerian navy bombarded Freetown in the name of Ecowas, no such consultation had taken place.

Nigeria convened a meeting of Ecowas Foreign Ministers in Conakry on June 26. It seemed, however, that they were forced to this decision only after their forces had proved unable to topple the junta on June 2 when 310 of their soldiers were taken prisoner. Moreover, the fate of another military offensive could not be determined with any degree of certainty. So they turned to diplomacy to buy time. Subsequent meetings in Abidjan, Conakry, Abuja, New York and Lome followed this meeting.

Thus, after the first attack on Freetown, it took a whole month before a meeting of Ecowas Foreign Ministers was convened in Conakry to consider the crisis. This may be compared with the remarkable promptitude with which Ecowas reacted to the *coup* in Cote d'Ivoire that toppled President Konan Bedie on December 24, 1999. It took only four days to convene a meeting of the Ecowas Mediation and Security Council in Bamako. No less noteworthy is the fact that whereas only the exiled government of President Kabbah was invited to the Conakry meeting, the delegations of both the deposed government and the military junta in Cote d'Ivoire were allowed to attend the Bamako meeting and make representations.

That is not all. Although the Bamako meeting condemned the *coup*, it rejected any notion of military intervention to reverse it, urging instead the establishment of a transitional administration to be followed by free and fair general and presidential elections by June 2000. In the case of Sierra Leone, Ecowas recommended a three-pronged strategy: negotiation, sanctions/embargo and force. It was envisaged that all three measures may be applied simultaneously in order to achieve three objectives: (a) to reinstate the legitimate government of President Kabbah; (b) to return the country to peace and security; and (c) to stem the flow of refugees and displaced persons. On the question of the use of force, the Ministers introduced a caveat that no such action should be taken until there had been further consultation "at the highest level".106 It then set up a Committee of Four, later enlarged to Five then to Seven,107 and charged it with responsibility for monitoring developments in Sierra Leone and ensuring "the implementation of decisions resulting from the recommendations". It was also asked to open dialogue with the AFRC and report back to the Ecowas Chairman within two weeks.

But the strategy was not well focused. It beats the imagination how it was possible to combine all three measures at one and the same time. History is replete with instances where dialogue has been pursued *pari passu* with sanctions or the *threat* of force but never with the actual *use* of force; the two are simply incompatible. The Foreign Ministers probably had this problem in mind when they insisted on the caveat. Not also far from their thinking was the fact that the crisis was a purely internal one and, in accordance with the provisions of the Protocol on Mutual Assistance in Defence 1981, armed intervention by the Community in such situations is barred.

On what authority then did the Foreign Ministers contemplate the use of force? Was this their understanding of the OAU's mandate to Ecowas to "assist the people of Sierra Leone to restore constitutional order"? If so, all that can be reasonably said is that it was a most extraordinary interpretation, because the OAU itself did not even pretend to have such authority. *Nemo dat quod non habet.*

The absence of any such authority did not apparently deter Chief Tom Ikimi, Nigeria's Foreign Minister. On July 11, he claimed before the United Nations Security Council that the OAU had "endorsed the action taken by Ecowas" on June 2 to reverse the situation in Freetown. And he tried to fudge an explanation for the use of force in these terms: "In the course of the deliberations, concern was expressed by delegations about the use of force as a means of resolving the present crisis in Sierra Leone. However, it was recognised that the other two options, including negotiations and sanctions/blockade, could not be achieved without the use of military force. For example, if Ecowas would mount a credible sanctions regime against the illegal authorities in Sierra Leone, the air, land and sea borders of Sierra Leone would have to be militarily blocked while negotiations would be enhanced by a show of force and a sustained military build-up in the area. The Foreign Ministers therefore recommended that all three measures would require consultations at the highest level among Ecowas countries. They have therefore suggested that the Ecowas Chairman should initiate these consultations."[108] This was a *non sequitur par excellence.*

Most of his colleagues disagreed. Nor did his interpretation sit well with the understanding of his own boss, who, while on a visit to Abidjan on August 18, admitted that force could only be used as a last resort. "The dialogue is still open," Abacha said, "but if the leadership in Sierra Leone is not reasonable, will not look at things objectively --- then we will look at so many other options like the issue of sanctions, the issue of embargo, and, where necessary, force can be used."[109]

Another problem with the Foreign Ministers' recommendations was that they did not consult the people of Sierra Leone either before or after their deliberations. The visits undertaken by individual ministerial delegations from Ghana and Guinea were outside the aegis of Ecowas. Nor did the Ministers seem troubled by the fundamental principle of *audi alteram partem*. They had apparently reached their conclusions relying solely on evidence tendered by the representatives of Kabbah's exiled government in Conakry. By any standards, this falls short of their mandate, and by contemplating the use of force, they clearly exceeded it. The underlying assumption throughout was that President Kabbah's government was a democratically-elected government and that alone justified any measures Ecowas and its members might wish to take to oust the illegal military regime in Freetown.

To say the least, this argument was threadbare and brazen and could only lead, as indeed it did, to a long drawn-out conflict. The Alliance for Peace and Democracy had cautioned against this on August 25. It said that the use of force could produce "unintended repercussions on the war-weary civilian population and on the already ravaged economy, especially its infrastructure, and indeed on the intervention force itself which would almost inevitably become embroiled in a long-lasting urban-type guerrilla war. The end result would be to make worse an already bad situation and postpone indefinitely the prospects of achieving a durable peace." The Alliance went on to advise that: "What is needed now is the adoption of a Peace Plan that would contribute to the consolidation of peace and the restoration of constitutional order. Such a Plan should bring to centre-stage, as acknowledged by the OAU itself, the Abidjan Peace Agreement of November 30, 1996 and should call on all concerned to update the Agreement and renew their efforts to implement its terms to the fullest, while also recognising the new realities on the ground. Of course, this cannot be achieved without the release and participation of the leader of the RUF, Corporal Foday Sankoh."[110]

Consisting of concerned Sierra Leoneans in London, the Alliance was not alone in this. The International Crisis Group (ICG) made a similar warning: "The effort to return the country to democracy will at worst fail and at best provide very short-lived results as long as it is pinned exclusively to the return of the previous government, intact. Demobilisation and, critically, reintegration, of all armed elements is a prerequisite to both sustainable security and sustainable democracy and ensuring Sierra Leone has a government that tackles these issues should, for now, be the strategic goal of international policy."[111]

Neither Kabbah nor Abacha paid heed. They continued to pressurize the international community into ratifying their military campaign in Sierra Leone, regardless of the consequences. Any proposal, therefore, that fell short of this was considered by them to be anathema.

The United Nations Security Council reacted to the Ecowas recommendations. It gave its full support to the objectives but not the strategy, particularly the use of force. Instead, it called on the coup leaders to cooperate with Ecowas and agreed to continue its monitoring of "the progress of measures aimed at a peaceful resolution of the crisis". It also promised to consider other "appropriate measures" if the junta failed to restore constitutional order.[112]

Obviously, this was not what Abacha and Kabbah had hoped for. Ikimi put on a brave face when he expressed satisfaction that "all the elements that we would want are contained in the

Council's statement". Then, he added his own spin: "We depart New York fully satisfied that the international community and the Security Council are in full support of the actions that we are taking as a sub-region on Sierra Leone, which has been supported fully by Africa at the summit of the OAU."113

(b) The Abidjan Meetings of July 1997

Following the meeting with the Security Council, the Committee of Four met with a delegation of the AFRC in Abidjan on July 17 and 18. The Minority Leader of the Sierra Leone Parliament, Dr John Karefa-Smart, and I attended in our private capacities as concerned citizens and made representations for a peaceful resolution of the conflict. From the outset, we had expressed opposition to the use of violence, arguing that the crisis in Sierra Leone was rooted in political and socio-economic factors and that its solution must perforce bear those essential elements. Accordingly we had deplored the *coup* just as much as we had condemned the Nigerian military intervention, and campaigned instead for a political solution founded on dialogue and national reconciliation.

But the format at Abidjan was far from conducive to dialogue. While the AFRC delegation said it had come to Abidjan in the hope of negotiating, Ikimi was not in the mood. He never missed the opportunity to remind the AFRC delegation of his mandate. For him, there was nothing to negotiate about and the AFRC had only one option: to pack out and run while they could.114 His attitude was uncompromising. Unsurprisingly it was in unison with remarks made by James Jonah, then Sierra Leone's Ambassador to the United Nations, a fortnight earlier. Jonah had warned the *coup* leaders that they would be missing the point if they expected that negotiations would take place in Abidjan. The Committee's only mandate was to clear the way for Kabbah's regime to return, he emphasised.115

The "Concluding Statement" issued at the end of the Abidjan meeting confirmed the tilted nature of the meeting. It studiously avoided the word "negotiation," employing instead the phrase "decisions of the meeting" of the Committee of Four. Nevertheless, the AFRC delegation was ecstatic and the residents of Freetown took to the streets in jubilation. For them, the value of the meeting lay in the fact that an agreement was reached, first and foremost, on a cease-fire; and, secondly, on a peaceful resolution of the remaining issues. The meeting also decided to work towards the early restoration of constitutional order and gave the AFRC a couple of weeks to prepare detailed modalities towards that end.

At the end of the meeting, Ikimi enthusiastically declared: "We feel we have made substantial progress and the atmosphere exists for a substantial breakthrough" after describing the atmosphere as "friendly, cordial and brotherly."[116] Paolo Bangura, the leader of the AFRC delegation, shared his optimism.

When the parties met again in Abidjan for a follow-up meeting on July 29 and 30 – this time Karefa-Smart and I decided not to attend -- the talks foundered due to an unexpected announcement by the junta leader in Freetown that they intended to stay in power until November 2001. Although he subsequently reversed himself, the damage had been done. The Committee of Four responded by denouncing the junta's decision as "totally unacceptable".[117] The Commonwealth Secretary-General, Chief Emeka Anyaoku added his own moral weight to the condemnation and called on West African leaders "to take every necessary step to see legitimacy, constitutionality and democracy reinstated in Sierra Leone."[118] The deadlock, which inevitably ensued, was not broken until late in October 1997.

Before this second round of meetings, a group of patriotic citizens, ardent advocates of political dialogue, had worked long hours in Freetown and, independently of the junta, had produced a blueprint for peace. It was in three parts: (a) the restoration and consolidation of peace and security; (b) the foundations for genuine national reconciliation and (c) the re-establishment of civil and constitutional government. The last proved the thorniest and most controversial. Yet the group mustered the courage to confront the junta leader with proposals on July 26 the gist of which was that a Kabbah-led transitional government of national unity should be established to replace the AFRC after six months. The six months' timetable was designed to enable the AFRC to consolidate peace by way of disarmament and demobilisation, with assistance from the United Nations. After that, the transitional government was to take over for an agreed period, followed by democratic elections to be held under international supervision. These proposals were to be ratified by a Bintumani-type national conference consisting of representatives of the key stakeholders, political parties and civil society.

The fundamental principles implicit in these proposals were the recognition that, first and foremost, however passionate the concern of friends might be, it was the duty of the citizens of Sierra Leone themselves to take full ownership of their tragedy and its solution. Secondly, that a solution arrived at in this way stood a better chance of commanding the support and respect of all the stakeholders and of strengthening the foundations of lasting peace and national reconciliation.

As it happened, the junta leader himself had given a similar assurance to the visiting Ghanaian Ministerial delegation a month earlier that they would demit power after six months. He had said that that amount of time was needed to complete the process of disarmament, demobilisation and reintegration of ex-combatants into civil society, which they had already begun.

However, as became evident at the second Abidjan meeting, these proposals had not found favour with the AFRC. Although they tried to justify their attitude as purely one of tactic, the meeting aborted following the unexpected announcement by the junta leader. The AFRC delegation returned to Freetown empty-handed and without its leader.

In the hope of winning back his Foreign Secretary and appeasing Ecowas, the junta leader wrote to him on July 31. He acknowledged that his broadcast the previous day "had not gone down well with a number of enlightened citizens" and conceded that he had "over-reacted" and " for this I am sorry. As human beings we all make mistakes and I am no exception. I am willing further to admit this much – that I erred in making such a broadcast at the time the negotiations were in progress in Abidjan and the impression might have been created that our delegation was not acting in good faith throughout. To that extent the distinguished Foreign Ministers were right in coming to the conclusions they arrived at without the benefit of our assessment of the situation from a distance. In hindsight, however, I now realise that I may have put my Secretary of State for Foreign Affairs, Mr Alimamy Paolo Bangura as leader of our delegation, in an unenviable position as he was neither fully briefed nor was he aware of the contents of the said broadcast of yesterday, the 30th of July, 1997."119

Reacting to the breakdown of the talks, the Security Council convened on August 6 and issued a Presidential Statement in which it pinned responsibility for the failure entirely on the junta. It condemned as unacceptable the junta's attempt to set pre-conditions for the restoration of the ousted government and demanded that it resume negotiations with Ecowas immediately. It again declared its readiness "to take appropriate measures with the objective of restoring the democratically-elected government of President Kabbah" if the junta failed to make a satisfactory response.120

(c) *The Conakry Meeting of October 22-23*

The next meeting of the Ecowas Committee (this time enlarged to five members following the inclusion of Liberia) with the AFRC took place in Conakry on October 22 and 23. The real purpose of this meeting, so far as Nigeria was concerned, seemed to be to unlock the doors to the Commonwealth biennial summit in Edinburgh, which had been closed to its delegation. In the months leading to the summit, agitation had mounted for the expulsion of Nigeria from the Commonwealth. In reply, Nigerian jet fighters had bombarded residential suburbs in eastern Freetown, thereby shattering the lull in the fighting and provoking the junta into renewed hostilities. This bombing continued into October and was only momentarily halted when an Ecowas Peace Plan was announced in Conakry on October 23. No sooner it became apparent that this had failed to impress the Commonwealth summit than the accord was thrown to the wind and the Nigerian army in Sierra Leone once again resumed business as usual. In language that smacked of sarcasm, the Commonwealth exhorted the Nigerian military junta to try and match its support for democracy in Sierra Leone with compliance at home with the Harare principles.

Like the Abidjan Peace Accord before it, the main burden of the Conakry Peace Plan was the re-establishment of lasting peace through dialogue and reconciliation, to be followed by the reinstatement of the constitutional government within a six-months' time-frame. There was mutual recognition by the AFRC of the need to make way for the reinstatement of Kabbah's government on the one hand and on the other by Ecowas and

Kabbah's government of the continuation of the AFRC as a government for a further six months. The Peace Plan also contained political and military provisions as well as a humanitarian programme to accommodate this new arrangement.

On the military front, the parties agreed on an immediate cease-fire, to be monitored by Ecomog and verified by UN military observers. In addition, a process of disarmament, demobilisation and reintegration of ex-combatants was to be put in place starting from December 1997, again under Ecomog supervision; and incentives were to be provided, through international financial assistance, to facilitate the process.

On the political front, the parties agreed on the need to restore constitutional order after creating the appropriate climate for the government to regain effective control of the country. As a prerequisite, however, the parties agreed to evolve "an all-inclusive government" which would accommodate "the interests of the various parties in Sierra Leone". Accordingly, the new cabinet was to be "a cabinet of inclusion"; appointments to boards of parastatals and senior cadre of the civil service were to "reflect the broad national character"; and that these power-sharing formulae was to come into effect not later than April 22, 1998. It was believed that these measures would "enjoy the support of the majority of Sierra Leoneans" as well as "the confidence of the sub-region". The parties further agreed to allow Foday Sankoh "to play an active role and --- participate in the peace process" and that, in the spirit of both the Abidjan and Conakry accords, he would be allowed to "return to his country to make his contribution to the peace process". At the time Sankoh was in detention in Nigeria. Finally, it was agreed to extend "unconditional immunities and guarantees from prosecution ...to all those involved in the unfortunate events of May 25, 1997 to take effect as from April 22, 1998".121

The Conakry Peace Plan was hailed as a significant breakthrough partly because its tenor was pragmatic and conciliatory but mainly because it attempted to redesign the political architecture in order to put the country back firmly on the road to genuine national reconciliation. It also recognised special responsibilities for the people of Sierra Leone, to be assisted by Ecowas and the United Nations.

Given this strikingly innovative approach to the resolution of the conflict, the Alliance for Peace and Democracy in Sierra Leone welcomed it. The Alliance advanced the view that it was necessary, first and foremost, for the parties to accord primacy to the political arrangements within the framework of a national conference. As experience elsewhere had shown, both the deployment of Ecomog and the disarmament process could have been considerably strengthened if the management of the political aspects of the plan were both efficient and effective.122 However, to the utter disappointment of the people, the Peace Plan was never put into effect.

(c)   Further meetings of the Ecowas Committee of Five

As envisioned by the Conakry Peace Plan, the Committee of Five was due to undertake an assessment mission to Sierra Leone on November 20, 1997. It never took place. Instead, from November 11 to 12, the ECOMOG Field Commander held technical meetings with representatives of the AFRC at Kossoh Town, on the outskirts of Freetown, to discuss modalities for the implementation of the Peace Plan. Another meeting followed in Freetown on November 27, this time with both the Ecowas Executive Secretary and the UN Special Representative for Sierra Leone present. Throngs of war-weary citizens, waving banners demanding peace, had greeted them.

The technical discussions ranged over 17 items, including the choice of venue, who was to be disarmed, who was to do the disarming, the timing of the release of the RUF leader from detention in Nigeria, the de-mining of the international airport and other locations, the re-opening of the air and seaports and the re-commencement of humanitarian assistance. Provisional agreement was reached on the re-commencement of humanitarian assistance, set for November 14; the immediate re-opening of the seaports and airports; the exchange of prisoners of war through the ICRC and the Catholic Mission; the de-mining of the airport; and the dismantling of unnecessary roadblocks. There was also agreement to set up three committees to deal with disarmament, cease-fire violations and humanitarian assistance.

However, three major issues were unresolved. First, who was to be disarmed? The junta had stoutly argued that the national army, being the legally constituted army, should be exempted from disarmament. The Nigerians disagreed. Later they insisted that an understanding had been reached at Conakry that disarmament should apply to all combatants without exception, but there was no independent confirmation of this. It is interesting, however, that the Nigerians did admit to agreeing to "joint security patrols" for certain strategic sites, which clearly suggests that the parties did indeed envisage that a part of the national army would continue to operate normally and play a role alongside the Nigerian troops during the six-months' transitional period,[123] It is well to remember also that the Abidjan Accord of 1996 had simply referred to the "restructuring and reorientation of the military as well as its leadership" and to the "down-sizing of the armed forces of Sierra Leone, taking into account the security needs of the country" (Articles 9 and 10). Where it talked about "disarming", the reference was only to private militias like the RUF, the *kamajors* and civil defence forces. In the case of the RUF, it was agreed that it could convert itself into a political movement provided it had disarmed (Article 13).

The second point of disagreement concerned Nigeria's domination of the "sub-regional forces" in Sierra Leone. The AFRC contended that while they were "not opposed to Nigerian troops" *per se*, nevertheless they were opposed to their dominating the peace process. They therefore called for a reconfiguration of the sub-regional forces with Nigerian involvement but not Nigerian domination.[124]

This was reminiscent of the powerful argument that Charles Taylor of Liberia had advanced at the Ecowas negotiations at Yamoussoukro in 1992, to the effect that his forces could not reasonably be expected to disarm to an army against whom they had been fighting almost regularly. To insist on that, he had further argued, was tantamount to inviting them to surrender. Ecowas had accommodated these arguments by reconfiguring Ecomog through the introduction of new troops, which hitherto had not participated in Ecomog, initially from other Ecowas countries, and subsequently from Uganda and Tanzania.

The third point of disagreement concerned the modality and timing of the release of the RUF leader. The RUF fighters insisted that unless their leader was released from detention in Nigeria and allowed to play a part in the peace process, they would not agree to disarm. They also warned that if President Kabbah were returned to power by force, it would only lead to a prolongation of the conflict as their forces, along with many others, would flee into the bush once more to continue their rebellion interminably.

While the stalemate persisted, the junta leader protested in a BBC interview on December 18: "The disarmament should have started on December 1, but up to now nothing has been done. So, naturally, I think we will not meet the time that is stated."[125] Kabbah interpreted this as a requiem for the Conakry Peace Plan and for the principle of dialogue: "All peaceful means now seem to have been shattered. Events of the last few weeks have brought the problem to a stalemate. I am therefore compelled to face reality and come to this sad and realistic conclusion that the resolution of this problem can only be achieved through other means."[126]

This prompted another meeting of the Committee of Five. It was their seventh. The Committee not only reaffirmed the centrality of the Conakry Peace Plan; it emphasised the importance of adhering to the hand-over date. It therefore asked the Security Council to accelerate the deployment of UN military observers to enhance the implementation of the disarmament process, and urged Ecowas countries to help upgrade Ecomog's operational capability. This was necessary because apart from Guinea and Nigeria, no other Ecowas country had agreed to send troops to Sierra Leone.

The Committee then travelled to New York on February 5, 1998. It first met with the United Nations Secretary-General and then briefed members of the Security Council in an informal meeting. Chief Ikimi informed the Council that the junta had refused to implement the Conakry Peace Plan and had busied itself introducing new conditions for compliance. He also reported the junta's unwillingness to hand over power on April 22, emphasising that Ecowas was not ready to countenance any of these demands. He concluded by pleading with the Council to deploy the promised UN military observers without further delay.[127]

Although the Council issued no statement, the Committee of Five did. On February 6, it claimed, *inter alia*, that the Council had supported its actions in Sierra Leone and had promised to strengthen its support, including the creation of a trust fund.

Ikimi's briefing stopped short of telling the whole truth, particularly the fact that on that very day his country's forces were already engaged in an all-out offensive on Freetown.

Being preoccupied with the resurgent crisis in the Gulf following Saddam Hussein's refusal to allow UN weapons inspectors to do their work, the Council had had very little time for the Ecowas delegation. They had met under the "Arias formula". While this was going on, a new Ecomog Field Commander, Major-General Timothy Shelpidi, arrived in Freetown, declaring an all-out war on the junta. "We are moving with full force and we are not joking. I can tell you if we are going to take Freetown, we will take it when we want to," he declared. On February 12, the Nigerians reached the centre of Freetown, recaptured State House and forced the junta to retreat and seek sanctuary in the interior, ominously without even a fight.

This Nigerian assault seemed to have surprised even the Security Council, which had then ordered an immediate cease-fire. On February 10, the President of the Council recounted that they had never authorised anyone to use force and angrily accused the Ecowas delegation of misleading members of the Council at their briefing of February 6.128 Chief Ikimi had merely characterised the offensive as a "skirmish" when questioned by the press but, as observed by a diplomat in New York, "it was obvious that while they were white-washing in New York, they were planning to topple the junta by military means" contrary to the decisions of the Security Council.129

This rebuke so angered Ambassador Jonah of Sierra Leone that he spared no breadth in conveying his displeasure. "I do not understand the new jurisprudence that I have been hearing in the corridors," he said. "Some say that the Ecowas Ministers, when they were in New York recently, deceived the Security Council. First of all, we have to remember that there was no formal meeting of the Security Council on Sierra Leone. The meeting, which was closed, was requested by the five Foreign Ministers, under the Arias formula. They came to find out what the UN Security Council was prepared to do. All they were told was that the Secretary-General had recommended ten military liaison officers to go to Sierra Leone. That was all the Security Council was preparing to ask for, ten military liaison officers. Just ten! If there was anyone who should have been frustrated, it was the five

Foreign Ministers, and not the Security Council and those who talked about being deceived by the Foreign Ministers," he added.130

It is obvious, however, that the assault on Freetown did not happen suddenly. In fact, it had been delayed in order to give Kabbah and Abacha time to work on members of the Security Council who were opposed to the use of force. It is obvious too that by the end of 1997, the patience of the two leaders had worn thin and were now resolved to taking the military option whatever the cost. When they spoke about dialogue, they were merely playing for time. For Abacha, he had become obsessed about getting a big foreign policy success in order to deflect attention away from his international pariah status and get his Western tormentors off his back. For Kabbah, the waiting game in Conakry had become unbearable. It was beginning to look like eternity. What is more, the *kamajors* were growing restive especially after being made battle ready by the Nigerians and Sandline International, the mercenary firm that had supplied them with weapons. They were all now anxious to prove their worth.

Of course, there had been many previous attempts at peaceful settlement, none of which had come to fruition. It is also true that there can be no promise of peace or policy of patience without limits, though some might say that prior to the Conakry accord, there had been no genuine offer of dialogue from both sides. All that one could really see was continuous posturing, manoeuvring and false pretences; hardly a genuine attempt at dialogue from either side. There was thus no hope for the durability of any previous peace plan.

The battle readiness of the pro-Kabbah forces did not fail to induce a militaristic posture within the Kabbah camp. Earlier he had delegated powers to the Ecowas Committee of Five to negotiate on his behalf and to agree to any peace proposals for him and for themselves. When the Committee briefed him on the outcome of the Conakry meeting, he welcomed it as evidenced in a statement he issued from the Commonwealth summit in Edinburgh on October 24. Four days later he repudiated two key demands in the Peace Plan, namely the granting of amnesty to the *coup* leaders and the six-months' timetable for the transfer of power. His objections were that the rebels had destroyed his private home in Freetown. Like many other citizens who had lost their homes and loved ones during the rebel war, his emotion was understandable. However, if that argument were allowed to prevail, then presumably thousands of other people, relatives of those who had been killed, and those whose properties had been destroyed, could reasonably demand that they too were entitled to retributive justice. Ultimately, it would look like telling the junta not to hand over power or not to stop fighting because they could not be certain of avoiding criminal prosecution.

It is also not easy to reconcile many of Kabbah's utterances. For example, his rejection of amnesty for the coupists cannot be reconciled with his promise of "genuine and lasting reconciliation". He first made that promise to the United Nations on October 1 and confirmed it at the London conference on Sierra Leone on October 20, just three days before the Conakry Peace Plan was signed. He even promised to set up a truth and reconciliation commission á la South Africa.131 Again, on November 5, Kabbah urged his countrymen to embrace the Conakry Peace Plan, describing it as an instrument that "contains a number of positive elements .. [for] the resolution of the crisis."132 A week later, on November 12, he reversed himself. He was reported as ruling out power-sharing with the junta, saying this was not justified by the Constitution. "My Constitution prevents me doing a number of things and I am not interested in that kind of compromise," he said. He again repeated his riposte to amnesty for the coupists, saying that "the cruelty witnessed in the first days of the *coup*, even if I had promised an amnesty for the coup-makers, I would come under great pressure to punish them in an exemplary manner". Then, in an amazing *volte face*, Kabbah declared his willingness to work with Foday Sankoh. "We all make mistakes. If he recognises his and promises to work for the good of the country, I cannot rule out forgiving him and considering him a compatriot, associating him with the future of this country," he said.133 But he said he would not work with the leader of the AFRC. Apparently he ignored the fact that the RUF had committed atrocities which made those of the AFRC look picayune. But all this was before his reinstatement. No sooner he was restored to power in February 1998 than he was immediately struck down by selective amnesia, conveniently forgetting most of his promises and putting Foday Sankoh and many others on trial for treason.

2. The Ecowas Authority

On August 28, 1997, Ecowas leaders met for the first time to consider the Sierra Leone crisis, almost three months after Nigeria had fired its first shots on Freetown. They had before them the recommendations of the Conakry Meeting of the Ecowas Foreign Ministers. The leaders deplored the *coup* and imposed wide-ranging economic and military sanctions against the junta but failed to exempt humanitarian assistance.134 They then established what they designated as "sub-regional forces" for Sierra Leone and gave them responsibility "for applying the measures contained in the Final Communiqué" of the Conakry meeting. They authorised the sub-regional forces to "employ all necessary means to impose the implementation of this decision--- to monitor closely the coastal areas, land borders and airspace of the Republic of Sierra Leone, and to inspect, guard and seize any ship, vehicle or aircraft violating the embargo imposed by this decision."

That decision was based on the belief that other Ecowas countries would promptly provide troops to constitute the "sub-regional forces", and that Abacha's forces could be relied upon to act within the ambit of their limited mandate. Neither of these things happened. Abacha's forces behaved much the same way when they had a mandate as when they did not.

The Ecowas mandate had been limited to enforcing an embargo on Sierra Leone. But, according to Article 53 of the UN Charter, even this needed authorisation from the Security Council. That Article provides that "no enforcement action shall be taken under regional arrangements or by regional agencies without the authorisation of the Security Council." The meaning of this injunction is clear. No regional or sub-regional forces can lawfully engage an enforcement action, still less use force, unless and until it has been properly authorised by the Security Council. So it was rather incongruous for the Ecomog Field Commander to think that the Ecowas mandate by itself was sufficient authority to apply force in Sierra Leone. If the sub-regional forces applied force without proper authorisation, they ran the risk of violating the Charter and international law as well as the sovereignty and territorial integrity of Sierra Leone. Aware of this limitation on their power, the Ecowas leaders had specifically instructed the

Ecowas Committee of Five to "solicit the assistance of the Security Council to render these sanctions universal and mandatory in accordance with the UN Charter."

Renewed mediation by Ecowas

The routing of the AFRC junta from Freetown by the pro-Kabbah forces did nothing to bring the conflict to an end; it merely drove the rebels from the seat of government to allow President Kabbah to return. They retreated into the hinterland from where they continued to launch attacks particularly against defenceless civilians, contrary to the laws of war. Kabbah further complicated matters when, out of vengeance, he angrily announced the disbandment of the entire national army.

When the situation got worse, particularly after the rebels marched effortlessly into Freetown in January 1999, Ecowas became alarmed. The Committee of Five, now expanded to Six with the inclusion of Togo, met and appealed to the rebels to stop fighting, lay down their arms, recognise the legitimacy of President Kabbah's government, participate in dialogue and accept the government's offer of amnesty. It urged the international community to leave the rebels in no doubt that they would never receive recognition even if they succeeded in seizing power again by force. Ecowas countries, which had promised troops, were called upon to redeem their pledges and the international community was asked to expedite the provision of logistical support, particularly transport and communication equipment, in order to improve the mobility and effectiveness of the sub-regional forces. The Committee condemned the countries that were supporting the rebels and requested the Chairman of Ecowas to embark on initiatives that would bring about true and genuine rapprochement between the leaders of Sierra Leone and Liberia. Finally, the Committee resolved to resume work and to seek to re-establish dialogue between the Sierra Leone government and the rebels, as envisaged by the peace accords.135

Consequently, on January 7, 1999, the Chairman of Ecowas, President Eyadema of Togo, called on President Kabbah and Foday Sankoh to halt the fighting and agree to reopen dialogue between them with a view to securing a definitive settlement of the crisis. He despatched his Foreign Minister, Joseph Kokou

Koffigoh, joined by his Ivorian counterpart, Amara Essy, who had had considerable experience from the Abidjan mediation in 1996, to begin a fresh round of diplomatic contact. These initiatives received the support of the Security Council, which, under resolution 1231 of March 11, 1999, encouraged the Secretary-General to facilitate dialogue between the warring parties.

None of these developments had, however, impressed Kabbah. In a seemingly vexed tone, he issued a statement on February 21, rejecting the Council's conciliatory approach and urging it instead "to consider the possibility of taking further action, not excluding the threat of force, against the rebels and their supporters, in order to give effect to the Council's previous demands that they [the rebels] 'cease all violence and seek genuine dialogue for the restoration of lasting peace and stability in Sierra Leone.'"136

He also raised the spectre of foreign involvement in order that the crisis could be transmuted from being a civil war to now being characterised as a war of foreign aggression.137 James Jonah was the architect of this new strategy. On January 29, he boldly claimed in New York that the conflict had ceased to be "an internal conflict" and had become "a regional one, being waged by a group of countries and individuals bent on denying the democratic right of the people of Sierra Leone.138

So, the government side did not appear to be very keen on a peaceful solution. It seemed not to have abandoned its militaristic posture. Nigeria was persuaded to reinforce its troops while Mali promised to send a battalion139 and Britain supplied logistical equipment. This buoyed hopes within the government's camp and inspired a surfeit of new proposals. One of them was the proposal to raise a 15,000-strong civil defence force pending the formation of a 5,000-strong national army. So disclosed by James Jonah during a visit to London on January 21, 1999. He asked Britain to provide training and weapons for the proposed militia. He also demanded to know what Britain proposed to do about the alleged complicity of the Liberian government in the Sierra Leone conflict.140

But Jonah's plan was not new. A similar plan had been put forward by Executive Outcomes to the SLPP government just before the 1997 *coup*. Under that plan the *kamajor* militia was to have been discreetly integrated into the national army so that it could have become its linchpin. The announcement that each district would provide 1,000 men for the proposed militia was therefore nothing but hogwash. With most districts still struggling to recover from the war's ravages, it was simply impossible to raise that number of fighters.

Another proposal had come from outside the government. Writing from Freetown, Sam Kiley of *The Times* (London) called on the British government to finance mercenaries in support of Kabbah's government, because "Sierra Leone is once again teetering between democracy and criminal dementia." He goes on and I quote him in extenso:

"Whether or not Sandline was implementing British policy then, it is quite clear that it should be now. The Foreign Secretary should learn from the events of last year. The redeployment of mercenaries in this blighted nation would be an act of genuinely ethical foreign policy.....

"This is where Mr Cook can salvage a little honour from the Sandline affair. This week, while the British Government continued to put pressure on President Kabbah to negotiate with the rebels, British forces have been keeping a weather eye on matters. A brigadier, David Richards, carried out reconnaissance in Freetown and has returned to brief Mr Cook's Cabinet Committee. He is likely to convey the message from both Mr Kabbah and his West African allies in Ecomog that a cease-fire and negotiations are out of the question while the rebels hold the diamond-rich east.

"It is clear that jaw-jaw will not work if the rebels are allowed to maintain their grip on the diamond mines. The gems can be mined by anyone with a shovel. The rebels can generate tens of millions of pounds to fund their massacres. Talks while the rebels remain in possession of these resources will only strengthen the rebels' hands. What the legitimate President and his allies need is air support to hit rebel bases from the rear. Without air support, Ecomog's armour and infantry can fight only a limited war of attrition, unable to strike behind the rebel lines.

"It is in Britain's interest to see that air support, and additional military muscle, are supplied. We have a moral duty to maintain the President whose election we backed. But the crisis affects more than one country. If Ecomog forces were to lose on the battlefields of Sierra Leone, a domino effect could harm the cause of progress throughout West Africa.....

Britain and her Western partners can now help Sierra Leone by hiring a company like Executive Outcomes, Sandline, or any one of a number of British security firms operating in Africa. Such an organisation can bring badly needed helicopters to fight in Freetown and beyond. The Sierra Leone Government cannot afford to do so. In all honour, we cannot afford not to. At no risk to British soldiers and equipment, Mr Cook can practise private-sector peacekeeping. He should authorise the deployment of mercenaries to help Ecomog to drive the rebels out of Sierra Leone. That, after all, is what the Foreign Office thought was a good idea a year ago."[141]

Kiley's recommendation for air support did find favour with Britain, for not long after it was published, two helicopter gunships, allegedly financed by Britain, arrived in Freetown. But the proposal for mercenary support did not find approval. Earlier on, Cook had endorsed the observation of the Parliamentary Select Committee on Foreign Affairs when it said that "the aim of lasting peace in Sierra Leone is 'hardly likely' to be helped by the activities of mercenary forces."[142]

Kiley's proposal for mercenaries is unacceptable for a number of reasons. First, what was really being recommended was not peacekeeping but peace-enforcement by mercenaries. Second, as the Angolan and Sierra Leonean experiences had shown, there is no monopoly over the hiring of mercenaries, aside from their apparent inability to prosecute a sustained guerrilla war. Third, if Kiley is right that the conflict in Sierra Leone was being fuelled by mercenaries from Liberia, then driving them out of Sierra Leone was not going to solve the problem; it would only shift it to another location but still within the region. And, lastly, Kiley's proposal offers no guarantee that the pro-government forces would have succeeded against an enemy who was better motivated and knew the terrain well. Indeed, his proposal would have had the effect of giving pre-eminence to the military option and prolonging the agony of the people of Sierra Leone indefinitely without any guarantee of lasting peace. All the same, while the belligerents were on the warpath, diplomacy was forced to take a back seat.

Kabbah slams and re-opens the door of diplomacy

When the rebels re-entered Freetown in January 1999, President Kabbah immediately sued for peace. The man who, barely three months prior, had flatly turned down international pleas for clemency for a group of convicted soldiers and Foday Sankoh, was now promptly offering a pardon to Foday Sankoh in exchange for a cease-fire and a promise to revive the Abidjan Peace Accord. This offer was interpreted as willingness by Kabbah to restart the moribund peace process and get the beleaguered country out of its quagmire. The Ivorian and Togolese Foreign Ministers flew into Lungi International Airport, where they met with President Kabbah on January 10. They returned to Conakry where they talked to Sankoh on January 12. Francis Okelo, UN Special Representative, and Sama Banya, Sierra Leone's Minister of Foreign Affairs, also participated. The Ministers reported that Sankoh, still clad in the uniform of a condemned prisoner, had demanded his freedom and official recognition for the RUF before agreeing to a cease-fire.143

The lead role taken by the two Francophone countries stirred the ire of Nigeria. Although undertaken on the directives of the current chairman of Ecowas, Nigeria was irked by the fact that, in spite of its massive military presence in Sierra Leone, it had not been invited to take part in the latest diplomatic moves. A hiatus soon emerged: the country with the largest number of troops on the ground was asked to take a back seat while those with no troops took the front seat. Besides, these diplomatic moves were being made at a time when the Nigerian military was still reeling from its severely bruised reputation as a regional military power. Never before, in the whole history of the conflict, not even when Freetown was under the protection of the ill-equipped Sierra Leone army, had the capital been allowed to fall into the hands of rebels as happened in January 1999 when the Nigerian army was in charge. Ignatius Olisiemeka, Minister of Foreign Affairs after the demise of Abacha, voiced Nigeria's discomfiture. "Those who do not even have a soldier in Sierra Leone are pretending to be peacemakers," he protested. "I would ask them to stop it. We cannot be taken for a ride. When we are ready for peace we shall let them know," he added.144 The question on everybody's mind was when would the Nigerian military be ready for peace in Sierra Leone?

This outburst effectively suspended the Ecowas mediation effort and put its solidarity at risk. It also eroded any pretence that still remained of the Nigerian military intervention in Sierra Leone being a pan-Ecowas affair and not a unilateral Nigerian adventure, not to speak of undoing Kabbah's autonomy over the management of the conflict. The Nigerians were now openly calling the shots. What also baffled a lot of people was how Nigeria, a leading belligerent in Sierra Leone, could have concurrently played the role of peacemaker and expect the rebels to give its peace offerings an unquestioning acceptance.

Olisiemeka's disdainful and intemperate remarks forced a genteel response out of an otherwise reluctant government in Abidjan. On January 17, the Ministry of Foreign Affairs issued a statement, recalling the fact that it was the extraordinary meeting of the Ecowas Committee of Six on Sierra Leone that had called for the reinforcement of the sub-regional forces as well as for the resumption of dialogue between the government and the rebels. It also recalled the fact that the "involvement of Cote d'Ivoire in the settlement of the crisis in Sierra Leone [was] the result of an urgent request made in this regard by former Sierra Leonean leader, Maada Bio, and President Kabbah to President Henri Konan Bedie, who had made great efforts towards the signing of the Abidjan Peace Accord on 30 November 1996, an Accord which had received the support of the entire international community."145

Olisiemeka was in Freetown a week later. He was accompanied by the Nigerian Chief of Defence Staff. Kabbah came out of their meeting with renewed confidence in a military solution and slammed the door on dialogue and diplomacy. "Now there is only a military solution. We have to push the rebels far, far from Freetown," he said. Like a pendulum, Kabbah swung from promising Sankoh his freedom in exchange for a cease-fire on January 7 to espousing only a military solution barely a fortnight later. To push the rebels as far away from the city as possible was correct but to proclaim that only a military solution was acceptable was a different matter altogether; it was substantiated neither by the nation's experience nor by the chivalry of the pro-government forces.

But the biggest surprise of all was yet to come. On January 27, 1999, no sooner the Nigerian Commander reported that his forces had pushed the rebels out of Freetown than the new Nigerian leader, General Abdulsalami Abubakar, was assuring Lloyd Axworthy, the visiting Canadian Foreign Minister, in Abuja that his "ardent wish was for the restoration of peace and normalcy in Sierra Leone so that Nigerian troops in the country could be withdrawn before 29 May 1999" - the date he had promised to hand over power to an elected government in Nigeria.

Thus, while in Abuja the Nigerian leader was talking to the Canadian Foreign Minister about the need for a negotiated settlement in Sierra Leone, in Freetown his Foreign Minister and his host were planning for war. No breakdown in communication between a Foreign Minister and his boss could be more patent. Olisiemeka gave the impression of an official who was totally oblivious of the unpopularity of his country's military expedition in Sierra Leone and of the unacceptably high level of its material and human costs. Between January and February 1999 alone, Nigeria had reportedly lost some 780 soldiers[146] while at the same time the financial cost had escalated to between $1 million and £1 million a day. "A large sum for a government who are wrestling with their legacy from years of abuse and corruption by the previous military junta," were the remarks of the British Foreign Secretary.[147] This level of expenditure was being incurred at a time when revenue was declining sharply as a result of drastic falls in oil prices. Oil had been the life-blood of the Nigerian economy, contributing 75 per cent of government revenue and, typically, over 95 per cent of export earnings.[148] The collapse in prices from mid-1998 onward had brought about a balance-of-payments crisis and severe cuts in public spending, leaving a deficit of $3 to $4 billion in early 1999.

It was therefore not difficult to understand why General Abubakar was calling for a negotiated settlement. This was endorsed by no fewer than seven Ecowas leaders who were in Conakry for the second swearing-in ceremony of President Lansana Conte on January 29. They accepted the dual-track policy, which the British government had propounded, though they believed that greater emphasis should be laid on dialogue.

These developments notwithstanding, President Kabbah, backed by James Jonah, now turned Minister of Finance, remained adamantly opposed to dialogue. This even though he had no army of his own, having disbanded the entire national army, nor any effective control of his country. At the same time two of his Ministers, Julius Spencer and Allie Bangura, were preoccupied with luring the civilian population into a false sense of security. They did all but imprison the residents of Freetown in their houses when they ordered them to stay indoors or else risk being shot at as rebels. Those who obeyed and stayed in their homes ran the risk of being burnt alive in their houses by marauding rebels for refusing to come out and demonstrate support for their peace offerings, while those who ventured into the streets were bombed by Ecomog warplanes. The result was an unprecedented loss of civilian life and property. Freetown, the last safe haven for the civilian population, became the new frontline.

Kabbah's uncompromising stance puzzled a lot of people. Could it be that he was unaware of the yearnings of his citizens even when they took to the streets in jubilation upon hearing news of a cease-fire accord between him and Sankoh?[149] Could it also be that Olisiemeka did not brief Kabbah about their plans to withdraw Nigerian troops from Sierra Leone to coincide with the transfer of power to a democratically-elected government in Nigeria? Even if he was not briefed, it could not have been a surprise.[150] In London the week before, Jonah was already contemplating that possibility. If, on the other hand, Kabbah did know of the planned withdrawal, could not his subsequent declaration that he was ready to continue fighting be interpreted as a deliberate act of deception? Or was there something sublime, outside the public gaze, that was helping Kabbah to keep faith so resolutely with the military option?

Many had also wondered just what guarantees Kabbah had for his people that, after eight years of failed attempts to secure a military victory, he would succeed this time around, especially after the Nigerians would have withdrawn. Just what he relied upon was unclear apart from his bland declaration that his government was "now committing substantial additional resources to national security, and that this stance has received the support of the major international financial institutions."[151] Can a policy be more misguided than that which advocates for a multiplicity of armed militias within the same country? How can such a nation survive without perpetual conflict?

Clearly, any leader with this kind of thinking needs help, and plenty of it. General Abubakar came to the rescue. He asked the Libyan leader, Colonel Moammar Kadhafi, to intercede between Kabbah and Foday Sankoh. Colonel Kadhafi agreed, and, on February 2, sent an invitation to the two belligerents in Sierra Leone to meet with him in Libya.[152] This invitation was renewed on February 11, again through the Nigerian leader. Again he sent an emissary to Freetown.[153] By approaching the Libyan leader, General Abubakar must have directed his mind to the fact that Libya had once played host to Sankoh where he and many of his followers had trained in the late eighties. A second offer to mediate also came from Togo, current chairman of Ecowas.[154]

All these offers presented Kabbah with only one option, negotiation. The Western Powers, too, weighed in making it abundantly clear that they no longer had the stomach for a military solution. Thus, with ill-concealed reluctance, Kabbah had to swallow his pride and put on the velvet gloves of diplomacy. On February 7, 1999, he informed the nation of his government's willingness "to continue its efforts for dialogue – this time, using the Abidjan Peace Accord, which Foday Sankoh and I had signed, as a frame of reference," provided the RUF first recognise the legitimacy of his government, cease hostilities and present no pre-conditions for peace. He promised to allow Foday Sankoh to have a face-to-face meeting with his colleagues in a third country so that they could develop a coherent set of political demands to form the basis for subsequent negotiations.[155]

External pressure thus played an important role in generating the impetus for dialogue. If only it had come months earlier, thousands of lives could have been saved. But there was domestic pressure also. Belatedly Kabbah acknowledged this when he confessed to a growing collaboration between civilians and rebels, spurned by the folly of relying too much on foreign troops to deliver victory in an unfamiliar terrain. Foreign troops usually have very little way of knowing who is friend and who is foe until the first shot is fired, and often they do end up committing unintended atrocities against innocent civilians.

116

Eventually, the government declared a willingness to negotiate but remained thoroughly confused about when to call a cease-fire. Given the scale of atrocities perpetrated by the January 1999 attack on Freetown, one might be forgiven for thinking that the need for a cease-fire was immediate. However, this was not the thinking in government circles. They wanted to regain control of the diamond deposits first before calling for a cease-fire. So once more it prevaricated. This was why there was an incredibly long silence about a cease-fire. On February 22, the government was forced to circulate official guidelines on the matter: "The President and members of the government should refrain from making any public statements on the issue of cease-fire, at least until such a proposal is formally put to the government or until the government arrives at a definitive decision on the matter." In an apparent warning to over-zealous diplomats busy misrepresenting the official line, the circular stated: "It is dangerous for a government official to publicly state or write that 'the government will not accept a cease-fire' or that 'the rebels [must] first lay down their arms before dialogue'." That stage had been passed, added the circular, and any such statement "would give the impression that the government is intransigent, and would only encourage others to place additional pressure on us and compel us to lay down our arms as well under a premature cease-fire arrangement. In other words, they would call on both sides to suspend hostilities."

It is difficult to characterise this circular otherwise than to say it was at least obfuscatory or stultiloquent. It portrayed the government as still incomprehensibly dragging its heels over the issue of war and peace, forgetting that good governance is about the ability of government to provide adequately for the security, peace and welfare of its citizens. If it was not able to provide this, then pressing for a cessation of hostilities was only a recognition that that was the most reasonable thing to do; after all, the armed conflict in Sierra Leone was not about the acquisition or loss of national territory. A government cannot be described otherwise but an utter failure if it cannot guarantee the welfare of its citizens in an atmosphere of tranquillity. Worse still, if it is almost totally dependent on foreign powers to guarantee its own security.

Within 24 hours the RUF gave the government's peace offer a "cautious welcome". Its Spokesman, Mr Omrie Golley, said: "We would wish to receive proposals as to how the government wishes to proceed with these matters within the shortest possible time in order for us to carefully study them and respond."156

Encouraged by this gesture, the Security Council instructed its Special Representative to offer his good offices to the parties and to report back to it by March 5.157 This led to a meeting between them in Abidjan from February 19 to 21. A communiqué issued at the end of the meeting said that the rebels had called for the release of their leader, Foday Sankoh, whose appeal against conviction and sentence of death on charges of treason was then pending. They demanded that, after their internal consultations, Sankoh should not return to jail but that those consultations should be immediately followed by substantive negotiations. They also agreed to announce a cease-fire upon the release of Sankoh, the only condition being that there should be enough United Nations military observers on the ground to monitor and verify compliance.

On the question of venue for the internal RUF consultations, the government agreed to release Sankoh to a neutral and safe venue where he would meet his colleagues. They offered him a British or American frigate inside Sierra Leone's territorial waters. The RUF countered by offering Ouagadougou, Abidjan or Lome. Ultimately, agreement was reached on Lome, necessitating the lifting of the UN travel ban imposed under resolution 1132 (1997).158

The next question was the date for the release of Sankoh to proceed to Lome. The Attorney-General had insisted that the law should run its course, arguing that the appeal process had to be completed first. However, the Court of Appeal stepped in and agreed to suspend hearing as a gesture to the peace process. Kabbah, in a national broadcast on March 27, promised to allow Sankoh to travel to Lome "on or about April 18". He demanded an undertaking from the RUF that their internal consultations would not last more than a week so that the nation would celebrate the return of peace concurrently with the commemoration of its 38th independence anniversary on April 27. Events were later to prove him overly optimistic.

Thus, by the time Olusegun Obasanjo took over the Nigerian presidency in May 1999, Sierra Leone had become something of an albatross around Nigeria's neck and one that was getting heavier and heavier by the day. More than a quarter of its army had been deployed there and it was the single most expensive foreign enterprise for the Nigerian treasury after Liberia. If the proposed peace talks had failed, the new Nigerian civilian administration would have had to choose between remaining to fight a war that most conceded could not be won and pulling out with very little glory. President Obasanjo therefore invested his personal prestige in the negotiations. Before the election, he had promised to withdraw Nigerian troops; subsequently he qualified it by saying it would be a managed exit, linked to the progress of the negotiations. Obasanjo lamented that: "The amount we are wasting in peacekeeping in another country is enough to provide infrastructure in this country."

After his election, he came under international pressure to modify his stance. He now said the troops would remain until peace was restored. "We will not abandon Sierra Leone without ensuring there is peace and stability there," he remarked during a visit to Kenya. "If the rebels think that once there is no more military government in Nigeria, Nigeria will withdraw Nigerian troops and then they'll overrun the country, they are making a very serious mistake." But he warned that the Sierra Leone government must work towards peace and reconciliation with the rebels because Nigerian troops "cannot remain indefinitely in Sierra Leone."159 The meaning of this was clear. The Nigerian troops would definitely be withdrawn, though their exit would be a managed one, linked to progress in the peace process.

The cease-fire agreement

At the conclusion of the RUF's internal consultations, the delegations of the parties assembled in Lome on May 25. Solomon Berewa, Attorney-General and Minister of Justice, led the government side while Foday Sankoh headed the RUF delegation. Before that, the parties had signed a cease-fire agreement on May 18, effective May 24, under which they agreed to maintain their military positions, refrain from any further hostile acts that might undermine the peace process, and start substantive negotiations not later than May 25. By this time, the rebels controlled more than three-fourths of the country while the government's writ barely ran outside the capital, Freetown. Jointly President Eyadema of Togo and Reverend Jesse Jackson, United States

Special Envoy for the Promotion of Democracy in Africa, played a key role in achieving this cease-fire. On July 7, the parties signed a Peace Agreement, pledging, among other things, to make the cease-fire permanent and to bring the eight-year-old civil war to a final end.

The Liberian fly in the ointment

With the help of NPFL fighters in Liberia, the RUF had invaded Sierra Leone in March 1991. Not much was heard from the Sierra Leone government by way of protest, presumably because the Interim Government of National Unity (IGNU) in Liberia, headed by Dr Amos Sawyer, was itself powerless to stop it. It had no army of its own and the national army (AFL) had joined the fray as a separate warring faction.

However, when, in January 1999, Liberia was accused of complicity in the rebel attack on Freetown, Charles Taylor and his NPFL had become the government of Liberia. As the daredevilry of the rebels stunned the country, so accusatory fingers were pointing at the Liberian government. Nigeria, Britain and the United States supported the Sierra Leone government in making the accusation.[160] While the British spoke generally about the rebels receiving "Liberian support", avoiding any direct accusation against the Liberian government itself,[161] the Americans were not so restrained. They claimed they had solid evidence to back their allegation but declined to make it public.[162]

For its part, the Liberian government never denied involvement by its citizens but maintained that this was not official. On December 29, 1998, it issued an indignant denial and revealed that "successive regimes in Sierra Leone, from that of President Joseph Momoh to the elected government of President Tejan Kabbah, have used Liberian mercenaries, usually associated with former warring factions in Liberia, to augment their national security capacity. Even now, the *kamajor* militia are using Liberian mercenaries to assist in their fight against the Junta/RUF forces. We view the constant arming and use of these mercenaries as a threat to our national security and to the stability of the sub-region."[163]

In a subsequent letter to the UN Secretary-General dated February 23, 1999, President Taylor reiterated his government's denial of official support for the rebels in Sierra Leone. "Liberians," he said " have been used as mercenaries in Sierra Leone for a long time by all governments of Sierra Leone. They have always been there.....about 3,000 of them. But they are there on their own."164 Challenging his accusers to produce concrete evidence of his government's complicity, Taylor asked the Security Council to conduct an independent investigation as well as to deploy United Nations monitors along the common frontier between the two countries.165

There is no doubt that the Liberian government was greatly troubled by the allegations. A week before Taylor's letter to the Secretary-General, the Liberian Ministry of Foreign Affairs issued an "Official Statement on the Sierra Leone Crisis" on February 19.166 It outlined the measures the Liberian government was prepared to take to curtail the involvement of Liberian fighters in the Sierra Leone conflict, including the granting of amnesty, provided they returned home within 45 days. After that, they would become liable to arrest and prosecution in Liberia. It appealed to the United Nations to help it identify, document and process an organised repatriation of Liberian fighters in Sierra Leone, as well as assist with their reintegration into Liberian society in order to prevent them from being recycled as mercenaries elsewhere in the region. It emphasised that it was taking these measures in order "to discourage Liberian citizens from complicating the crisis in Sierra Leone, and to ensure compliance with the laws and conventions relating to mercenaries."

Two days later, the Liberian government ordered the deportation of two out of ten persons it had arrested the previous week on suspicions of collaborating with rebel forces in Sierra Leone. The two deportees were a British and a Sierra Leonean national. It also declared as *persona non grata* the Information Officer of the Sierra Leone Embassy in Monrovia. All three were accused of mercenarism and of fabricating evidence against Liberia.167

Although the Security Council did ask the UN Secretary-General to consider the practicality and effectiveness of deploying international monitors along the Liberia-Sierra Leone border, no such action has been taken. Nor was retribution against Taylor considered prudent especially as it would have had the effect of undermining the very fragile democratic transition that the international community had worked so hard to install in Liberia. The only feasible solution was either a voluntary or an organised repatriation of Liberian mercenaries from Sierra Leone. Mercifully, the Lome Peace Agreement of July 7, 1999, did envisage this kind of repatriation.

CHAPTER 4

The Role of the United Nations

UN attitude to unauthorised use of force

Abacha's bombardment of Freetown on June 2, 1997 marked a watershed in the Sierra Leone tragedy. At the time of the bombardment, the capital was overflowing with displaced citizens from all parts of the country, and it takes little imagination to visualise the massive outflow of refugees that it engendered. I felt compelled to write to the United Nations Secretary-General on June 4, drawing attention to the unlawfulness of the Nigerian military intervention and pleading with him to bring the matter to the attention of the Security Council. I also proposed that, in the meantime, Nigeria should be asked to halt its assault on the people of Sierra Leone. The letter then goes on:

"I know there is a minority which supports the military *coup* but the overwhelming majority of the people of Sierra Leone oppose Nigeria's military intervention and are calling for the immediate withdrawal of her troops. This also reflects my own personal position. Calling for the withdrawal of Nigerian troops is therefore not an expression of support for the *coup*, which I have already opposed publicly. I believe strongly that the chances of restoring civilian rule by way of a negotiated settlement have not been exhausted, and that Sierra Leoneans should be given the opportunity, without foreign military interference, to continue to pursue this veritable option. They demonstrated a capacity to resolve their own internal problems last year, to the commendation of the world, when, faced with a military government intent on entrenching itself in power, they successfully pressed for civilian rule through elections. I believe the people of Sierra Leone can do it again if given the chance to seek a peaceful negotiated settlement of their crisis based upon a consideration of all available options including the restoration of President Kabbah.

"A framework for such a negotiated settlement already exists under the Abidjan Accord of November 30, 1996. The view is widely held in Sierra Leone that the Government of Cote d'Ivoire, the United Nations, the OAU and the Commonwealth, as the moral guarantors of that Accord, reinforced by other disinterested states, could help Sierra Leoneans develop a peaceful solution. This alternative is certainly more welcome than the military option being pursued by Nigeria. Already, the RUF rebels have integrated themselves into the regular army. Although this poses a myriad of problems of its own, it does at least provide some guarantee against the recurrence of hostilities by the RUF against the people of Sierra Leone……..

"Nigeria's intervention in Sierra Leone has also been compared with that of the United States in Haiti. In my humble opinion, there are material differences. In Haiti, Father Aristide, who had invited foreign intervention to restore democracy, clearly continued to enjoy the support of the overwhelming majority of his people. In Sierra Leone, the failure to implement the Abidjan Peace Accord had not only alienated public opinion but had made various sections of society, not least the military, to become disenchanted. Further, the United Nations Security Council did not authorise military intervention in Sierra Leone, as it had done in the case of Haiti after all non-military options had been thoroughly exhausted. But there is another crucial difference: a country whose democratic credentials were not in doubt anywhere had led the intervention in Haiti."

This advice went unheeded as the Nigerian assault continued until frustrated by the military junta. The Conakry meeting of June 26 had contemplated the use of force. Britain did not approve and took this into account when it drafted and sponsored resolution 1132 in the UN Security Council. On July 11, 1997, the British Foreign Secretary made it plain that the use of force was unacceptable to his government and repeated this on numerous occasions.168 For example, on May 6, 1998, he reminded the House of Commons that: "There was no Government policy or UN support for military intervention to restore President Kabbah.

Resolution 1132 and consistent ministerial statements on Sierra Leone stressed that we supported President Kabbah, but wanted him to be restored through diplomatic negotiation, not military intervention."169 The British Prime Minister had earlier confirmed this policy when, in his reply to President Kabbah in June 1997, he had stressed that his government did not consider armed intervention as the most appropriate response to the *coup*.

Unanimously adopted on October 8, 1997, resolution 1132 constitutes the seminal basis for United Nations involvement in the conflict. Its operative paragraph 3 reads:

> "[The Security Council] expresses its strong support for the efforts of the Ecowas Committee to resolve the crisis in Sierra Leone and encourages it to continue to work for the peaceful restoration of the constitutional order, including through the resumption of negotiations."
> 170

Clearly, the language in the first part of the paragraph is expressive of "strong support" for the efforts of Ecowas. However, cognisant of Nigeria's unauthorised use of force on June 2, and the recommendation of the Conakry meeting, the Council wanted to leave no ambiguity about what it intended. So in the second part of the paragraph, it limited its support to encouraging Ecowas "to continue to work for the peaceful restoration of constitutional order, including through the resumption of negotiations." It could not have been otherwise.

Mandating the use of force is most exceptional and, wherever this is contemplated, clear and unambiguous language is required and is often used. This is because every authority to use force is an exception to the fundamental prohibition against the use or threat of force under the UN Charter. A few random examples will suffice. In resolution 221 (1966), the Security Council authorised Britain to ensure "by use of force if necessary" the enforcement of an economic embargo against the illegal Ian Smith regime in Southern Rhodesia. Another example is resolution 1270 (1999), by which the Security Council mandated UNAMSIL to "take the necessary action", within its capabilities and areas of deployment, to ensure the security and freedom of movement of its personnel as well as afford protection to civilians under imminent threat of physical violence. Further examples are resolution 794 of December 3, 1992, on Somalia; resolution 836 of June 6, 1993, on

Bosnia; resolution 940 of July 31, 1994, on the situation in Haiti; and resolution 1264 of September 15, 1999, relating to the situation in East Timor. All these examples show that where the Security Council is desirous of authorising enforcement action under Chapter VII of the Charter, it almost invariably uses unambiguous language. It is quite a different matter whether the enforcement action is carried out at all or whether it is effective for attaining or sustaining the desired goals, as demonstrated by the situations that occurred in Somalia, Rwanda and Bosnia.

Moreover, authorisation to a regional body to take enforcement action under Chapters VII and VIII of the Charter is rare and is in the nature of a delegated power. As such it can be withdrawn as necessary. Article 53 of the Charter makes this clear. It stipulates that before a regional agency can take enforcement action, it must first obtain the authorisation of the Security Council. In the case of Sierra Leone, the Security Council may have felt uneasy about giving such a mandate to Ecowas, dominated as it then was by General Abacha's military junta, whose despotic rule had itself attracted international opprobrium and sanctions. The Council therefore limited its mandate to the taking of peaceful methods only save for the imposition of an embargo on arms and fuel.

Embargo on Sierra Leone

Ecowas leaders had asked for comprehensive sanctions against the AFRC junta in Sierra Leone. They had two objectives in view. One was to mark the disapproval of the military junta by the international community and force it to retreat to the barracks; the other was to secure future compliance with its decisions. But the United Nations Security Council did not agree to comprehensive sanctions. Under resolution 1132, after deploring the *coup* in Sierra Leone and demanding a return to constitutional order and the reinstatement of President Kabbah, it decided to impose only a limited set of sanctions under Chapter VII of the United Nations Charter.

The Ecowas draft had been prepared by Kabbah's government. Under it Kabbah had wanted the United Nations to extend its sanctions to cover such things as fuel, arms and ammunition, military vehicles and equipment, police equipment, spare parts, and commercial trade in all commodities and products. He also wanted travel restrictions imposed on members of the junta, military officers, members of their families and "other entities directly or indirectly connected with the regime" as well as a freeze of their financial assets and those of "civilians directly and indirectly connected with the regime." Thus he wanted punished not only the members of the junta but also the so-called junta collaborators as well.

Mercifully, the Security Council did not agree. It approved only a limited range of sanctions on the supply of "petroleum and petroleum products and arms and related matériel of all types, including weapons and ammunition, military vehicles and equipment, paramilitary equipment and spare parts". Travel restrictions were imposed but only on "members of the military junta and adult members of their families." It exempted travel that was authorised by the Sanctions Committee, for example, travel undertaken in connection with negotiations aimed at ending the conflict. Moreover, unlike the Ecowas draft, the Council specifically exempted humanitarian assistance from its embargo.

The limited nature of the UN embargo should come as no surprise. The main sponsor of the resolution, the United Kingdom, had deliberately circumscribed its scope and effect. As observed by Sir Thomas Legg, the British Government only wanted to "reduce the military capability of the rebels, bring about their quick removal, and secure the return of the legitimate government."171 This is why the embargo approved by the Council was restricted to arms, fuel and travel by junta members and their families. More circumspect than Ecowas, the Council did not like being used as a Trojan Horse to victimise the democratic opposition as well as the military junta. Put simply, it savoured of undemocratic behaviour.

The embargo on arms was imposed on Sierra Leone as a geographical entity. No exception was made for the constitutional government or for the sub-regional forces. Whereas Ecowas had proposed an exemption for weapons intended for the exclusive use of its sub-regional forces in Sierra Leone, the United Nations' policy was aimed at drying up arms supplies to all combatants in the country, be they pro-government or rebel forces. But this aspect was not much publicised; in fact the sponsors of the resolution had deliberately downplayed it. To cite Sir Thomas Legg again, it was "partly because of the sensitivities about the possible role of Ecowas, which, unlike Her Majesty's Government, had explicitly contemplated the use of force, and about the role of Nigeria within Ecowas and Ecomog."[172] The British Government was not going to let the United Nations reward General Abacha's junta for its role in Sierra Leone by permitting it to circumvent its own arms embargo by the European Union.[173] So, when Tony Lloyd informed Parliament that resolution 1132 had "imposed sanctions on the military junta" alone,[174] the Parliamentary Select Committee on Foreign Affairs had rebuked him sharply for telling a "half-truth", adding that "half-truths are a dangerous commodity in which to trade."[175] The Committee regarded his remark as a misdescription and a misstatement of the scope of the arms embargo in that it disguised the fact that it applied to the whole of Sierra Leone, not merely to a part of its territory or to a selected entity.

The embargo on oil, on the other hand, was different. Exceptions were provided for under a no-objections procedure. These covered fuel imports by the "democratically-elected government of Sierra Leone, by any other government or United Nations agencies for verified humanitarian purposes or for the needs of the sub-regional forces", subject to acceptable arrangements for effective monitoring of delivery.[176] On March 16, 1998, the oil embargo was terminated under resolution 1156 following the restoration of constitutional rule.

It may be observed that the scope of these sanctions was wider than those imposed on the NPFL in Liberia in 1992. At the height of that faction's intransigence, Ecowas had made a similar request for the imposition of comprehensive diplomatic, economic and military sanctions. The Security Council had again declined. Its resolution 788 of November 19, 1992, restricted the embargo to the supply of "weapons and military equipment"[177] intended for the warring factions in Liberia. It applied neither to the Interim Government of National Unity (IGNU) nor to Ecomog. On that occasion, the Council was particularly mindful to target only those responsible for the bloodletting in Liberia - the warring parties - and to avoid collateral damage to the blameless civilian population. Consequently, the Ecowas Executive Secretary gave specific instructions to the Ecomog Field Commander to enforce only the very limited military sanctions approved by the Council and to ignore those adopted by Ecowas.

Travel restrictions

Similarly, with regard to travel restrictions, none waš imposed on any person in Liberia even though Ecowas had canvassed for them. In contrast, travel restrictions were imposed on the military junta in Sierra Leone in the very first resolution the Council adopted and at a time when negotiations for a peaceful settlement were pending. So there is no consistency in the Council's practice.

Another example is Haiti. Even though the *coup* had taken place in 1991, travel restrictions were not imposed on the military junta until 1994 and only after several warnings had gone unheeded.[178] Similarly, it took more than six years from the date the Council became seized of the situation in Angola before a travel ban was imposed on senior officials of the National Union for the Total Independence of Angola (UNITA) and adult members of their immediate families.[179]

In the case of Sierra Leone, travel restrictions were imposed on members of the AFRC junta without any prior warning. On January 8, 1998, the Sanctions Committee, established under paragraph 10 of resolution 1132, approved a list of banned individuals. Strangely, though, this list was not published until three weeks later, on January 28.[180] Even more incomprehensible is the fact that the exiled government of President Kabbah submitted a secret list of banned persons to the Sanctions Committee in November 1997. This list contained not just names of members of the junta but much more, including names of members of the democratic opposition. It was never officially published. Yet, some countries took the imprudent step of instituting a travel ban on the civilians named therein without notifying them or giving them an opportunity to rebut the allegations against them, a procedure manifestly contrary to the fundamental principles of due process or natural justice. Nor were procedural protections designed to minimise the risk of receiving governments erring or committing erroneous deprivations observed. Two particular cases may be cited.

(a) *Phillip Sesay's Case*

The first case is that of Dr Phillip Sesay,[181] a Sierra Leonean middle-level career civil servant of 18 years' standing of which 12 were in Washington, DC, as a diplomat. In his bid to rejoin his family in the United States, he arrived at the JFK International Airport in New York on December 20, 1997 with a valid visa that the United States Consul in Freetown had issued to him in 1996. He was arrested and detained by the United States Immigration and Naturalisation Service (INS) on the grounds that he was a member of the military junta in Sierra Leone and therefore barred from entering the United States under a Presidential Proclamation. His visa was also cancelled. The State Department confirmed that determination in a letter to the INS dated February 12, 1998, even though his name was not on the United Nations ban list, adopted on January 8.

As already mentioned, Dr Sesay was a career civil servant. The Civil Service in Sierra Leone, modelled on the British Civil Service, was underpinned by hallowed, centuries-old traditions according to which civil servants are duty-bound to serve the state regardless of the complexion of the government in power, civilian or military, constitutional or extra-constitutional. They do not make policy decisions. Even if Dr Sesay had occupied the highest position in the Civil Service, in law and in practice, he was not, and could not have been, a member of the executive, neither was he a member of the legislature. His substantive rank was that of Acting Director of Protocol in the Ministry of Foreign Affairs, a post offered to him by the government of President Kabbah prior to the *coup*. In October 1997, he was transferred to act as State Chief of Protocol for the military junta, a post he apparently left to return to his family in the United States, where, on arrival, he applied for political asylum. Notwithstanding, he was determined by the American authorities as a member of the banned junta, implying thereby that he was a member either of the executive or legislative branch of government, which he plainly was not.

As regards the possible justification for this determination, two perspectives may be considered. First, that Sesay was detained by virtue of United States policy and second that his detention was grounded on the United Nations resolution. The President of the United States made proclamation 7062 on January 14, 1998, pursuant to section 212(f) of the Immigration and Naturalisation Act. It was entitled "Suspension of Entry as Immigrants and Non-Immigrants of Persons who are Members of the Military Junta in Sierra Leone and Members of their Families." Section 1 of the

Proclamation suspends entry into the United States for members of the military junta in Sierra Leone and members of their families. Section 2, however, gives a wide discretion to United States officials not to apply the provisions of Section 1 to any individual who, though caught by its provisions, it would not be contrary to the interests of the United States to allow to enter. The Secretary of State was given responsibility to determine the persons who are to be affected.

As an instrument made in furtherance of binding resolution 1132, the Proclamation cannot but be read in conjunction with that resolution. Indeed the resolution itself emphasises its binding character as it enjoins "all states and all international and regional organisations to act strictly in conformity" with its provisions. The United States voted for the resolution. The question is whether an inconsistent designation made pursuant to a national proclamation can override a designation made by the Security Council?

Even if the Proclamation were meant to further United States foreign policy objectives in Sierra Leone, designating a person as a member of the military junta although not on the United Nations list, is not devoid of problems. Can it lawfully be done without adequate safeguards, enabling an aggrieved person to rebut the allegations made against him? To say otherwise smacks of arbitrariness and offends the fundamental right to due process.

Quite apart from the Proclamation, there are other difficulties if the designation of Sesay as a member of the junta is based on anything other than the United Nations list. Sesay arrived in New York in December 1997. The United Nations list was adopted on January 8, 1998. Therefore the decision of the INS could not have been based on that list. Could it have been based on the "secret list" prepared by President Kabbah and circulated to the members of the Security Council in November 1997? If so, what is its legal status? A ban on any individual that is based on some secret list hardly meets the requirements of due process. Having voted for resolution 1132, defining the basis on which all members of the United Nations should deal with the junta in Sierra Leone, it was unnecessary for any state to establish its own unilateral criteria for dealing with the junta. To argue contrariwise is to render multilateralism, which resolution 1132 represents, redundant and to put politics ahead of justice, which, in every such case, should be over-arching.

Lastly, it is to be observed that the government of Sierra Leone has granted amnesty to rebels and their collaborators under the Lome Peace Agreement of July 7, 1999. If Sesay were regarded as a rebel collaborator, he would benefit under that amnesty. Save where he has committed a crime under international law, what possible justification could there still be for the United States to continue to deny him his freedom? Can the US afford to ignore these issues merely because Sesay had applied for political asylum? After all, the problem stemmed from an improper determination by the State Department that Dr. Sesay was a member of the military junta as well as from its refusal to correct itself in spite of many representations by Congressmen and others on behalf of the detainee.

(b) *Abass Bundu's Case*

The second case concerns this author. He was detained by the British immigration service for several hours at Heathrow Airport in London on June 19, 1999. No reasons were given but, from the line of questioning, it appeared that the British immigration officer had believed him to be a banned person under resolution 1132. Following representations, it was disclosed that his name had indeed appeared in Kabbah's secret list of November 1997 though not in the final UN list of January 8, 1998.

On September 20, 1999, Peter Hain, who had succeeded Tony Lloyd as the new British Minister of State for African Affairs, replied to an inquiry from Lord Avebury in these terms: "As Tony Lloyd explained in his letter of 27 July, there was a failure of communication between the Foreign and Commonwealth Office and the Immigration Service in January 1998 which resulted in the Immigration Service being unaware that the final UN list, without Dr Bundu's name, had issued. I can only repeat Tony Lloyd's apologies for the inconvenience caused to Dr Bundu by this. Strengthened procedures have now been put in place to ensure that the Home Office has fully up-to-date information on all travel ban regimes in force. This is done through immediate notification of changes rather than through compilation of consolidated lists." Then came this curious revelation: "We applied a travel ban on the basis of the draft list provided by the Permanent Mission of Sierra Leone to the UN Sanctions Committee, pending agreement by the Sanctions Committee on a final list. If we had not acted as we did, leaders of the junta or their key associates would have been free to visit the UK at a time when the junta was quite rightly attracting universal condemnation from the international community for appalling human rights abuses."182

The Minister's apology was accepted, but there are still serious errors of judgment, to say the least. Was there any reasonable justification for using Mr Kabbah's secret list, which obviously included names of the democratic opposition? Familiar as they were with the political landscape, the British government ought to have advised itself against applying the ban to the democratic opposition in Sierra Leone. Furthermore, resolution 1132 did not prohibit the "associates" of the junta, whatever that meant. The prohibition was on "members of the junta and adult members of their families." In another letter dated November 9, the Minister implicitly acknowledged that it was indeed wrong to have used Kabbah's secret list and promised that in future travel bans, they would ensure that "there are no secret lists."

Contrary to what the Foreign Office stated, persons banned under the resolution were obviously not "free" to visit the United Kingdom at any time. Citizens of Sierra Leone holding Sierra Leonean passports are subject to visa requirements for entry into the United Kingdom and have been since September 1994. The granting of visas is a matter in which British Consuls enjoy almost unfettered discretion. A junta member could be refused a visa at any British Consulate on the simple ground that his entry into Britain would not be conducive to the public good. Thus, by its visa regulations, the British authorities could easily have prevented the entry of junta members and their families. It was therefore not necessary to have acted with undue haste by adopting Kabbah's secret list as the basis for exclusion. Besides, a secret list prepared by President Kabbah and circulated to the Council can hardly qualify as a "designation" within the meaning of paragraph 10(f) of resolution 1132, a term that connotes some act of public identification.

The use of Kabbah's secret list raises further questions. By what procedure does the UN Sanctions Committee designate prohibited persons? Are designated persons permitted to make representations to the Committee to establish their innocence or at least to rebut the allegations against them? If so, at what point can they do so? What evidence is admissible? Who carries the burden of proof and what is the standard of proof in such matters?

Nor is the power of the Security Council to impose penalties on individuals merely because they are *persona non grata* with their home governments free from difficulty. While there might have been good reasons for getting at members of the military junta in Sierra Leone, the same cannot be said for the democratic opposition, if the *raison d'etre* of resolution 1132 was the protection of democracy. The Council may be commended for resisting Kabbah's cunning attempt to use it as a stalking horse. Had he succeeded, it would have created a potentially dangerous precedent that other despotic regimes could exploit in future. To take an example, what would be the Council's attitude if the Sudanese government were to ask it to impose travel restrictions on John Garang and his SPLA movement?

Surely, it is a fundamental principle of justice that sanctions ought not to be applied without the usual procedures and safeguards in place, such as the presumption of innocence, due process and reliable evidence. It is therefore important that the Security Council give urgent consideration to the adoption of coherent rules in this area. Such rules should embody natural justice principles that guarantee a designated person the right to rebut any *prima facie* allegation that he or she falls within the category of persons restricted in a relevant resolution of the Council.

Interpreting the embargo

Paragraph 6 of resolution 1132 enjoined all states to prevent "the sale or supply to Sierra Leone by their nationals or from their territories or using their flag vessels or aircraft [of] arms and related matériel of all types" whether originating in their territory or not. Paragraph 8 enjoined Kabbah's government to cooperate with Ecowas in the implementation of the embargo. Because of this, it was argued that the arms embargo was not aimed at Kabbah's government but "only at the illegitimate regime". "President Kabbah could hardly have been asked to police a regime that was directed against him," so the argument ran.[183] The answer to this is two-fold. First, it was not Kabbah's government, but Ecowas, that was authorised to police the embargo. Second, if the Council had intended to exempt Kabbah's government from the scope of the arms embargo, it would have said so explicitly as it did for the oil embargo.

Applied to Sierra Leone as a geographical entity, it mattered not where the arms came from or for whom they were intended or whether they arrived too early or too late for the purpose for which they were intended. "Sierra Leone," for the purposes of the embargo, was defined in the British Order in Council to include the government of Sierra Leone or any other person in or resident in Sierra Leone. Under this formulation, it is sufficient to constitute an offence in Britain that the arms were supplied to any person in or connected with Sierra Leone; it was a violation of British law as well as international law.[184] This formulation of the British law was all the more important, because Britain was the architect of resolution 1132. In a sense, therefore, Britain is the keeper of the shrine!

President Kabbah, of course, believed that the arms embargo did not apply to his government in exile. This was also the understanding of the UN Legal Adviser, who opined that there was an implied exception in favour of the sub-regional forces in Sierra Leone for the purposes defined by the Council in the resolution. "Any other interpretation," he had argued, "would lead to a paradoxical situation in which the Council, while entrusting Ecomog with important responsibilities, at the same time deprived it of the means to carry out those responsibilities."185

Enforcing the embargo

Paragraph 8 of resolution 1132 empowers Ecowas to halt and inspect inbound maritime shipping to verify that they are not carrying prohibited cargoes into the country. Beyond that, Ecowas has neither a general mandate to apply force nor any other role from the Council. It is also specifically enjoined to respect applicable international standards in discharging this responsibility, and to report every thirty days to the Sanctions Committee established under the resolution.

So formulated, all arms shipments by Nigeria to its forces in Sierra Leone, over and above what was strictly required for implementing this mandate, were contrary to the resolution. Recognising this, and desiring to exempt such shipments from the embargo, President Kabbah wrote to the Secretary-General on May 21 to ask that an amendment be made to resolution 1132 to enable those forces to import arms into the country.186 This was granted under resolution 1171 adopted on June 5, 1998. It terminated paragraphs 5 and 6 of resolution 1132 and reimposed a new arms embargo, but this time only on the rebel forces. This amendment would have been unnecessary if the opinion of the UN Legal Adviser had been correct.

Under paragraph 18 of resolution 1132, the Council urged all states to provide technical and logistical assistance to enable Ecowas carry out its responsibilities under the resolution. Is this permission to provide any type of logistics to Ecowas or is it limited to the strict requirements of policing the embargo? Giving logistics to the government of Sierra Leone on a bilateral basis is not affected, but can they also be given to the Nigerian troops in Sierra Leone?

State practice on the matter looks inconclusive. The British government felt no restraint when it supplied vehicles and communications equipment to the sub-regional forces in Sierra Leone, knowing fully well that they might be used for the suppression of internal rebellion. Similarly, on February 11, 1999, Susan Rice, United States Assistant Secretary of State for African

Affairs, announced that her government was asking Congress for US$4 million for logistical support for the Nigerian forces in Sierra Leone. She justified this in terms that those forces were "the only thing between the vicious atrocities of the RUF and the civilian population."187 Likewise, the Commonwealth Secretary-General, on February 2, 1999, called on the member states of his organisation to provide military assistance to the sub-regional forces to suppress the rebellion, because "the defence of Sierra Leone cannot and should not be left to the unaided efforts of a few of its neighbours. Ecomog.....desperately needs material and logistical support to discharge its mission fully and effectively."188 Canada, on the other hand, chose to channel its own assistance to sustaining the peace effort. It gave C$4.5 million to humanitarian aid for displaced persons and refugees, C$2.5 million to the World Bank Trust Fund for Sierra Leone, C$1 million to the United Nations Trust Fund, C$1.5 million to international and Canadian organisations to provide assistance specifically to children affected by war and to amputees, and C$0.5 million to a variety of peace-building efforts, with priority to assisting the demobilisation and reintegration of child soldiers.

British and American logistical assistance had come hard on the heels of the unprecedented sacking of Freetown by the rebels in January and February 1999. The UNOMSIL report to the Security Council spared no words in accusing all the combatants, though to a much greater degree the rebel forces, of serious violations of international humanitarian law.189 If, in spite of this report, the Western Powers still felt no constraint in delivering logistics to the pro-government forces, they may have been driven more by political and moral considerations than by any desire to adhere strictly to the rules of international law. They have repeatedly said, especially after the Somalia debacle, that they no longer have the stomach to commit their own troops to crises in Africa; therefore, helping an African army willing to step into the fray with logistics was the least they could do. After all, somebody else was doing a job, which would otherwise have fallen on their shoulders as permanent members of the Security Council.

Nigeria's difficulty in procuring weapons to prosecute its war in Sierra Leone had been a function partly of its own human rights record but mainly of the international disapproval of its military intervention in Sierra Leone. However, Britain did harbour some residual sympathy for Nigeria, which it wanted translated into an amendment to resolution 1132 to allow for arms supplies to its troops.[190] But the Nigerians did not wait. On February 6, 1998, they struck, four months ahead of the adoption of resolution 1171. Tony Lloyd did not conceal his anger. He said that "the military observer group of Ecowas did not await a United Nations mandate before intervening, [since] Britain worked very hard to ensure that it knew that we would support such a resolution if proper rules of engagement and a proper military plan were presented to the United Nations to give it legal legitimacy."[191]

While the proposed amendment was under contemplation, the Alliance for Peace and Democracy in Sierra Leone, resolute in its campaign for the restoration of constitutional rule by peaceful rather than by violent means, wrote to the British Foreign Secretary and the United Nations Secretary-General on June 1, 1998. It warned about the likely consequences that the lifting of the arms embargo would have, arguing that the West African sub-region was already awash with small arms and that the last thing Sierra Leone needed was an increase in arms supply. The letter went on to add: "Importing arms into Sierra Leone at any time will have the direct effect of increasing the supply of munitions in a country which is, by any standards, already saturated with weapons. It has other potential consequences as well. It would put more weapons in the hands of a private militia, the *kamajors*, which is made up predominantly of a single ethnic group in a multi-ethnic society, as well as in the hands of other combatants like the RUF and the former military junta. It would also open the prospect of increased weapons supply to Ecomog (and by implication Nigeria in breach of the EU arms embargo), thus bolstering its determination to pursue its military solution even though Britain had felt unable to endorse such military action in Sierra Leone. In all, any increase in arms supply could prolong the conflict indefinitely and worsen the suffering of the people of Sierra Leone, with the potential of endangering the peace of the sub-region as a whole."

The Alliance then made proposals for durable peace and stability in the country. "In our humble opinion, what is needed now, more than ever, especially after Kabbah's reinstatement, is the cessation of hostilities, political dialogue and genuine national reconciliation...., not more weapons and more fighting. This is why we welcome resolution 1162 of 17 April 1998 of the Security Council, which emphasises, in Article 3 thereof, 'the need to promote national reconciliation in Sierra Leone and encourages all parties in the country to work together towards this objective'. The time is long past when anyone could afford to be indifferent about what is happening in Sierra Leone or about what is needed to restore lasting peace and security. The time is also past when the international community could look to the parties to the conflict or to Ecomog (in reality, Nigeria) to take the necessary initiative for such reconciliation. The responsibility now falls squarely upon the United Nations to facilitate the process, and, in this context, we appeal to Britain to take a lead role just as she did in the drafting and sponsoring of resolution 1132. We cannot fail to recognise the successful policy of national reconciliation in Northern Ireland, which provides object lessons for Sierra Leone. Indeed, it would be but a natural and logical step in the search for a peaceful resolution of the crisis. No section of Sierra Leonean society is dispensable, nor is it ethical to consider any section as such; therefore all concerned must eschew the use of any more military force and work instead to bring about a permanent comprehensive settlement through peaceful means."

The British Government may not have been unaffected by the weight of this argument but remained undeterred in its plan to help Kabbah's government. As acknowledged by the British Foreign Secretary in February 1999, Sierra Leone was indeed "a country with too many forces too well armed" and that one way to secure its peace and stability was to "dry up the supply of firearms".192

In spite of this, the Security Council adopted resolution 1171, lifting the arms embargo against the government and Ecomog. It also terminated the travel ban imposed by resolution 1132 but renewed it for the "leading members of the former military junta and the RUF" as designated by the Sanctions Committee. These new sanctions would remain in operation until "the control of the government of Sierra Leone has been fully re-established over all its territory" and "all non-governmental forces have been disarmed and demobilised."

Exceeding the UN mandate

Notwithstanding the express limitations on the mandate of Ecowas, the so-called sub-regional forces or, in reality, Nigerian troops exceeded it. Baroness Symons, Parliamentary Under-Secretary in the Foreign and Commonwealth Office, informed the House of Lords: "Our Permanent Representative to the UN made clear at the first meeting of the Sanctions Committee that we expect Nigeria to operate strictly within the provisions of the United Nations Security Council resolution 1132."[193] She was replying to a question whether Britain would propose an extension to the Sanctions Committee's mandate to include a consideration of unauthorised military action by Nigeria, which had resulted in the death of civilians and damage to property in Freetown and elsewhere, and of the payment of compensation to the victims.

A comparison with the maritime blockade of Iraq in 1990 is apposite. When Iraq invaded Kuwait, the Security Council passed a series of resolutions,[194] condemning the invasion and calling upon Iraq to withdraw. When Iraq failed to comply, the Council called for economic sanctions which, in effect, amounted to a blockade of that state. A number of states, basing themselves on resolution 661 (1990), directed their naval forces to interdict trade with Iraq by intercepting neutral vessels, firing across their bows when necessary and diverting them with their prohibited cargoes. When war broke out between Kuwait and Iraq, those states, which had agreed to enforce the naval blockade, joined Kuwait in its defence. When, subsequently, the blockade proved inadequate, the Council passed resolution 678, setting a date by which Iraq must evacuate Kuwait, failing which it authorised "member states co-operating with Kuwait..... to use all necessary means to uphold and implement" all its resolutions on the matter. When this ultimatum expired, those nations comprising the Coalition commenced military action by way of enforcement of the various Security Council resolutions. So, despite occasional references to the contrary, the operations against Iraq were not, strictly speaking, a United Nations operations in the conventional sense. They were operations by a multinational force put together to enforce measures authorised by the Security Council.[195]

The question is whether Ecowas operated strictly within the terms of resolution 1132. It did not. In the first place, Ecowas is not synonymous with Nigeria. The mandate was given to Ecowas as a regional agency which, in turn, established what it called "sub-regional forces" to carry out its mandate. Those forces did not and could not have sub-delegated to Nigeria, because at that time they did not in fact exist. Nigeria had simply usurped the powers of Ecowas and the sub-regional forces. Secondly, commercial goods, food and humanitarian supplies, though not prohibited cargoes, were nonetheless refused entry into Sierra Leone, with dire consequences for the entire civilian population.

It is difficult not to blame the Security Council for these aberrations, because it ought to have known that the Nigerian forces were unlikely to respect any limitations on their mandate. Nigeria had acted unilaterally in Sierra Leone on June 2, 1997, and again and again after that. No sooner the Ecowas summit ended on August 29 than the Nigerian Commander started again to take the law into his own hands. According to eyewitness accounts, Nigerian artillery and warplanes had bombed residential areas of Freetown indiscriminately and persistently, including Mabella and Magazine Wharf. One such bombardment reportedly killed 50 civilians, with many more wounded on September 4. The Nigerian forces had also aimed their fire at international shipping, preventing them from berthing in Freetown. On September 20, a vessel, which was trying to discharge a cargo of rice, was bombed by Nigerian warplanes. All these violations were committed in the name of Ecowas.

These antecedents were sufficient to put the Security Council on notice that the Nigerian forces were unlikely to comply with any restrictions on their military activities. They had waxed, so to speak, so much eloquence that it required no further evidence about what they could do next if given enforcement powers. Having flagrantly disregarded international law once, the probability was great that they would do it again and possibly again.

As stated, the mandate is limited to intercepting and inspecting incoming vessels to ensure that they are not carrying prohibited cargo. The moment the Council passed its resolution on October 8 Nigerian Alpha jets started bombing the headquarters of the Sierra Leone national army in Freetown in an attempt to kill its leaders, then scheduled to hold a meeting there at the time. They went on to bomb other residential locations in the city, provoking an all-out military confrontation that lasted until the Conakry Peace Plan was signed on October 23. As far as the Nigerian forces were concerned, their mandate in Sierra Leone was plainly Nigerian, and the United Nations resolution provided only a fig leaf when required.

The excesses were many and varied. Yet, no attempt was made to stop them. On the contrary, strenuous attempts were made at various times to obfuscate. For example, on November 27, Baroness Symons, in the same written answer from which we quoted earlier, stated that "the circumstances of military action in Sierra Leone are unclear and are disputed by both sides." Whatever the disputed circumstances might have been, one thing is incontrovertible. Outside of UNOMSIL, only the pro-government forces, particularly the Nigerians, had air capability. There is also admission on their part that their shells did fall on ships bringing food into Freetown though they denied taking a deliberate aim at residential areas. Yet the shells that fell in those areas were shells belonging to the Nigerian military. It was clearly a case either of military incompetence on a scale difficult to imagine for a professional army or the aim was deliberate since most of the shells landed in the same vicinity in a firing that lasted several hours. If the first shots had been a mistake, the gunners had all the time in the world to have adjusted their aim.

The conclusion therefore seems inescapable that in their desire to get rid of the junta, anything and everything was game. Britain somehow felt compelled to protect Nigeria against criticism of breaches of international law, because it was the only military power willing to do a job no one else wanted. Robin Cook confessed that the policy of his government was "to look to African states, through Ecowas in West Africa, and the OAU for elsewhere in Africa, to supply troops for peacekeeping purposes."[196] Only when the junta had been ousted did Britain publicly admit that the Nigerian military intervention in Sierra Leone was not "covered by a Security Council mandate."[197]

Can the Security Council also be held responsible? However charitable one might want to be, it is difficult not to point a finger at the Council and its members, in the light of the huge catalogue of misjudgements, miscalculations and transgressions. Their attitude even smacks of acquiescence, if not downright indifference, which contributed in no small measure to the prolongation of the conflict and to the huge suffering of the civilian population. Each time a strong disapproval was called for to compel compliance, the Council turned the other way. It adopted a policy of see no evil, speak no evil. The defenceless citizens of Sierra Leone were thus caught between three evils: the tyranny and brutality of the illegitimate military junta, the terror of the unauthorised military intervention of Nigeria and the insensitivity or cynicism of the international community. What is worse, no one is ever likely to be held accountable.

Embargo on commercial and humanitarian goods

Equally reprehensible is the unilateral extension of the scope of the United Nations embargo to commercial imports and humanitarian goods which, by no stretch of the imagination, come within its scope.

(a) Commercial imports

The Nigerian army extended the embargo to prevent ordinary commercial goods, including food, from entering Sierra Leone. In his Second Report on the Situation in Sierra Leone dated December 5, 1997, the United Nations Secretary-General wrote: "In Freetown, commercial food stocks have dwindled considerably and prices have started to rise as the sanctions take effect. These price increases have affected most the vulnerable groups with limited purchasing power but they are also affecting the majority of the capital's population. It is projected that the remaining commercial food stocks will be severely depleted in approximately two weeks."[198]
Commercial food stocks did run out shortly afterwards. And the price of the main staple, rice, soared from US$20-25 to US$65-75 for a 50-kilogram bag by the time the Secretary-General's Third Report was published two months later.[199] Which *sanctions* was the Secretary-General's Report talking about? If the reference was to UN sanctions, then these applied only to petroleum products and arms. If they were being extended to commodities other than arms and fuel, as the passage above seems

to suggest, why did the Secretary-General not take immediate steps to end such an unlawful extension of the sanctions? If that was not possible, why did he not report the matter to the Security Council?

As no disapproval came from the Security Council, the Nigerian army assumed it had a *carte blanche* in blocking almost anything from reaching the country. The Kabbah government, which had *locus standi* as the only recognised government, did not complain nor was it even inclined to, because the Nigerians were acting in its name and on its behalf. On the other hand, the entity that complained, the AFRC, had no *locus* because it was not recognised as a government. The result was that millions of hapless Sierra Leoneans, caught in the fray and with no money to escape to foreign lands or buy expensive contrabands, were rendered hopeless, voiceless and hungry.

(b) *International humanitarian assistance*

At the end of November 1997, there were fewer than 2,000 metric tons of food aid in stock in the whole country. By February 1998, these stocks were "almost exhausted."200 Throughout the interregnum, the sub-regional forces in Sierra Leone did not hesitate to make unauthorised extensions of the scope of sanctions to prevent international humanitarian assistance from entering the country. Resolution 1132 had expressly obligated "all those concerned, including Ecowas, the UN and other international humanitarian agencies, to establish appropriate arrangements for the provision of humanitarian assistance and to endeavour to ensure that such assistance responds to local needs and is safely delivered to, and used by, its intended recipients".201

Notwithstanding, the so-called sub-regional forces prevented humanitarian supplies from entering Sierra Leone, claiming this was in keeping with the Ecowas embargo.202 They insisted that all humanitarian supplies must first be taken to Liberia or Guinea for inspection. The international aid agencies complained but to no avail. General Malu insisted, saying: "Either they are cleared or they do not come at all."203

With great respect, this was more than an error of judgment. It looked more like an insouciant disregard for the United Nations. Once the limits of resolution 1132 were exceeded, the tendency was to take refuge behind a so-called Ecowas embargo. This was so, despite the oft-repeated assurances by the Nigerian Foreign Minister that Ecowas would not constrain humanitarian relief operations into Sierra Leone.204 As far as the Nigerian military was concerned, there were two embargoes, one imposed by the United Nations and the other by Ecowas. The latter was claimed, albeit erroneously, as a convenient cover for their military excesses.205 The result was that food aid stocks ran out, food prices soared, and the poor masses starved, giving rise to a humanitarian emergency. It did not take long before the emergency spiralled into a crisis. And, in spite of all the Nigerian assurances, not a grain of rice or a tablet of aspirin was allowed into Sierra Leone.

In truth, there was only one lawful embargo on Sierra Leone, the one imposed by the Security Council. The so-called Ecowas embargo needed prior Security Council authorisation the absence of which made it unlawful under international law. The Council did give authorisation but it was expressly limited to the two commodities mentioned therein, fuel and arms; it was certainly not an open-ended embargo.

Such was the pathetic situation in Sierra Leone despite unequivocal assurances by members of the Council that sanctions would never be used to punish the civilian population. Ambassador Bill Richardson of the United States, for example, had assured the international community that "the resolution does not limit shipments of food, medicines and other basic necessities. It contains provisions for regular review of the implementation and impact of sanctions. The sanctions are designed to have maximum impact against the junta in Sierra Leone while imposing a minimum burden on the civilian population." His Japanese counterpart made a similar promise: "[T]through the implementation of these provisions, the negative impact of the sanctions on the civilian population will be kept to a minimum. We look forward to the Secretary-General's report on the situation in Sierra Leone and will be interested in its evaluation of the humanitarian conditions there."

Two weeks after the Secretary-General's Second Report, the United Nations Department of Humanitarian Affairs admitted that the medical emergency response capability in Sierra Leone had been drastically reduced, contributing greatly to the spread of disease. It concluded with the following chilling revelation: "UN and humanitarian agencies are challenged to maintain even the most basic health and nutrition services without additional supplies being brought in from Guinea immediately. Even on-going humanitarian operations inside Sierra Leone by NGOs such as MSF, ACF and MERLIN are now experiencing difficulties in restocking. This is primarily due to the fact that the procedures for the sanctions exemptions mechanisms are not in place and thus relief goods exempted from the embargo according to agreed-upon DHA recommendations to Ecowas, are not moving across the border as expected. Ecowas will clear operations to begin after the fielding of an inspection team at the border."[206]

No sooner the junta was chased out of the capital than the Nigerian soldiers tried to pass the buck, blaming the aid agencies for being too slow in responding to the crisis. "The aid agencies have been slow in getting food to the needy. We have assured them many times this week that Lungi is safe," said the Nigerian Commander.[207] Still, members of the Security Council did not feel able to stand up to these abuses. For example, in reply to a question in the House of Lords in January 1998, Baroness Symons said: "We support UN Security Council resolution 1132. The UN Sanctions Committee, of which we are a member, is aware of the problems with processing humanitarian shipments on the border and efforts are being made to address this problem through contacts between the UN and Ecowas."[208] The question was whether, as a permanent member of the Security Council, Britain would take steps to stop the Nigerian forces from unlawfully extending the embargo to prevent the delivery of humanitarian relief supplies to Sierra Leone.

Only much later, after the junta had been evicted from Freetown, did the British government publicly admit that the delivery of humanitarian assistance had been a serious problem. It issued a declaration as President of the European Union on February 20, 1998, a week after the fall of the junta, acknowledging that "the need now is for targeted humanitarian operations to start as soon as possible to relieve the suffering of the people. We urge Ecomog to co-operate with the United Nations, European Community Humanitarian Office and other aid agencies to facilitate this process, to ensure that international humanitarian law is upheld and to assure the security of those engaged in providing such relief." 209

This came after the UN Inter-Agency Assessment Mission to Sierra Leone published its interim report on February 10.210 It warned of a possible food crisis if a rapid humanitarian intervention was not undertaken. The report then put the blame squarely where it belonged: "The difficulties encountered by those operational agencies to ship their humanitarian consignments into Sierra Leone has revealed that Ecowas lacks the capacity to administer an exemptions process. The recent blockade of medicine by Ecowas confirms that the overall procedure needs to be reviewed urgently."211 On February 26, the Security Council responded by requesting Ecomog as well as all those concerned "to ensure safe and unrestricted access to those in need".212

If only the Council had acted sooner, by standing up to its responsibility, much of the suffering that it was now trying to alleviate could have been avoided.213 The apparent lapses have led to criticisms of the United Nations, to the effect that it condoned the use of food as a weapon of war, contrary to Article 14 of Protocol II of 1977 or as part of a wider strategy to dislodge the junta. It is not that humanitarian relief should have been delivered at all cost, but that, at least, the United Nations could have adopted prudent and pragmatic measures to minimise possible abuse, if this were a major problem, by developing effective mechanisms to ensure transparency and accountability.

The Sierra Leone situation also provides a classic example of how *not* to delegate enforcement powers to a regional organisation, especially where it is evident that its decision-making process is dominated by a single member whose respect for the principles of transparency and accountability is not assured or whose national agenda is different from that of the United Nations.

(c) *Complaints by humanitarian agencies*

These infractions were not for want of protest. Several NGOs did complain about the Nigerian excesses. One of them, ActionAid, a British NGO, did not just complain to the UN and Ecowas; it took the matter right up to its national legislature. On

May 15, 1998, it submitted a brief to the British Members of Parliament in which it stated as follows:

"From the *coup* in 1997 until the restoration of President Kabbah in March 1998, the UK's Department for International Development (DFID) greatly limited its funding of all aid programmes in Sierra Leone. It appears that the restriction of aid was a deliberate component of a wider political strategy to dislodge the military junta. This raises the question about the extent to which the FCO was instrumental in limiting humanitarian relief to Sierra Leone.

"At a time when basic services were collapsing and needs were increasing, aid agencies were unconvinced by the government's attempts to justify this decision. The consensus among aid workers was that the delivery of well-targeted humanitarian assistance would not have compromised the broader political aims of the international community. Moreover, it would have helped to reduce suffering of many civilians in a country that is already one of the poorest in the world.

"ActionAid welcomes the growing recognition by the international community, post-Rwanda, that the political aspects of conflict need to be addressed. Yet in this case it appears that political objectives were pursued at the expense of humanitarian action. Civilians caught up in conflict have a right to receive relief regardless of politics. This principle provides the basis for humanitarian responses in complex emergencies...

"ActionAid believes that the government should review its humanitarian aid policies to ensure that it can address both the political context of conflict situations as well as respond to humanitarian needs as they develop. It should also actively support the development of effective protocols for humanitarian operations to enhance the protection of vulnerable communities, to contribute to existing coping mechanisms and to reduce the potential for the delivery of humanitarian aid to fuel conflict. This will help to prevent a similar scenario taking place again."

In a defiant reply, Clare Short, British Secretary of State for International Development, said: "[We] did not reduce humanitarian aid to Sierra Leone to put pressure on the *coup* leaders. I personally met my officials and supervised everything that we did on that. That allegation has been made by one NGO and it just is not so; some of my officials have written to it on the matter. There was real trouble getting resources in and not feeding the fighters. That is always a serious problem but, through NGOs and the Red Cross, we put in as much relief as we could get through to people. We also funded a radio station so that people could gain access to the truth. We funded many refugees and prepared the government to return. We did not cut resources to hurt people."214

Be that as it may, the Minister failed to offer any statistics of food and medical supplies that got through to the people during the interregnum. There could hardly have been any from Guinea, where the sub-regional forces studiously refused to allow anything to pass through the land borders, to say nothing about access through the port of Freetown.

Enforcement action under Chapter VII of the UN Charter

Resolution 1132 was adopted under Chapter VII of the Charter but at a time when the avenues for a peaceful settlement under Chapter VI had not been entirely exhausted, as exemplified by the subsequent adoption of the Conakry Peace Plan barely a fortnight later. Moreover, the authority of the Security Council to impose a blockade is contained in Article 42 of the Charter (Chapter VII) the application of which is predicated upon a prior determination that the measures provided for under Article 41 would be inadequate or have proved to be inadequate. Was there such a determination under Article 41?

Even before that, the Council is required to make a preliminary determination, this time under Article 39, that the situation in Sierra Leone did constitute a "threat to international peace and security". This is the peg upon which crises of many colours have been hung. Can the unlawful overthrow of a constitutional government by itself trigger an Article 39 determination? Can the outflow of refugees by itself trigger such a determination? Is the Council bound, consistent with modern principles of probity, to offer reasons for its determination?

When the Council first considered the crisis in July and again in August 1997, it had merely expressed "concern about the grave crisis in Sierra Leone," which it said had endangered the peace, security and stability of the whole region. It also expressed worry about the likely negative impact it might have on the on-going electoral process in neighbouring Liberia.215 All these were Chapter VI determinations, requiring the situation to be resolved by peaceful means only. The dramatic change came two months later. Without any explanation, and with the United Nations staff and other diplomats, who could have given direct evidence, away from the scene, the Council determined, on October 8, that the crisis was a Chapter VII crisis, a threat to international peace and security in the region.

Numerous examples of illegal usurpation of state power have taken place in Africa over the past three to four decades. In West Africa alone, out of the 16 member states of Ecowas, only two, Cape Verde and Senegal, have so far escaped a revolutionary change of government. Some countries, like Sierra Leone and Nigeria,216 have experienced it more than once. Yet, there had been no determination under Article 39, comparable to that made by the Council in respect of the events of May 25, 1997, in Sierra Leone.

The next question is whether the Council's determination under Article 39 must be transparent? Or is it sufficient if it rests entirely on the absolute discretion of its members? If so, then the Article can hardly escape obfuscation, and different standards will inevitably apply to different situations. Moreover, small, weak and impoverished states will be at the mercy of the permanent members of the Council while the strong, powerful and rich ones will go scotch free. Compare the Council's reaction to the *coup* in Sierra Leone with its inaction in the situation in the two Congos (Kinshasa and Brazzaville) and Guinea-Bissau, all happening within months of each other. Reconciling them can be most daunting, to say the least.

In the case of the two Congos, both mineral-rich countries, the inaction of the Security Council may not have been uninfluenced by certain extraneous factors. The United States' alleged complicity in the overthrow of Mobutu, its long-standing friend in Congo (Kinshasa), who had fallen into disfavour and possibly desuetude as well, cannot be ruled out in that it may have given the nod to Uganda and Rwanda to assist Kabila's insurrection against him.

In the case of Congo (Brazzaville), the fourth largest oil producer in sub-Saharan Africa after Nigeria, Angola and Gabon, General Sasso Nguesso had moved deftly and concluded deals with some 12 Western oil companies, including the French group, Elf-Aquitaine, which does 80 per cent of the exploration and mining activities in Congo Brazzaville. It was therefore not surprising that France was the first Western Power to establish official dealings with Nguesso. The United States had developed a new relationship with the Angolan government, whose direct military intervention led to the removal of both President Lissouba and President Mobutu from power. This has put Angola's large, experienced and well-equipped army in a strategic position in the region, thanks to the almost US$4 billion it is earning every year in oil revenue alone, to say nothing about its other mineral exports including diamonds. With the end of the Cold War went Western support for UNITA and its cause and all United Nations resolutions since have pointedly condemned it, the result of the United States switching its support to the dos Santos government in Luanda to protect its huge investments in the two Congos. According to *The Economist*: "When Madeleine Albright, America's Secretary of State, was in Luanda last month, she remarked that Angola now supplies America with seven per cent of its oil imports. As if to stress America's friendship with the government it once tried to overthrow, she added that this represented three times as much as America was getting from Kuwait just before the Iraqi invasion [in 1991]. The message to Mr Savimbi, once given a reception at the White House worthy of a head of state, was clear."[217]

On the other hand, Western economic interests in Sierra Leone are at best marginal and certainly bear no comparison to their assets in the two Congos. So, on the face of it, they have precious little to protect in Sierra Leone at the time. But there are other considerations, not least being their economic ties with Nigeria, whose military regime had made the forcible reinstatement of President Kabbah's government in Sierra Leone a high foreign policy objective, linked almost imperceptibly to the broader goal of redeeming its own tarnished international image. As admitted by Madeleine Albright, during her visit to Nigeria on October 19,

1999, the United States is "Nigeria's largest trade and investment partner" and relies on her for eight percent of its oil imports, even more than it is presently importing from Angola. These economic assets probably explain the somewhat half-hearted criticism of Nigeria's military intervention in Sierra Leone, and of Angola's intervention in the two Congos. Indeed, the United States was among the first to praise the Nigerian troops on their successful counter-coup against the AFRC. On February 13, 1998, the Department of State congratulated them, saying: "We have now received information that Freetown as well as most parts of Sierra Leone are now firmly under the control of Ecomog forces and are satisfied that this has been achieved with minimum loss of lives. We congratulate the new Force Commander of Ecomog, Major-General Timothy Shelpidi, and the Ecomog High Command for their professionalism, determination and commitment to implement the Ecowas mandate. We commend, in particular, Colonel Maxwell Khobe and his men for their courage and gallantry in carrying out their assignment."218

Thus, the protection of Western economic and strategic interests abroad has been developed into an art form, and can be seen at work *par excellence* in West Africa. Western attitudes also lend vitality to the old adage "nothing succeeds like success". The Americans, who, at the beginning, had expressed serious reservations about Nigeria's military intervention in Sierra Leone, were to make such a virtue of their success that the Security Council, which, only the week before, was chiding Ecowas Ministers for their inadequate briefing, now felt bound to follow suit. It commended "the important role that Ecowas has continued to play towards the peaceful resolution of this crisis" and "encouraged Ecomog to proceed in its efforts to foster peace and stability in Sierra Leone, in accordance with the relevant provisions of the UN Charter."219

So, when it comes down to it, what appeals to the Western Powers is not conscience; if it were so, it would probably be misconceived. What really matters is their national economic and strategic interests. How else can one rationally explain why the almost identical situations in the two Congos and Sierra Leone, involving as they did the illegal overthrow of an incumbent constitutional government, were not accorded the same treatment. Need one emphasise too strongly that the attitude of the Security

Council was largely defined by that of the Western Powers on the Council?

CHAPTER 5

The Role of Civil Society and the Effect of Non-Recognition

Non-co-operation of civil society

Civil disobedience can be a potent instrument for effecting peaceful political change. It first emerged in Sierra Leone in 1996. The NPRC military junta was showing reluctance to demit office and had to be pressured. This was done at two resounding National Consultative Conferences at the Bintumani Hotel Complex, where civil society asserted its moral weight. The military junta, taking advantage of the war situation in the country, had launched a campaign for peace before elections in order to have the elections postponed, but the mood in the country did not support them. The people overwhelmingly opted for the enthronement of democracy. So, when, in the course of the deliberations of the Bintumani conference, the junta sounded like not wanting to quit, civil society joined forces with the political parties to bring the matter to a head. It was a triumph for national dialogue as a powerful and effective arbiter in a beleaguered polity.

There was already this precedent when the military struck again on May 25, 1997, just fourteen months after the NPRC had been ejected from office. So, from the beginning, the *coup* was doomed. It also turned out to be one of the most brutal ever. Looting was rampant and the looters did not even spare the ramshackle homes of the poor. Exacerbated by convicts sprung out of prison, who combined with the unemployed to prey on affluent neighbours, anarchy gripped Freetown.

The environment for intervention by civil society thus existed. But the civilian population was rudderless as those who could lead were the first to decamp to overseas destinations, including politicians, lawyers, doctors, judges, public servants, business executives, bankers and administrators, to name a few. The Labour Congress was a noticeable exception. An amalgam of 21 affiliate labour unions, its relationship with the junta was anything but friendly. Public sector employees withheld their services when fear gave way to stunning defiance and non-co-operation. Backed by their respective unions, they ignored orders to return to work.

The teachers were particularly outstanding as most schools remained closed throughout the interregnum. The Labour Congress advised its members to stay at home using the state of insecurity and the non-payment of salaries to good effect. Even when salaries were paid, it still rejected overtures from the junta that its members return to work. Instead it presented a ten-point plan, calling on the junta, *inter alia*, to restore democracy and work toward a negotiated settlement.

Another factor that conduced civil disobedience was the very poor state of the economy. Official revenue fell by 90 per cent, while foreign aid, which before the *coup* accounted for upwards of 50 per cent of the national budget, plummeted to zero. Customs revenues also virtually dried up when the embargo, albeit illegal, began to bite. Apart from the government-owned banks like the Central Bank, the Sierra Leone Commercial Bank and the Sierra Leone Development Bank, no other bank opened for business, despite repeated calls by the military regime for them to do so. The Association of Sierra Leone Commercial Banks predicated its co-operation on several pre-conditions, including the completion of repairs to the physical structures of the banks that had been damaged during the *coup*; the provision of adequate security; the replenishment of liquidity by the Central Bank; and the retrieval of vehicles commandeered by the coupists. The closure of the banks had resulted in a severe liquidity squeeze, virtually paralysing the formal sector of the economy. In the manufacturing sector, the little that was being produced before the *coup* rapidly ground to a halt when shipment of raw materials and spare parts ceased.

Thus, towards the end of 1997, the junta's administration was not unencumbered. And the withholding of services contributed to this greatly. Imagine what it could have been if the entire spectrum of civil society had stood firmly.

The second time that civil disobedience made its mark was in January 1999. The unchallenged rebel attack on Freetown had resulted in substantial erosion of public confidence in the ability of the pro-government forces and a corresponding increase in public demand for a negotiated settlement. So, when President Kabbah looked like dragging his heels over the issue, civil disobedience again asserted itself. This was reflected in the withholding of services by public servants, teachers and students refusing to return to school, and the judicial system remaining dysfunctional.220 The result was a lame administration throughout the country, including the capital. A former American Ambassador has described the situation as one of "virtual collapse" of government.221

The situation also gave birth to a Human Rights Committee in January 1999. Initially operating from Conakry, its membership consisted of a coalition of local and international human rights and humanitarian organisations, including the National Commission for Democracy and Human Rights, the National Forum for Human Rights, Medecins sans Frontieres, OXFAM and Christian Aid. The Committee mandated the Sierra Leonean members to take the lead in promoting demand for a peaceful resolution of the conflict.

On March 2, the ARTICLE 19 organisation called on the international community to support the demand for the active involvement of civil society in the search for peace. It particularly endorsed the call for the creation of a truth and reconciliation commission. As opined by Andrew Puddephatt, Executive Director of ARTICLE 19, "There needs to be an honest reckoning with the horrifying human rights abuses which have occurred in Sierra Leone. We welcome the Human Rights Committee's recognition of this and call upon the international community and the Government of Sierra Leone to take on board recommendations from civil society. Every Sierra Leonean must feel that they have a choice, both in deciding what has gone wrong over the past decade and in rebuilding the country. ARTICLE 19 strongly urges the government to make public consultation an integral part of the peace process."222

Non-recognition of the military junta

    (a)   By sovereign states (other than the United Kingdom)

The international rules governing the recognition of regimes born of unconstitutional procedures are less well settled than those relating to the recognition of new states. This is generally because the decision whether or not to recognise such regimes is essentially an exercise of prerogative power often embedded in or driven by notions of public policy or national interest, spheres in which the courts are rightly chary to intrude. It is thus beyond the pale of judicial review. Nonetheless, it is instructive to see what international practice has been.

In the 1950s, the United States pursued a practice that was not only discretionary but also expressive of its disapproval of the unconstitutional character of the government. The domestic acceptability of a new regime and its willingness to comply with international obligations were also significant factors. However, by the close of the 1970s, recognition as a policy had faded away and was replaced by a simple test, which de-emphasised the recognition process. The question became one of how the United States perceived its national interest to be affected by the new situation that has arisen in the foreign country concerned.223 Thus, in defining its attitude to the Afghan *coup* of April 27, 1978, the State Department spokesman said that "the question of recognition under the formulation of the last few years does not arise *per se*" and that the important question was not recognition but "whether diplomatic relations should continue."224 It took a similar position with regard to the two Congos in 1997.

With regard to the Sierra Leone *coup* of May 25, however, with no major American interest at stake, the State Department promptly condemned the *coup* and called on the junta to return authority to the country's elected leadership and parliament.225 Subsequently, it denied the junta access to monies and properties in the United States belonging to the government of Sierra Leone. After the Conakry peace accord was signed in October 1997, the AFRC had attempted to access funds in America belonging to the government of Sierra Leone. The Federal Reserve Bank sent a message to the junta to say that the United States would only deal officially with Kabbah as President of Sierra Leone. Kabbah had advised the Bank not to do any business with the Bank of Sierra Leone and to ignore any instructions it received from it.226

For the French Government, its modern practice has been not to grant formal recognition to regimes which come to power unconstitutionally.227 The Latin American states follow a similar practice under the Estrada doctrine. That doctrine posits that once the state is recognised, formal recognition of any change of government therein is immaterial.228

(b) United Kingdom practice

In the 1950s and 1960s successive British governments followed a policy enunciated by Mr. Herbert Morrison, British Foreign Secretary, in terms that it was international law which defined the conditions for recognising a government as *de jure* or *de facto* and that it was a matter of judgment in each particular case whether a regime has fulfilled the conditions. *De facto* recognition was given where the new regime was in effective control of most of the state's territory and seemed likely to continue. *De jure* recognition, on the other hand, was reserved for a regime that not merely had effective control over most of the state's territory, but was able to show that that control was firmly established. Recognition was granted automatically once the conditions specified by international law were fulfilled; it did not depend on whether or not the character of the regime was to the liking of the British government.229

These were the criteria adhered to when the British government recognised the unconstitutional regime of China in 1951, the Kadar regime in Hungary in 1956, the military junta in Greece in 1967, the Pinochet government in Chile in 1973, and the Rawlings government in Ghana in 1979, for example. Each was found to have fulfilled the criteria and it mattered little that the manner in which they had come to power had attracted adverse publicity in the British press. For example, the British Government continued to recognise the Pol Pot regime in Kampuchea until December 1979 when it accepted it had lost effective control, even though it had been under investigation for human rights violations.230

English courts, as a general rule, follow the executive branch in order to avoid speaking with discordant voices on the matter. Questions like the legal *persona* of a revolutionary regime or its *locus standi* were determined by the English courts according to whether it has been recognised by the British government either as the *de facto* or *de jure* government of the state concerned. If it was not recognised, it did not get *locus* in the courts and its acts had no effect in England. Thus, recognition by the British government was the decisive factor and the courts generally resolved such issues by reference to the executive certificate of the Foreign Office.

This was the practice up to April 28, 1980, when Lord

Carrington, as then British Foreign Secretary, announced a new policy. He said: "We shall no longer accord recognition to governments. The British government recognise states in accordance with common international doctrine." Then he enunciated the new policy as follows:

"Where an unconstitutional change of regime takes place in a recognised state, governments of other states must necessarily consider what dealings, if any, they should have with the new regime, and whether and to what extent it qualifies to be treated as the government of the state concerned. Many of our partners and allies take the position that they do not recognise governments and that therefore no question of recognition arises in such cases. By contrast, the policy of successive British governments has been that we should make and announce a decision formally 'recognising' the new government.

This practice has sometimes been misunderstood, and, despite explanations to the contrary, our 'recognition' interpreted as implying approval. For example, in circumstances where there might be legitimate public concern about the violation of human rights by the new regime, or the manner in which it achieved power, it has not sufficed to say that an announcement of 'recognition' is simply a neutral formality.

We have therefore concluded that there are practical advantages in following the policy of many other countries in not according recognition to governments. Like them, we shall continue to decide the nature of our dealings with regimes which come to power unconstitutionally in the light of our assessment of whether they are able of themselves to exercise effective control of the territory of the state concerned, and seem likely to continue to do so."231

When asked how, in future, it may be ascertained whether, on a particular date, the British government regarded a new regime as the government of the state concerned, the Foreign Secretary replied:

"In future cases where a new regime comes to power unconstitutionally, our attitude on the question whether it qualifies to be treated as a government will be left to be inferred from the nature of the dealings, if any, which we may have with it, and in particular on whether we are dealing with it on a normal government-to-government basis."232

The dealings, which matter, are governmental dealings. What is not altogether clear, however, is whether it is the courts alone that should draw the inference entirely from the facts and circumstances of each case, completely unaided by the executive branch of government. Some jurists think that the criteria have not much changed and that in effect it is still a matter of recognition by the government, the only difference being that, whereas before 1980 a public announcement was necessary, nowadays it is left to be ascertained as a matter of inference; a sort of theory of "inferred recognition".233 However, in at least one case, the phrase "left to be inferred" has been interpreted as one "designed to fulfil a need for information in an international or political, not a judicial, context".234

The new British policy was first announced on April 25, 1980, two weeks after Master Sergeant Samuel Kanyon Doe overthrew the Tolbert government in Liberia. At that time the Doe junta had still not been recognised. Under the new policy, no formal announcement was required and none was made. Diplomatic relations was maintained through the British Embassy in Monrovia and the Liberian Embassy in London. In September 1980, a new British Ambassador to Liberia was appointed, agrément for which was sought and obtained in the usual way, notwithstanding the international condemnation of the Doe junta for its flagrant violations of human rights, including the summary execution of President Tolbert and several other top officials of the deposed government.235 Similarly, in September 1980, the British government did not make any announcement about recognition following the military *coup* in Turkey that was accompanied by extensive domestic violence. The Foreign Secretary subsequently participated in a joint declaration by the Foreign Ministers of the EEC, which noted with concern the military take-over in Turkey and called for a speedy return to democratic government. It neither condemned the *coup* nor asked for a recall of European Ambassadors in Ankara.236

Again, in May 1997, when President Mobutu of Congo (Kinshasa) was violently overthrown in a rebellion led by Laurent

Kabila, assisted by foreign troops from neighbouring countries, Western Governments had no difficulty establishing official dealings with the new government. This was so even though the human rights record of the new regime and its lack of progress towards democratisation were under severe scrutiny. This attitude of the Western Powers was mirrored in the United Nations Security Council when it glossed over Charter violations resulting from the armed intervention of neighbouring countries. It merely called for the withdrawal of all external forces and for an agreement to be reached rapidly on a peaceful transition, including the holding of democratic elections.237 No condemnation was made of any foreign military intervention.

A month later, in June 1997, heavy fighting erupted in the neighbouring state of Congo (Brazzaville) between the armed forces of the constitutional government of President Pascal Lissouba and a private militia led by General Denis Sassou-Nguesso, a former Head of State, and supported by Angolan forces and foreign mercenaries. By mid-October, Sassou Nguesso had claimed effective control of most of the country. By the end of October, the fighting had become extremely bloody and had assumed ethnic dimensions. The UNHCR estimated that approximately 500,000 of the 858,000 inhabitants of Brazzaville had fled the city either into the interior of the country or to neighbouring Congo (Kinshasa). President Lissouba himself was forced to relocate outside the country. He eventually received asylum in the United Kingdom, having been rejected by France.

Again, in keeping with its new policy, the British government made no official announcement of recognition. In reply to a Parliamentary question whether the British government recognised the new government of Sassou Nguesso, Baroness Symons, Minister of State in the FCO, said that though her government deplored the violent overthrow of the constitutional government and unlawful military interventions, "it is the practice of [the British Government] to recognise states (including the Republic of the Congo), not governments."238 Again, on April 8, 1998, she said: "The European Union has noted Sassou Nguesso's creation of a National Forum for Unity, Democracy and the Reconstruction of the Republic of the Congo and his plans for the re-establishment of democracy. The European Union remains concerned both at the continued presence of Angolan troops and about the proposed transition programme. The European Union will press Sassou Nguesso on the need for an inclusive political progress."239 She was answering a question about the attitude of the European Union Foreign and Security Policy Working Group to alleged human rights abuses in Congo (Brazzaville).

At that time, doubts existed in many quarters about the ability of the new regime to exercise effective control of the country on its own. Although evidence of official dealings between Britain and the Nguesso regime were rare, neither it nor the United Nations Security Council condemned the unconstitutional overthrow of the legitimate government of President Lissouba. The Presidential Statement of the Security Council of October 16 only condemned external military interference in the Republic of the Congo and called for the immediate withdrawal of foreign troops.240 Angola did not comply.241

The French Government, for its part, wasted no time in establishing formal links with President Nguesso, who paid an official visit to Paris in December 1997. France's attitude may have influenced Britain and the rest of the EU.242 By April 1998, the EU, with British participation, was already "taking note" of official decisions of the new regime.243 On March 8, 1999, when a story broke in London, allegedly implicating Lissouba in a conspiracy to organise a counter-*coup* against Sassou Nguesso, *The Mirror* newspaper in London, in an editorial, opined strongly as follows:

> "As the democratically elected President of Congo Brazzaville, he introduced essential human rights to his country. We have every sympathy with his desire to get back into office after being overthrown in a bloody military *coup*. But the means by which he plans to return to power are abhorrent...... It will not just be enemy soldiers who will suffer if Lissouba blasts his way back to power. Innocent civilians, as always, will be caught in the cross-fire. There will be death, destruction, famine, disease and homelessness. This private war, which has no backing from the international community, is being planned from London. Yet, again, it is Britain that is being used as the base for overseas intrigues. By refusing to take action against Lissouba, the Foreign Office is giving tacit approval for his machinations. This is utterly

unacceptable. Britain can be proud that it gave refuge to a deposed democratic leader. But if that leader abuses British hospitality, the Foreign Office must make it absolutely plain that he will be kicked out."244

Unlike Sierra Leone, there was no breach of any United Nations sanction because there was none. Only British law was at stake. The question was whether the alleged conspiracy, if made in England, amounted to statutory conspiracy and therefore punishable under the Criminal Justice (Terrorism and Conspiracy) Act, 1998. However, no prosecution was brought against anyone.245

But Britain took a radically different view of the May 1997 *coup* in Sierra Leone. As in Congo (Brazzaville), that *coup* had resulted in the unlawful overthrow of the constitutional government and the coupists were in effective control of the country. But, unlike Congo, the Sierra Leone *coup* was purely internal, unaided at the material time by any foreign army. Although the Carrington doctrine did not define "effective control," Lord Atkin's dictum in *The Arantzazu Mendi* offers persuasive authority. "By 'exercising *de facto* administrative control' or 'exercising effective administrative control'," His Lordship understood to mean "exercising all the functions of a sovereign government, in maintaining law and order, instituting and maintaining courts of justice and adopting or imposing laws regulating the relations of the inhabitants of the territory with one another and with the government."246

There was evidence enough that the junta in Sierra Leone was doing all of these things. Yet, the British government declined to have any governmental dealings with it, choosing instead to close its diplomatic mission in Freetown and relocate its High Commissioner to Conakry where he continued to attend to the exiled President. This British reaction probably had more to do with political disapproval of the junta than with the application of foreign policy criteria. The British Minister of State in the FCO told the House of Commons, on July 11, 1997, that as far as they were concerned: "There is no new government in Sierra Leone. We condemned the military *coup* which took place there on May 25, 1997 and consistently called for the restoration of the legitimate government of President Kabbah." His rationale was that "those who led the *coup* have no support from their own people or from the international community. International stability and respect for human rights are core parts of the Foreign and Commonwealth Office mission statement. They have an evident relevance to the situation in Sierra Leone."247

Thus, regardless of the situation on the ground, which in many respects bore a resemblance to that in Congo (Brazzaville), the position of the British government was that Sierra Leone did not have a new government as President Kabbah's legitimacy had not vanished. Baroness Symons underlined this when she said: "We decide the nature of our dealings with regimes which come to power unconstitutionally in the light of our assessment of whether they are able of themselves to exercise effective control of the territory of the state concerned, and seem likely to continue to do so."248

Can these differing attitudes of the British government be reconciled? In Sierra Leone, on the one hand, a deliberate decision was taken, regardless of the situation on the ground, to withhold substantive official dealings from the military junta. In Congo (Brazzaville), on the other hand, the Carrington doctrine was applied even though the regime seemed unable of itself to exercise effective control. If "global support of democracy"249 is truly now part of British foreign policy, as is so often claimed, necessitating the withholding of official dealings from unelected military juntas, it is difficult to understand why this was not done in the case of Congo (Brazzaville). There, the constitutional government was not only overthrown unconstitutionally; it was done illegally with the help of foreign troops on whom the new regime came to depend for survival. Baroness Symons tried to distinguish between the two situations, contending that Kabbah had remained the legitimate leader of Sierra Leone even after the *coup*, while "the outbreak of civil war in June in Congo (Brazzaville) [had] resulted in the cancellation of the presidential election and the subsequent expiry of President Lissouba's mandate in August 1997."250

With respect, this distinction is fatuous. If the outbreak of civil war in Congo (Brazzaville) had resulted in the cancellation of the presidential election and the expiry of the incumbent President's term of office, then surely there was a vacuum. Could it be filled by the victor of the duel between the incumbent and the challenger? Was this so prescribed by the Congolese constitution?

In any case, is it proper to use undemocratic means to change a government? Is it ethical?

What really could be argued was that, in principle, the conflict brought about a suspension of the election. As such, the legitimacy of President Lissouba, like that of President Kabbah, could be considered as continuing until either Sassou Nguesso makes way for the restoration of President Lissouba or is replaced by an elected constitutional government. Alternatively, the British government could have reincarnated its policy on Kampuchea in 1976-79. There it chose to continue to recognise the Pol Pot regime even after it had lost effective control of the country to the Heng Samrin regime, on the grounds that the latter had been installed illegally by foreign intervention.[251] Either approach would have lent greater consistency to a policy regime that is all too often fraught with contradictions and volatility.

Be that as it may, and putting the Congolese crisis aside, what the Sierra Leone situation definitely shows is that it is not sufficient for an unconstitutional regime to claim effective control over national territory. To qualify for official dealings, it must additionally prove that it has legitimacy in the sense of being democratically representative of the people it purports to govern. In other words, a confluence between effectiveness of territorial control and legitimacy of authority is necessary before foreign states can do official business with a revolutionary regime. Otherwise they will not. Thus non-recognition is still a powerful deterrent against military *coups* provided the international community is consistent in its practice. It can still send a strong message, particularly to rebels still fighting constitutional governments in Africa and elsewhere, that whatever the justice of their cause, they must seek redress only through constitutional procedures.

The Sierra Leone crisis before English courts

Before the demise of the AFRC junta in Freetown, the validity of its acts came for determination before the English courts in the case of *Sierra Leone Telecommunications Company Limited (Sierratel) v. Barclays Bank plc*.[252] Sierratel, the plaintiff, was a wholly-owned parastatal incorporated in Sierra Leone. It held a US dollar account at the Barclays Bank at Knightsbridge in

London. After the overthrow of President Kabbah by the military *coup* of May 25, 1997, he fled to neighbouring Guinea where he tried to function as a government-in-exile. The British government, which had condemned the *coup*, continued to have dealings with him.

Before the *coup*, a bank mandate had been issued on July 31, 1996, authorising four signatories to sign payment requests on behalf of the plaintiff. After the *coup*, on December 24, 1997, the bank received a letter purporting to come from the plaintiff's headquarters in Freetown, stating, *inter alia*, that a new board of directors had been appointed and that that board had taken a decision to suspend three of the four 1996 signatories. The minutes of the meeting were enclosed. Upon receipt of this letter, the bank declined to honour further payment instructions issued by the original signatories. This was the action that was being challenged in the English courts by way of a declaration. In effect, the bank was faced with a difficult choice of ignoring completely the instructions of the new management or those of the original signatories.

Under Sierratel's Articles of Association, only the government of Sierra Leone could appoint its directors. Furthermore, section 70 (e) of the Constitution of Sierra Leone provided that the appointment of directors of government-owned parastatals must be made by the President and approved by Parliament. The questions before the court were (a) whether the new board of directors had been appointed by the "government of Sierra Leone"; and (b) whether its purported acts were valid.

There was no express choice of law in the contract between Sierratel and Barclays Bank. Mr. Justice Cresswell decided that the law governing the contract was English law, being the law of the country where the account was kept, and that the law governing the appointment of Sierratel's officials was the law of Sierra Leone. He then turned to the main question before the court, namely whether the original board appointed by the "government of Sierra Leone" had remained valid or whether it had been superseded by the new board appointed by the military junta.

The court said this raised the question of recognition of foreign governments. Relying on the judgment of the court in *Republic of Somalia v. Woodhouse Drake and Carey (Suisse) SA and Others (The Mary)*,253 His Lordship spelled out the modern legal criteria for determining whether or not a government exists as the government of a particular foreign state as follows: (a) whether it is the constitutional government of the state; (b) the degree, nature and stability of administrative control, if any, that it of itself exercises over the territory of the state; (c) whether the British government has any dealings with it and, if so, what is the nature of those dealings; and (d) in marginal cases, the extent of international recognition that it enjoys as the government of the state.

(a)   Was   the   military   junta   the   constitutional government?

Unlike the case of *Adams v. Adams* in 1970, there was no jurisprudential determination of whether or not the usurper government was a constitutional government. To have pronounced on that question so that the validity of the acts of the junta becomes the *res* of the *res judicata* in the suit would have been tantamount to the court asserting jurisdiction over the internal affairs of Sierra Leone. That would have been contrary to international law.254 Instead, it treated the question as if it were a variant of the third element of the criteria, namely whether the British government had had any official dealings with the military junta in Freetown.

On the evidence before it, the court observed that the British government's policy had been to continue to have dealings only with the government of President Kabbah, and to have none with the military junta in Freetown whose *coup* it had consistently condemned. On June 27, 1997, Tony Lloyd, Minister of State at the Foreign and Commonwealth Office, issued a statement on Sierra Leone in terms that: "The British government has followed the events in Sierra Leone since the illegal overthrow of President Kabbah's government on 25 May with serious concern. It has been actively involved in attempts to find a peaceful resolution which will lead to the restoration of the legitimate government of President Kabbah. In this regard it welcomes the meeting of Ecowas states held in Guinea on 26 June, and looks forward to the report of the Committee established by Ecowas to take the process forward. In recognition of the close ties which have always existed between the United Kingdom and Sierra Leone, the government

167

underlines its continued support to the courageous people of Sierra Leone who have so steadfastly rejected this attempt to reverse the progress to democracy achieved last year. It looks forward to recommending its assistance to the reconstruction, rehabilitation and development of Sierra Leone, but until constitutional order has been restored."[255]

Again, on 28 November 1997, the FCO wrote to the plaintiff's solicitors, stating, *inter alia*, that: "We continue to deal with the democratically elected government of Sierra Leone under President Kabbah. We have no dealings with the military junta in Freetown."[256] This was again confirmed in a written answer to the House of Lords on January 12, 1998, by the Parliamentary Under-Secretary, Baroness Symons of Vernham Dean, in terms that: "Where democratic governments have been overthrown by violence we have often worked with them in exile as part of our global support for democracy. Tejan Kabbah is not the 'former' President of Sierra Leone; he remains the legitimate leader of that country."[257]

From the above statements, the court concluded that the government of President Kabbah was the government of Sierra Leone, because it was the only one with which the British government had had dealings even though it was not physically within the territory of Sierra Leone. Therefore, the board of directors of 1996, appointed by it, continued to be valid for the purposes of appointing the signatories to the London account.

(b) *What was the degree, nature and stability of the administrative control of the military junta?*

The focus here was entirely on the military junta. Having decided that the Kabbah government was, in the eyes of the British government, the government of Sierra Leone, the court concentrated only on examining whether the administrative control of the AFRC had been effective. How relevant this issue was to the court's decision is unclear. Once the court found for the plaintiff, on the grounds that the deposed government was the only government capable of representing Sierra Leone in the United Kingdom, it became unnecessary to examine the effectiveness of the administrative control of the military junta. If this were a relevant factor, then the court ought to have examined also the effectiveness of the administrative or territorial control of the government of President Kabbah.

Be that as it may, the court admitted various depositions by officials of Kabbah's exiled government. In sworn affidavits, those officials made a number of assertions. First, that "the military junta presently has no control whatsoever over the country outside of Freetown" and that even in the small enclave it allegedly controlled, "there are civil unrest problems". In the rest of the country, the affidavit further asserted, the "defence units loyal to President Kabbah" were operating "throughout the country" and had "imposed an internal blockade". Second, that only about a quarter of the nation's civil service had stayed behind in Sierra Leone and that none of the departments was functioning properly, if at all. Third, that the junta's aim had been "to coerce the civil population to collaborate with them" but that they had "failed in this aim" to such an extent that there were significant defections from the army and police to the intervention force and the civil defence militia. Fourth, that the infrastructure of the country had collapsed, with water and electricity virtually non-existent, hospitals barely functioning, the majority of schools remaining closed, fuel extremely short in supply, airports and ports under Ecomog control as were the main transport arteries to and from the capital. And, fifth, that the junta had "no control over more than two-thirds of the country" while "forces loyal to President Kabbah [were] in control of the most important areas up-country."[258]

The issue of control is a question of fact, but the only evidence before the court was that tendered by officials of the exiled government. No other evidence was taken or requested. Nor was cross-examination directed at testing the veracity of their depositions. So, the court did not have the benefit of corroboration or otherwise of the evidence submitted to it. Yet, as stated by Lord Justice Hobhouse in the Somalia case, factual matters that relate to the actual situation in a foreign country are matters of "legal characterisation" for the court alone to determine, and for this it is entitled to look at various sources of evidence. It is therefore arguable that although the result of the court's judgment was politically desirable, jurisprudentially speaking, it was not entirely flawless.

(c) *What was the extent of international recognition?*

Again, with respect, this question was unnecessary. As already stated, it was not only the acts of the junta that were in the dock but also the acts of company directors appointed by a government which had been overthrown and whose effectiveness ought to have been put under scrutiny.

The first case in which English courts considered the legal effect of the Carrington doctrine was *Republic of Somalia v. Woodhouse Drake & Carey (Suisse) SA and Others (The Mary)*.259 The facts are as follows. In January 1991, the Republic of Somalia bought and paid for a consignment of rice, shipped on a vessel called *The Mary*, to be discharged at Mogadishu. When the ship arrived off Mogadishu, the master refused to enter the port because he considered it unsafe on account of the fighting that was going on there. Disputes arose as to what should be done with the cargo and the shipowners issued an originating summons on March 12, 1991 in the English courts naming as the defendants the charterers of the vessel. On the same day the court ordered that the cargo be sold and that the net proceeds of sale be paid into court. It also ordered that the net proceeds be treated as if they were the cargo for all purposes. The question before the court was who was the rightful owner of the proceeds?

From December 1990 to January 1991, there was an uprising in Somalia in the course of which President Siad Barre was overthrown. Somalia consists of a number of areas each of which was dominated by a different tribal group or clan. Following the uprising and the overthrow of the constitutional government, whatever common interest there was between the tribal groups ceased as they began to fight each other. The central government ceased to exist. Various groups put themselves forward as entitled to control or govern either parts or the whole of Somalia. In the north-west the Somali National Movement (SNM) attempted to set up a separate state. The north-east was under the control of the Somali Salvation Democratic Front (SSDF). The area around and to the north of the capital, Mogadishu, was controlled by the United Somali Congress (USC) group; but this soon splintered into two factions, one led by General Mohamed Aidid and the other by Ali Mahdi Mohamed. Some of the bitterest fighting took place between these two factions in and around Mogadishu, particularly since November 1991, with neither gaining control over the other. Further south, different areas were under the control of the Somali Democratic Movement (SDM) and the Somali Patriotic Movement (SPM) and the followers of Siad Barre. No one group established control over the country. The capital had remained an area of open fighting between armed bands under the control of no one faction. The USC had remained split.

In July 1991, after a continuous period of widespread fighting between the various groups, including the two USC factions, a conference was called at Djibouti under the chairmanship of the President of the Republic of Djibouti. It was attended by the Presidents of Kenya and Uganda and representatives of the governments of Germany, the United States, France, Italy, Saudi Arabia, Egypt, Libya, Yemen, Nigeria, Ethiopia, Sudan, Oman, USSR, and China and of the Arab League, OAU and the EEC. From within Somalia six of the political groupings were represented. The SNM declined to attend and it seems that General Aidid did not attend either. After protracted negotiations, the conference reached an agreement. This was set out in a communiqué on 21 July 1991. It included as follows:

"Organisation of State: (A) The Conference had decided to adopt the 1960 constitution for a period of not more than two years from the date of signature of the present Agreement, the formation of the Government shall be agreed between the various movements. (B) The Conference had decided to set up a National Assembly composed of 123 members based on the number of constituencies existing before 1969 with a Speaker and two Deputy Speakers. (C) The Conference had agreed to introduce regional autonomy in the country which entails an amendment to the constitution....(E) The Conference nominates Ali Mahdi Mohamed as provisional president of the Somali Republic for a period of two years from the day on which he takes the oath. (F) Two Vice Presidents of the Republic shall be nominated, the first put forward by the SDM and the second by the SSDF and SPF. (G) The Prime Minister shall be a native of the north-west of the country....(J) The provisional government is charged with preparing a draft electoral law for the organisation of

[a] free and democratic election of the president of the National Assembly, with forwarding a policy of respect for human rights and public liberties on the basis of the universal declaration of human rights and to introduce into the country an organisation based on regional autonomy....."

Under this Djibouti accord, Mahdi became the interim President, and on August 6 he appointed Omer Arteh Qalib as Prime Minister. Qalib then appointed Ministers to serve under him. However, this interim government was unable to operate in Mogadishu and Qalib himself was compelled to operate from a hotel in Riyadh, capital of Saudi Arabia. On January 14, 1992, he wrote a letter confirming his earlier instructions for the Interim Government of the Republic of Somalia to be joined as a plaintiff in the proceedings.

There was no dispute that the money paid into court was the property of the Republic of Somalia. The question was whether the interim government was the government of the Republic of Somalia, entitled thereby to claim the money. If the court was not satisfied that it was such a government, the money would remain with the court unless a proper claimant came forward.

Lord Justice Hobhouse considered what criteria to apply if recognition by the British government is no longer conclusive of the question of *locus standi* of a foreign government in the English courts. He then set out the four criteria listed earlier.

(a) Is the claimant the constitutional government of the state?

The court found that the constitutional government headed by President Siad Barre had been overthrown in January 1991, and that it no longer existed anywhere. Since then, the various parties had been unable to agree upon a new government and their relationship was characterised by tremendous distrust and incessant infighting between and within the clans, with each claiming hold over a particular region of the country.

His Lordship drew a distinction between a regime that is the constitutional and established government of the state and one that is seeking to establish itself as such either by displacing a former government or filling a vacuum. The court then made the observation that "a loss of control by a constitutional government may not immediately deprive it of its status, whereas an insurgent regime will require to establish control before it can exist as a government."260

The Djibouti Agreement, His Lordship observed, was not constitutional, nor did it create a *de jure* status for the interim government in Somalia. "The interim government was not and did not become the constitutional successor of the government of President Siad Barre," said the court, adding: "Accordingly, if the interim government is to be treated as the government of Somalia, it must be able to show that it is exercising administrative control over the territory of the republic. That it is not able to do."261

In reaching this conclusion, the court was not entirely uninfluenced by the fact that the regime purporting to be the government of Somalia was in fact not operating from Somali territory but rather from a hotel room in faraway Riyadh. It might well have been different if it had been *in situ* and exercising a substantial degree of administrative or territorial control over Somalia.

(b)   The degree, nature and stability of administrative control, if any, that it of itself exercises over the territory of the state.

In other words, whether the regime in question "is able of itself to exercise effective control of the territory of the state concerned and is likely to continue to do so".

His Lordship referred to three letters written by the FCO in reply to inquiries by solicitors. In the second of these letters, dated August 5, 1991, it was stated that "the interim government does not command nation-wide acceptance. We support efforts to establish one that does". Then the letter concluded: "In these circumstances, it is very difficult to judge, for the purposes of your case, who is the government of Somalia."262 This letter was written after the Djibouti conference and despite its communiqué. Thus, in the eyes of the British government, which, incidentally, was not represented at the Djibouti conference, that conference had changed nothing and no legitimate or recognisable government had flowed from it.

In another letter, dated February 20, 1992, the British government stated: "The comment [in the letter of August 5, 1991] has been somewhat overtaken by subsequent events, in particular fighting between rival elements of the USC which broke out in November 1991 and in which thousands of people have been killed and injured. On 23 January the United Nations Security Council adopted Resolution 733 requesting the Secretary-General to increase humanitarian assistance to Somalia and to cooperate with regional organisations....in seeking the Mogadishu factions' agreement to a cease-fire, the distribution of humanitarian aid and the promotion of a political settlement. The UN and regional organisations met representatives of the Somali factions in New York on 14 February......However, fighting in Mogadishu has continued since the New York meeting. The United Kingdom maintains informal contact with all the factions involved, but there have been no dealings on a government to government basis."

Thus, it was the view of the British government that none of the factions claiming to be the government of Somalia was worthy of the name, as they exercised no effective control of the country. The interim government was just as much in that position as the other clan factions. It is significant to note here too that the attitude of the British government was based not on any political disapproval of the interim government's policies or conduct but rather on the fact that it was not in effective territorial and administrative control of Somalia.

The next question was what the particular weight should be given to the attitude of the British government? His Lordship said: "Once the question for the court becomes one of making its own assessment of the evidence, making findings of fact on all the relevant evidence placed before it and drawing the appropriate legal conclusion, and is no longer a question of simply reflecting government policy, letters from the FCO become merely part of the evidence in the case...... In so far as the letters make statements about what is happening in the territory of some foreign state, such letters may not be the best evidence; but as regards the question whether Her Majesty's Government has dealings with the foreign government it will almost certainly be the best and only conclusive evidence of that fact. Where Her Majesty's government is dealing with the foreign government on a normal government to government basis as the government of the relevant foreign state, it is unlikely in the extreme that the inference that the foreign government is the government of that state will be capable of being rebutted and questions of public policy and considerations of the interrelationship of the judicial and executive arms of government may be paramount.....But now that the question has ceased to be one of recognition, the theoretical possibility of rebuttal must exist."263

In other words, the question whether the British government has had official dealings with a foreign revolutionary regime is a matter solely for the FCO and its certificate on such matters may be conclusive and determinative of that fact. Where, on the other hand, the question involves a determination whether a revolutionary regime is exercising administrative or territorial control over the state it purports to rule, the FCO certificate may not be conclusive. Such a question is to be treated as a factual matter relating to "legal characterisation" and, as such, is one for the courts alone to decide. The determination of actual developments within Somalia was considered as falling within this latter category, and the court said it was justified to look beyond the Foreign Office letters. Accordingly, it went on to look at a situation report, prepared by the Agency for International Development of the United States Government on January 30, 1992. However, it found that the views contained in the report were on all fours with those of the British government. As to what the court would have done if the two views had been divergent, must remain a moot point.

(c) *Whether the British government has any dealings with the claimant government.*

The key questions here are (i) what is the evidence of the attitude of the British government as inferred from the nature of its official dealings, if any, with the claimant regime? Having ascertained the attitude of the British government, how much weight would the courts give to it?

Where official dealings exist, any evidence adduced by the Foreign Office is likely to be conclusive on the matter. On the other hand, "[t]he non-existence of such dealings cannot ...be conclusive because their absence may be explained by some extraneous consideration - for example, lack of occasion, the attitude of the regime to human rights, or its relationship to another state."264

(d)   In marginal cases, what is the extent of international recognition?

The court held that while the degree of international recognition by foreign states may be a "relevant factor" for assessing whether a regime exists as the government of a state, that recognition must, however, relate to the exercise of effective administrative control over the territory of the state concerned. On the other hand, where there is no administrative control over territory, international recognition alone may not suffice.265

CHAPTER 6

Force in Defence of Democracy and Human Rights

Force in defence of democracy

Renewed determination in the First World to shore up democracy world-wide is a familiar theme nowadays. It confirms truly that the Cold War is now a thing of the past. Indeed the international support given to President Kabbah derives from the basic assumption that his presidential credentials were legitimate and that that legitimacy was well founded in democratic elections. Even General Abacha was not afraid to claim that his military adventure in Sierra Leone was to defend democracy. The question is whether in this twenty-first century democracy can be defended by force, considering that one is the very antithesis of the other. Clare Short, British Secretary of State for International Development, has observed somewhat coruscatingly: "The paradox of the return [of the government of President Kabbah] is that it was led by the Nigerians, which means an undemocratic government helped to restore a democratic one. That is the biggest irony."266

European history of the nineteenth century was replete with episodes of gun-boat diplomacy, by which strong naval powers meddled in the internal affairs of weak nations in order to subvert their will or promote their own interests. The United Nations Charter 1945 consigned that nefarious practice to the attic of history by giving primacy, in its Articles 2(4) and 2(7), to the principles of non-use of force in inter-state relations, national sovereignty and non-intervention in internal affairs.

In more recent times, however, intra-state armed conflicts have been on the increase, arousing deep passions everywhere. Consequently, there have been attempts to re-invent the wheel. Protagonists appeal to the phenomenal growth of globalisation and international cooperation. They argue that the doctrines of national sovereignty and non-intervention serve the international community less worthily nowadays as despotic regimes resort to them to shield themselves from international scrutiny for domestic violations of fundamental human rights. They therefore call for a redefinition of these concepts if only to take account of the new forces of globalisation and international cooperation. They are also dismissive of the counter-argument that this might open the floodgates for states, which, by dint of wealth and military power, are able to subdue others in the name of protecting democracy and universal human rights. In other words, it is like advocating for a return to the nightmares of the gun-boat era.

That said, the present state of international law is still governed by a presumption against unilateral application of military force. This is encapsulated in the prohibition on the use of force as contained in the United Nations Charter. Save for self-defence or authorisation by the Security Council under Chapter VII of the Charter, forcible action by one state against another is impermissible. More specifically, there is as yet no general doctrine of democratic necessity in international law. In this regard, three episodes that occurred during the Cold War era and four cases after the end of that period will be examined. Only Haiti comes closest to supporting the existence of such a doctrine. Even so, it was unexceptional as it was governed essentially by express authorisation of the Security Council.

State Practice during the Cold War

(a)   *Dominican Republic 1963*

In 1963 a civilian junta overthrew the democratically-elected government of President Bosch. Three years later, it too was overthrown in a military revolt that led to the fragmentation of the army and inter-factional fighting. On April 28, 1965, United States landed troops in the country on the pretext of protecting and evacuating American citizens. Its Ambassador tried to justify his government's action on the basis of protecting democracy: "We believe that the Dominican people, under the established principle of self-determination, should select their own government through free elections …Our interest lies in the re-establishment of constitutional government and, to that end, to assist in maintaining the stability essential to the expression of the free choice of the Dominican people."267 However, this was not supported by other states, which viewed the American military action as a violation of the principle of non-intervention in internal affairs.

(b)   Grenada 1979

The new Jewel Movement, led by Maurice Bishop, ousted Prime Minister Eric Gairy in 1979, and formed a new leftist-leaning government under the title of People's Revolutionary Government. After increasing disagreement among members of the new government, an armed revolt by the Grenadian People's Revolutionary Army resulted in the ouster of Maurice Bishop from power in October 1983. In its place a new government was formed under the rubric of the Revolutionary Military Council. On October 25, 1983, the United States, supported by Jamaica, Barbados and member states of the Organisation of Eastern Caribbean States (OECS), launched Operation Urgent Fury. They sought to justify their military action on the need to restore constitutionality as a prelude to restoring democracy in Grenada. President Reagan talked about the need "to assist in the restoration of conditions of law and order and of governmental institutions to the island of Grenada, where a brutal group of leftist thugs violently seized power..."[268]

Other countries were not impressed. By resolution 38/7, the United Nations General Assembly condemned the military intervention as a "flagrant violation of international law and of the independence, sovereignty and territorial integrity" of Grenada, and called for an "immediate cessation of the armed intervention and the immediate withdrawal of the foreign troops."

(c)   Panama 1989

General Noriega nullified the election of the opposition candidate, Guillermo Endara, in May 1989. This, coupled with Noriega's alleged participation in drug trafficking, strained relations between Noriega's government and the United States, and on December 20, 1989, the United States sent 14,000 troops to join its other troops already stationed in Panama under the terms of the Panama Canal treaties. They invaded Panama and arrested General Noriega.

The United States put forward the defence of democracy as justification for its military action in Panama. Its representative to the Organisation of American States said: "Today we are once again living in historic times. A time when a great principle is spreading across the world like wildfire. That principle, as we all know, is the revolutionary idea that the people – not governments – are sovereign.... [This principle] has in this decade – and especially in this historic year 1989 – acquired the force of historic necessity .... Democracy today is synonymous with legitimacy the world over; it is, in short, the universal value of our time."269

Nevertheless, the intervention was roundly condemned by the General Assembly, in Resolution 240/44, as a flagrant violation of international law.

These three cases represent early attempts by the United States to advance the concept of pro-democratic intervention. However, they failed to convince the international community because there were no valid international precedents. Before then, the justification for similar interventions had been based upon the right of a state to protect its nationals abroad, self-defence, invitation by the lawful local authorities, and, in the case of Panama, a treaty right of intervention based on the Panama Canal treaties. Second, they represent attempts by the United States to advance its own foreign policy goal of preventing the penetration of communism into the Western Hemisphere.270 Besides, the United States was far from consistent in its own practice. For example, while making such powerful advocacy in the Americas in favour of democratic governance, it failed to extend the same principle to *apartheid* South Africa where a white minority was forcibly ruling the country against the wishes of the black majority population.

Post-Cold War State Practice

(a) Haiti 1994

In 1990, Jean-Bertrand Aristide became President of Haiti after internationally monitored and supervised elections. In 1994 he was overthrown by a military *coup*, forcing him to flee the country. The international community condemned the *coup* as illegal and refused to recognise the military junta. Instead it continued to regard Aristide as the legitimate head of state of Haiti.

The Security Council adopted resolution 940 on July 31 in which it decided to take enforcement action against the junta under Chapter VII of the Charter. The objective was to ensure "the

180

restoration of democracy in Haiti and the prompt return of the legitimately elected President, Jean-Bertrand Aristide, within the framework of the Governors Island Agreement." The Council then adopted the following strategies. A regional multinational intervention force was to be organised, under the leadership of the United States, a country with impeccable democratic credentials, to implement the decision. Second, to respect the UN Charter scrupulously. Accordingly, the deployment of the force was delayed until September 19.271 Third, the military intervention was authorised under Chapters VII and VIII of the Charter only after the Security Council was satisfied that all relevant pacific settlement procedures under Chapter VI had been thoroughly exhausted and there had been no reasonable prospect of peaceful settlement after a year and a half of negotiation. Fourth, the mandate of the multinational force was limited in both time and scope in that it was to terminate as soon as a secure and stable environment had been established and democracy restored in Haiti. Fifth, the member states constituting the multinational force, as well as the Secretary-General, were required to report regularly to the Council. The Council also established a United Nations Mission in Haiti (UNMIH) part of whose mandate was to monitor the operations of the multinational force. As will be seen shortly, none of these safeguards was applied to the situation in Sierra Leone.

(b) *Sierra Leone 1997*

Like Haiti, a constitutional government was overthrown in Sierra Leone in May 1997. But that is where the similarity ends. The differences are stark. First, the Security Council approved only a limited embargo under resolution 1132 and authorised Ecowas, as a regional organisation, to implement it. Notwithstanding this, the Nigerian military hijacked the mandate and turned it into its private agenda in Sierra Leone. Second, save for what was strictly necessary to enforce the embargo, in conformity with international standards, the resolution authorised no other force to be applied in Sierra Leone. Third, before 1999, the intervention force was neither regional nor multinational in composition; it consisted entirely of forces from the Nigerian military,272 whose reputation in the world of justice, democracy and human rights was most unflattering.273 Pointing to the obvious paradox of his crusade against the military junta in Sierra Leone, Abacha, in a characteristic *non sequitur*, said: "There are some cynics who would wonder why a military regime in Nigeria should denounce a military putsch in Sierra Leone. Let me remind such cynics that this military regime came to power at a critical moment of Nigeria's history to avert disintegration."274

The differences between the two situations are clear. In the case of Haiti, the execution of the enforcement action was delegated to a force that was unquestionably multinational and under the leadership of a country governed by a democratic government. And the Council's monitoring of the implementation of its decision could not have been more meticulous. In the case of Sierra Leone, on the other hand, there was the most extraordinary delegation of enforcement powers, which, to all practical purposes, were usurped by a despicable military junta. And the Council did nothing to stop it.

So then, though the objectives were similar - to get rid of a military junta and restore constitutionality - the means used could not have been more different. Whereas in Haiti the United Nations did everything possible to exhaust pacific settlement procedures, the Nigerian military in Sierra Leone placed the highest premium on military power. For example, Kofi Annan, in his letter of October 7, 1997, to the President of the Security Council, had emphasised democracy as the "great issue of principle" at stake in Sierra Leone.275 On the other hand, Abacha played out his true agenda by warning the West to stay out of his country's domestic affairs. In celebrating his fourth anniversary in power on November 17, he informed his audience of "the growing tendency by some members of the international community to target Africa and other parts of the developing world for alleged non-compliance with their perception" of human rights and democracy. This he condemned as "patently unfair and unacceptable" and as a "ploy to interfere in the internal affairs of states."276 This was the same leader to whom the Security Council turned to champion the cause of democracy in Sierra Leone!

That was not all. The United Nations also faltered on the interpretation of constitutionality. In many respects, it made it appear as if the concept was coterminous with the reinstatement of the *persona* of President Kabbah. Yet, consistent with the principles of fairness and justice, which must surely be part of the *corpus* of United Nations law, it is at least arguable that constitutionality should have been related back to April 29, 1992. That was the date the NPRC junta overthrew the constitutional government of President Joseph Momoh. Whatever view one might take of elections under a one-party system, that had brought Momoh to power, the fact remains that he was the constitutional leader of Sierra Leone. Therefore, his overthrow by the NPRC in 1992 was, in principle, as illegal as the overthrow of President Kabbah by the AFRC in 1997. Reversion to the *status quo ante* in both cases faces the same constraint, namely would it, of itself, return Sierra Leone to lasting peace and security? A return to the *status quo* of either 1992 or 1997 would, of course, have restored constitutionality but not, short of a military victory or a political solution, durable peace and security. The intervening election of 1996 as a legitimating factor is of little value, because of the existence of fraud which tainted the result and removed the shine from it.

(c) *Congo (Brazzaville) 1997*

Barely two weeks after the *coup* in Sierra Leone, political and ethnic differences exploded into violence in Congo (Brazzaville), leading to the overthrow of the constitutional government of President Pascal Lissouba four months later. The rebels, led by the former head of state, Denis Sassou Nguesso, were heavily supported by foreign troops from the Democratic Republic of the Congo (Kinshasa) and Angola. Civilian casualties ran into the tens of thousands, while the internally displaced numbered more than 800,000. All the other scars of civil war were also evident, including extensive property damage, looting, food shortages, malnutrition and outbreaks of communicable diseases.[277]

On August 13, 1997, while the fighting was still going on, the Security Council issued a Presidential Statement, expressing concern about the plight of civilians caught in the cross-fire. Subsequently, it offered to send United Nations peacekeepers, proposed by the Secretary-General, or a multinational force, as proposed by the President of Gabon and the member states of the West African Economic and Monetary Union (UEMOA), subject to three conditions. First, that the warring parties accept a cease-fire; second, that they agree to the peacekeepers taking control of Brazzaville airport; and third, commit themselves to a negotiated settlement of the crisis.278

Believing that an agreement was imminent, the Secretary-General made contingency plans for securing the airport and ensuring that it operated as a neutral zone. He also made provision for a cease-fire, its maintenance and consolidation, the delivery of humanitarian assistance, the facilitation of political reconciliation and the holding of democratic elections. Before this plan could be implemented, however, General Sassou Nguesso launched a final assault and took control of the seat of government.

Foreign support for Sassou Nguesso more than justified a condemnation. None was made. Nor did the Security Council condemn the unlawful overthrow of the constitutional government. Instead, it issued another Presidential Statement on October 16 in which it stressed "the importance of a political settlement and national reconciliation" and the need for "agreement on peaceful transitional arrangements leading to the holding of democratic and free and fair elections with the participation of all parties."279

If the situation in Freetown was "unacceptable" to the Security Council,280 why was the one in Brazzaville accepted? It is puerile to suggest, as implicit in the Council's inaction, that President Lissouba's term of office had ended by the time Nguesso's forces struck. This surely flies in the face of the Constitution, which prescribes for succession to the presidency by means other than violence. Besides, it should have been plain to any objective bystander that durable peace in a country deeply divided by ethnic mistrust is impossible except by way of a return to constitutionality through the democratic process, and, preferably, under the supervision of the United Nations.

(d) *East Timor 1999*

If, by inaction, the United Nations intended to use the Congolese crisis to demonstrate the absence of a general doctrine of democratic necessity, the crisis in East Timor sealed it. East Timor had been invaded and forcibly annexed by Indonesia after the Portuguese colonialists pulled out in 1975. Some 250,000 people, a third of the territory's population, were killed by Indonesian troops, to say nothing about other gross human rights

184

abuses. While Australia openly recognised the annexation, neither the United Nations nor the other Western Powers seriously protested against it. For more than two decades, East Timorese demands for self-determination were greeted with deafening silence in Jakarta and the territory became a fiefdom of the Indonesian army. Not until May 1999 did Indonesia concede to a United Nations supervised referendum to determine the territory's future. In reality, it was the result of President B.J. Habibie, Suharto's successor, having to contend with a moribund economy and waves of popular demands for democratisation in Indonesia itself.

Viewed against this historical background, it was nothing short of naiveté not to anticipate Indonesian resentment if the referendum went against them. Instead of ensuring a strong international military presence to enforce the result of the referendum, as was done in Cambodia in 1993, the United Nations conceded security and law and order to Indonesia merely because, technically, it was still the local sovereign of East Timor. Furthermore, a vote for independence required Indonesian approval before sovereignty could be transferred to East Timor via a United Nations transitional administration.

Predictably, in August 1999, by nearly 80 per cent majority, the East Timorese people voted overwhelmingly for independence as against autonomy within Indonesia. Even in the face of violence from both the Indonesian army and Indonesian-supported anti-independence militias, the people turned up in droves to register and vote. But the potential for violence was always there, so the failure to provide adequately for the protection of the United Nations Mission in East Timor (UNAMET) and the civilian population can be attributed to no other than those who wield extraordinary powers in the Security Council. Here, as in Congo (Brazzaville), poor judgment and poor timing once again characterised the work of the Council, for only after East Timor had been virtually devastated did it decide to come to the rescue, even so not even with a force of its own.

No sooner the result of the poll was made public than a backlash of astonishing brutality from the Indonesian overlords began. Pro-Indonesian anti-independence militias and thugs of the Indonesian army on the island combined in a way that could no longer effectively conceal Indonesian complicity. These conspirators took the law into their own hands and within two weeks transformed East Timor into a smouldering shadow of its former self, with its entire population either politically-cleansed or displaced. Members of the pro-independence intelligentsia were hunted down like animals while the lucky ones who escaped were deported either to West Timor or Australia, or left to flee for their lives into the steep forested hills overlooking Dili, the capital. A state of total anarchy reigned in the entire territory, providing another example of man's beastliness to man. So flagrant, systematic, and widespread were the violations of international humanitarian and human rights law that war crimes looked too kind a term. Mary Robinson, the United Nations Human Rights Commissioner, could barely conceal her outrage when she demanded the establishment of a war crimes tribunal to investigate and try those responsible for the atrocities in East Timor.

The Security Council dispatched a fact-finding mission. It reported: "This massive forced relocation [of the population] outside of East Timor has been designed to give the impression of large-scale dissatisfaction with the vote, a situation of civil war, and to bring large groups of the population under Indonesian control away from the spotlight of international attention. But it cannot be ruled out that these are the first stages of a genocidal campaign to stamp out the East Timorese problem by force."[281]

Rejecting parallels with Kosovo, where the United Nations had been promptly sidelined as unequal to the challenge in hand, Western leaders insisted on respect for the United Nations authority and predicated international action upon Indonesia's prior consent. This negated any notion, if ever there was one, of democratic necessity being a basis for external military intervention either by the United Nations or its member states. It may be difficult to admit it publicly, but geography, military power, race and national self-interest considerations all surfaced as powerful defining factors. Indonesia's refusal to give consent meant that the United Nations dithered. All it could do was to remind Indonesia of its obligation to secure the territory and its population. Even when things were getting completely out of control, with some of its staff being brutally murdered by militias, all the UN could do was to evacuate the remainder of its staff and those Timorese who had taken refuge in its compound. Within hours of the evacuation, the compound was on fire, giving a foretaste of what an international peacekeeping force was to expect.

Behind this facade of adherence to principle lay huge Western economic assets in Indonesia. This was the main controlling factor. Indonesia is the world's fourth largest state with a population of 210 million, providing space for ever-increasing Western investments and arms sales. Size of economy thus vitiated moral outrage. Here, as elsewhere, the resolve of the Security Council was being shaped by national interests of its most powerful members rather than by principle. And one cannot but agree with *The Times* of London when it opined that: "Far from being a textbook case for new interventionism, East Timor has been a textbook case for the old realpolitik."282

For their own part, the countries of the Association of South-East Asian Nations (ASEAN) decided to stick to principle. Because they had openly criticised NATO's intervention in Kosovo, they could not do otherwise than insist on not taking part in any regional action except with prior Security Council authorisation. And Indonesia played out its mendaciousness when it blamed the violence in East Timor on the United Nations' conduct of the referendum. It refused to allow international peacekeepers to enter East Timor until after two complete weeks following the result of the poll. By that time, the main cities in the territory had been reduced to rubble and its population of 800,000 drastically displaced. Only then was the United Nations able to mandate an 8,000-strong Australian-led multinational force, dubbed the "coalition of the willing". The need for urgency had ruled out a formal United Nations peacekeeping operation, which would have required months of bureaucracy, including funding.

The multinational force was given a broad mandate with robust rules of engagement. Adopted under Chapter VII of the UN Charter on September 15, 1999, resolution 1264 authorised the multinational force "to take all necessary measures" to fulfill its mandate. This was "to restore peace and security in East Timor, to protect and support UNAMET in carrying out its tasks and, within force capabilities, to facilitate humanitarian assistance operations." It was to remain in the territory until replaced by a United Nations peacekeeping operation.

Force in defence of human rights

Human rights abuses have similarly aroused deep passions. Sometimes there is a call for action by the international community, going beyond mere expressions of concern. But the question is whether military intervention is justifiable in defence of universal human rights? In the absence of a definitive judicial determination, and state practice still in a state of flux, we must turn to juristic opinions.

Jurists too are divided. However, the preponderant opinion seems to be that ambitious as the doctrine of humanitarian necessity may be, like the doctrine of democratic necessity, it is not yet part of the corpus of international law, permitting one state to intervene militarily in another to defend human rights. Professors Ian Brownlie and Jimenez de Arechaga say it is at least doubtful whether such a right exists in international law while Professor Vaughan Lowe believes that "few lawyers would claim that the 'right' is at present clearly established in international law". Professor Christine Chinkin is similarly of the view that state practice is not yet sufficient for one "to conclude definitively that the right to use force for humanitarian reasons has become part of customary international law". And Professor Akehurst argues that claims of a right to use force by one state against another to prevent violations of human rights might make states become reluctant to accept legal obligations concerning human rights.

On the other hand, if such a principle exists in international law, then there is certainly no consistency in its application and it is not easy to find rational explanations for this. Humanitarian necessity has been claimed in some recent cases. To give an example, there is the Bosnian conflict in 1992. The minority Muslim population was made the object of attack by Serb forces. Muslim states claimed that it was legitimate for them to supply the Muslim population with arms to defend themselves against the Serbs, and even threatened to intervene on their behalf.

Another example is the "no go" areas in Iraq. With the acquiescence of the Security Council, the West created "no go" areas in northern and southern Iraq and barred Iraqi aircraft from overflying them in order to provide protection for Kurdish minorities.

Yet another example is NATO's unprecedented 78-day bombardment of Yugoslavia, which started on March 24, 1999. NATO claimed it was necessary in order to force the government of Slobodan Milosevic to agree to grant autonomy to the Yugoslav province of Kosovo, withdraw its forces from that province, and accept a NATO military presence to underpin a settlement and keep them all in order.

Although Kosovo is an integral part of Yugoslavia, on March 24, the British government justified the NATO's military action as "an exceptional measure" to prevent an "overwhelming humanitarian catastrophe". John Prescott, Deputy Prime Minister, claimed that their action was aimed at disrupting Serbian repression of the Albanian population in Kosovo. "Two United Nations Security Council resolutions, 1199 and 1203, underpin our actions," he contended. "Both demanded that the Serbs cease all actions against the civilian population and withdraw the security units used for civilian repression. Milosevic has been in breach of every single part of those resolutions," he added.[283]

When reminded that Russia and China had condemned the NATO action as illegal, Prescott replied: "I understand the concern of the Russians about the legal justification.... but the use of force is justified under international law to prevent an overwhelming humanitarian disaster. We believe that what is happening in Kosovo could be such a disaster, and that is the legal justification for our action on this occasion."[284] However, he admitted the qualification that it was an action of last resort, undertaken one year "after it became clear that the final diplomatic effort in Belgrade had not met with success and that all efforts to achieve a negotiated political solution to the Kosovo crisis had failed."[285] On March 28, the British Prime Minister called Milosevic a "brutal dictator" and added: "It is our job in the name of humanity and stability in the region to carry on until we have stopped."[286]

The questions are whether the concept of "overwhelming humanitarian necessity" is recognised in international law; whether it overrides other principles of international law; and, if so, how the circumstances in which it may do so are to be recognised by the international community? In reply to questions like these in the House of Lords on November 16, 1998, Baroness Symons said: "The prohibitions on the use of force contained in the UN Charter do not preclude the use of force by a state or group of states in self-defence in accordance with Article 51 or under the authorisation of the Security Council acting under Chapter VII of the Charter. There is no general doctrine of humanitarian necessity in international law. Cases have nevertheless arisen (as in northern Iraq in 1991) when, in the light of all circumstances, a limited use of force was justifiable in support of purposes laid down by the Security Council but without the Council's express authorisation when that was the only means to avert an immediate and overwhelming humanitarian catastrophe."287 She reaffirmed this answer on May 6, 1999.

On March 23, 1999, Dr. Javier Solana, the Secretary-General of NATO, said: "Our objective is to prevent more human suffering and more repression and violence against the civil population of Kosovo. We must also act to prevent instability spreading in the region..... We know the risks of action but we have all agreed that inaction brings even greater dangers. We will do what is necessary to bring stability to the region." This statement, reminiscent of the Ecowas justification for its military intervention in Liberia in 1990, places at least as much emphasis on the necessity of maintaining regional stability, a sort of pre-emptive collective self-defence, as it does on averting a humanitarian catastrophe.

However, whatever be NATO's legal justification, the fact remains that it was a Chapter VII enforcement action requiring prior Security Council authorisation under Article 53 of the Charter. There was none. This led the UN Secretary-General to lament the sidelining of the world body, while Russia and China accused NATO of flouting international law. Crucially, France, Canada and The Netherlands, known sticklers for legalism, abandoned principle for political expediency.288 Outside Europe and the United States, the NATO intervention received little support. Asian countries led the rest of the world in condemnation. The Hindustan Times of India wrote: "It is a ludicrous sight to watch the mighty NATO war machine preparing to tame a tiny nation whose only lapse has been its refusal to pawn its sovereignty."289

NATO's intervention in Kosovo was thus initially grounded on humanitarian necessity. The contention was that the systematic suppression by the Belgrade government of its own citizens in Kosovo was so repugnant to the norms of civilised behaviour and generally accepted principles of human rights that it amounted to a rejection of all humanitarian considerations, compelling other states to undertake humanitarian intervention. However, one may wonder why similar action had not been taken in Chechnya, Tibet and the other flash points in Africa. Interestingly, in August 2000, even the British Parliament was not at all confident that the NATO military action in Kosovo had been legally justified. The Foreign Affairs Select Committee of the House of Commons concluded that " at the very least, the doctrine of humanitarian intervention has a tenuous basis in current international customary law, and that this renders NATO action legally questionable."[290] However, the British government holds a different opinion. The Foreign Secretary said: "The Government has made clear that use of force is justified as an exceptional measure when it is the only means to avert an immediate and overwhelming catastrophe and is in support of objectives set by the UN Security Council, even if the express authorisation of the Council has not been possible. Such cases would in the nature of things be exceptional and depend on an objective assessment of the factual circumstances at the time and on the terms of relevant decisions of the Security Council bearing on the situation in question."[291]

Be that as it may, it seems that the doctrine of humanitarian intervention leans heavily on politics and morality. It also evokes a great deal of passion and subjectivity, and quite often it leads to double standards. All that can be reasonably stated is that, under the current state of international law, unless justified as self-defence or authorisation by the Security Council under the United Nations Charter, the use of force to defend human rights in a purely internal conflict situation is untenable. The so-called doctrine of humanitarianism is in effect a short hand for a reversion to nineteenth century nightmares of gun-boat diplomacy. As no country is perfect in the observance of human rights obligations, it would simply open the flood-gates for powerful states to pursue their political, economic and strategic national interests in the territories of less powerful states and thereby negate the absolute prohibition in Article 2(4) of the UN Charter against the use of force in international relations.

This is still the preponderant position in state practice. For instance, Article 3(2) of Additional Protocol II of 1977 to the Geneva Conventions of 1949, relating to non-international armed conflicts, precludes outside military intervention, whether it be on ideological grounds or in response to human rights abuses, either in the conflict or in the affairs of the state in whose territory the conflict is taking place. It follows from this that the parties to a non-international conflict cannot invoke even the United Nations Declaration on Friendly Relations to secure foreign assistance from a non-party to the conflict.292

In the absence of a definitive international judicial decision on the matter, reliance may be made on certain judicial *obiter dicta*. The International Court of Justice has opined that while violations of human rights do engender obligations *erga omnes*, they nevertheless do not give a state the right to forcibly compel their observance in another. In another case, the Court said it was illegal for one state to exercise by force its executive authority in the territory of another against its will. "The alleged right of intervention," said the Court in the *Corfu Channel Case*, is nothing more than "the manifestation of a policy of force, such as has, in the past, given rise to the most abuses and as such cannot, whatever be the present defects in international organisation, find a place in international law."293 And in *Nicaragua v. USA*, the Court said that "the use of force could not be the appropriate method to.... ensure .... respect" for human rights.

Thus seen, there is as yet no general principle of humanitarian necessity recognised by customary international law. The preponderant practice is to punish state officials who violate the rights of their citizens through the judicial process including war crimes tribunals or by other non-military means, for example, by imposing sanctions or withholding development assistance, though not humanitarian aid, for so long as the violation persists. For example, when asked to list the countries whose development assistance had been curtailed and suspended on grounds of human rights violations, Clare Short informed the House of Commons as follows:

> "Since May 1997, aid from my Department's budget to Sierra Leone has been suspended, although we continue to assist the elected government which is now in exile. Aid also remains suspended through the governments of countries such as Burma, Nigeria and Sudan. In these cases, the regime's records on human rights were one of the factors taken into account in our decisions..... In

Belarus, in accordance with EU policy, we will not work through state organisations in future and will provide only humanitarian or regional support or support which directly promotes the process of democratisation. In countries where aid through central official channels has been suspended, we retain our aim of helping to eliminate poverty and will pursue this by working through NGOs and local government. We thereby also show our solidarity with oppressed peoples. Where we retain official aid, we may also wish to modify the pattern of aid, including possibly curtailing aid, in response to a number of short or longer-term factors, including human rights. This is a continuous and general process and it is often difficult to draw out any one factor as critical to the outcome."294

Even where the violation amounts to a crime under international law, such as torture, genocide, war crimes or crimes against humanity, it is doubtful whether forcible humanitarian intervention is permissible. But it is legitimate to express international concern,295 and, of course, where the rule infringed is one of *jus cogens*, universal jurisdiction may be assumed by national courts. What this emphasises is that even in proven cases of gross violations of international humanitarian or human rights law, the proper remedy lies in the judicial realm, not in military action. And foreign courts, provided they have given themselves appropriate jurisdiction, have competence under international law to punish such crimes extra-territorially when committed by state officials against their own citizens within their own territories.

However, punitive executive measures, particularly military action, have not yet been recognised as legitimate measures that a state can take unilaterally outside the framework of the United Nations Charter. For this, an international treaty is required. I agree with Kofi Annan when he says that: "If the new commitment to humanitarian action is to retain the support of the world's peoples, it must be – and must be seen to be – universal, irrespective of region or nation. Humanity, after all, is indivisible."296

Commonwealth countries *inter se* no longer enjoy individual discretion in the matter of international recognition of regimes coming into existence by unconstitutional means, for example, by overthrowing democratically-elected governments. Each member has agreed to be bound by the decisions of the association in such matters, particularly where a member state is directly affected.

According to Chief Emeka Anyaoku, former Commonwealth Secretary-General, democracy is now the Commonwealth's "international political gold standard". The association has established rules by which each member has agreed to be judged by the others, particularly whether their policies and practices are consistent with this new standard. These rules were first propounded in the Declaration of Commonwealth Principles in Singapore in 1971 and later articulated in the Commonwealth Harare Declaration of 1991 and the Millbrook Action Programme of 1995. The last mentioned gave teeth to the Harare Declaration by setting up the Commonwealth Ministerial Action Group (CMAG) to deal with violations and to recommend collective Commonwealth action aimed at compelling the earliest possible return of the abuser to compliance with the Harare principles.

Under the Harare principles, each Commonwealth member has pledged to work, *inter alia,* for the promotion and protection of certain fundamental political values, including respect for democracy, democratic institutions that reflect national circumstances, fundamental human rights, the rule of law, the independence of the judiciary and just and honest government. Millbrook spells out the penalties to be imposed upon any member deemed to be in serious or persistent violation of the Harare principles.

The countries which have so far crossed the Millbrook Line are Nigeria (military *coup*, cancellation of democratic elections and gross abuse of human rights), The Gambia (military *coup* and denial of democratic right), Sierra Leone (military *coup*) and Pakistan (military *coup*). Nigeria was suspended from Commonwealth membership from November 1995 to May 1999, Sierra Leone from July 1997 to March 1998 while that of Pakistan commenced in November 1999. Though, in material terms, not a great deal is lost from Commonwealth exclusion, in political terms, a suspended member is generally treated as an international pariah.

It may be worthy to recite the measures stipulated in the Millbrook Programme of Action. They are as follows:

" Where a member country is perceived to be clearly in violation of the Harare Commonwealth Declaration, and particularly in the event of an unconstitutional overthrow of a democratically-elected government, appropriate steps should be taken to express the collective concern of Commonwealth countries and to encourage the restoration of democracy within a reasonable time frame. These include:

(i) immediate public expression by the Secretary-General of the Commonwealth's collective disapproval of any such infringement of the Harare principles;

(ii) early contact by the Secretary-General with the de facto government, followed by continued good offices and appropriate technical assistance to facilitate an early restoration of democracy;

(iii) encouraging bilateral demarches by member countries, especially those within the region, both to express disapproval and to support the early restoration of democracy;

(iv) appointment of an envoy or a group of eminent Commonwealth representatives where, following the Secretary-General's contacts with the authorities concerned, such a mission is deemed beneficial in reinforcing the Commonwealth's good offices role;

(v) stipulation of up to two years as the time frame for the restoration of democracy where the institutions are not in place to permit the holding of elections within, say, a maximum of six months;

(vi) pending restoration of democracy, exclusion of the government concerned from participation at ministerial-level meetings of the Commonwealth, including Heads of Government Meetings;

(vii) suspension of participation at all Commonwealth meetings and of Commonwealth technical assistance if accepted progress is not recorded by the government concerned after a period of two years; and

(viii) consideration of appropriate further bilateral and multilateral measures by all member states (e.g. limitation of government-to-government contacts; people-to-people measures; trade restrictions; and, in exceptional cases, suspension from the association), to reinforce the need for change in the event that the government concerned chooses to leave the Commonwealth and/or persist in violating the principles of the Harare Commonwealth Declaration even after two years."

Accordingly, the Millbrook Line, so to speak, is crossed only where the government overthrown is a democratically-elected government. This means that it is not enough that the overthrown regime had been the constitutional government of the state, for example, if it was elected under a one party or non-party system; it must be one that was democratically elected in accordance with Commonwealth standards. Nor is it a democratic government if it had come into being through vote-rigging or some other serious breach of electoral law. Second, the method employed for its overthrow must have been unconstitutional. The obvious example is a military *coup*. A fascinating case is that of the crisis in Fiji in June 2000. Compared to the previous Fijian crisis, it may be that the Millbrook Line was not crossed this time because there was no break in constitutional legal continuity; the head of state had merely resigned, albeit a forced resignation.

Under the Millbrook rules, the Commonwealth is essentially reactive and only to requests from governments seeking to entrench democracy, the rule of law and accountable governance. It is not proactive in that the rules are silent about what to do if there is no overthrow but only a threat to overthrow. Second, they do not cover the case where the incumbent government itself is guilty of subverting the national constitution, undermining democracy or abusing human rights. Such cases may well require Commonwealth action beyond the offer of good offices by the Secretary-General. Third, although suspension from the Commonwealth is an exceptional measure, the practice of the association does not appear to be consistent. For example, Nigeria had the longest record of military rule, yet it was not suspended until after it failed to comply and only after several warnings stretching over a reasonably long period of time. In contrast, Sierra Leone was suspended with remarkable dispatch, in the very first meeting convened by the CMAG to consider the crisis in that country. The suspension did not, however, prevent the British Prime Minister, as host and chairman, from taking the unusual step of inviting exiled President Kabbah to the Edinburgh Summit in October 1997 as his "special guest". As noted by Chief Emeka in his valedictory address in April 2000, "if the Commonwealth is to be a force for good in the world, it needs to be consistent about the principles which it proclaims."[297]

Lastly, taking activism in entrenching democracy and fundamental human rights from mundane monitoring of elections to greater heights, such as organising and supervising elections in its member states, is the new challenge facing the Commonwealth. This may best be achieved through a permanent international mechanism established specifically for that purpose.

CHAPTER 7

Observance of International Humanitarian Law

Violations of international humanitarian law

Like so many other internecine conflicts, the ten-year old civil conflict in Sierra Leone has been vicious, brutal and senseless. Estimates vary, but it may not be an exaggeration to put the casualty figure at 50,000 dead, more than one-half of the entire population displaced internally and more than half a million turned into refugees.

Unashamedly, abuses of human rights and international humanitarian law were rampant, bordering on the cruellest of conduct. They ranged from extra-judicial killings to mutilations of civilians of all ages to torture, rape and hostage taking. To a degree, they disconnected Sierra Leone from modern civilisation and reconnected her to a Dark Age of anarchy.

No belligerent party is immune. Unarmed civilians became their targets, viewing their protection as less than sacred. Accused of collaborating with the enemy, they almost routinely became soft targets for reprisals. Women and children, in particular, fared worst. While the former were pressed into service as porters and sex slaves, the latter were almost invariably conscripted as fighters and forced to commit horrendous atrocities against even their own families. Not surprising that most of them ended up being severely traumatised.

It is hard to fathom why unarmed civilians were made targets. Olara Otunnu, UN Special Representative for Children in Armed Conflict, who visited Sierra Leone from May 26 to 29, 1998, has opined that it was "part of the objective of warfare, not just indiscipline on the part of fighters". The aim was "to humiliate, wreak suffering, teach them a lesson and to demoralise as a tool of war."[298] Questions like who is responsible for particular atrocities or what should be done to the perpetrators are perhaps best left to the Special Criminal Court or the Truth and Reconciliation Commission. All that can be reasonably said is that, given the nature of the conflict and the scale of atrocities, no belligerent party can claim immunity from responsibility for gross abuses of both human rights and international humanitarian law.

Yet, from the start of the conflict till a long time thereafter, the impression given by the international media was that only the rebel forces were guilty of egregious abuses. Comparatively little, if any, was said about those committed by the pro-government forces. This was out of range with the thinking of ordinary Sierra Leoneans who believed that all belligerent parties partook of atrocities during the conflict. Sorious Samura's award-winning documentary, *Cry Freetown*, shown on television networks around the world, was also explicit about this and so were the victims of atrocities.

International human rights organisations should likewise be acknowledged for documenting human rights abuses. The American-based Human Rights Watch (HRW) was the first to publish a balanced account of the human rights situation in July 1998. About rebel atrocities, it says: "Many thousands of Sierra Leonean civilians have been raped; deliberately mutilated, often by amputation; or killed outright in a campaign by the AFRC/RUF between February and June 1998 alone. Men, women and children, probably numbering in the thousands, have been abducted by the AFRC/RUF for use as combatants, forced labourers, or sex slaves. Women have been actively targeted through sex violence, including rape and sexual slavery. Children have been targets of killings and violence and are forcibly recruited as soldiers. In addition to various forms of physical abuse, innumerable Sierra Leoneans suffer from psychological trauma due to intentionally cruel methods of inflicting harm against these individuals and their communities."

Civil defence forces were no less guilty: "The largest and most powerful of these groups, the *kamajors*, were responsible for the majority of the most serious abuses committed by those fighting on behalf of the Kabbah government since February 1998. In recent months, *kamajors* have also been responsible for obstructing humanitarian assistance and demanding money or compensation at roadblocks.... Groups providing assistance to the interior of Sierra Leone reported in June that the *kamajors* had become increasingly demanding at checkpoints, often insisting that they be compensated for having 'liberated' the country from AFRC/RUF," the report adds.

On summary executions, the report goes on to say: "The scale and nature of abuses committed by *kamajors* …differ significantly from atrocities carried out by the AFRC/RUF, but are often no less horrific. Many witnesses of abuses committed by *kamajors* spoke of the grotesque nature of killings, at times including disembowelment and followed by consumption of vital organs, such as the heart. Acts such as these were intended to transfer the strength of the enemy to those involved in the consumption. Killings by *kamajors* usually targeted people they believed to be members of the AFRC/RUF and their civilian supporters. A Sierra Leonean Catholic priest described how the *kamajors* reacted to the presence of the AFRC/RUF in Koidu in early February, just days following Ecomog's takeover of Freetown:

'On February 7th, they [the AFRC/RUF] started "Operation Pay Yourself". On Friday the 13th, I went back to the mission. The youths had called the *kamajors* who started arriving on the 11th, 12th, a day or two after "Operation Pay Yourself" had ended. They came from Sewafe, Punduru, Gondama....When they found AFRC, they would kill them immediately. The *kamajors* and youths started burning [AFRC/RUF] soldiers and collaborators. On about February 11th, they [the *kamajors*] called a meeting at the Town Council. They said it was to restore law and order – they said if anyone knows where they are, they should tell us. They decapitated one surrendered soldier and I saw them eat his raw liver and heart.....'

"Several foreign residents of Sierra Leone that had worked with or observed the *kamajors* in the field concurred that this 'take no prisoners' policy was widespread. One foreign trainer of the *kamajors* claimed that the fighters were as 'malicious as the AFRC/RUF', but committed fewer abuses due to their supervision, even though this was limited. Captain Samuel Hinga Norman, Deputy Defence Minister, who in recent months repeatedly stated that all CDFs were now under the control of ECOMOG, has led the *kamajors*. With their knowledge of the local terrain, *kamajors* are frequently relied upon by Ecomog as combatants and guides in unfamiliar rural areas."

HRW then concludes: "Civil Defence Forces, such as the *kamajors* and loosely organised bands of youths, represent a serious and growing human rights issue in Sierra Leone today. Like the AFRC/RUF, these groups are able to act largely with impunity. This trend, when considered in the context of past practices of armed groups in Sierra Leone, underscores the need to develop a comprehensive programme to disarm, demobilise and reintegrate all combatants into the new national army or Sierra Leone society. .... The reintegration aspects of the Disarmament, Demobilisation and Reintegration (DDR) programme must emphasise a respect for the laws of war and human rights. As combatants from rebel groups, CDFs and government forces have comprised the principal perpetrators of human rights abuses in Sierra Leone, the success of this programme could play a crucial role in preventing future human rights abuses."299

Apart from Human Rights Watch, similar reports have been compiled by Amnesty International for 1998300 and 1999,301 the United States Department of State's Annual Reports on Human Rights for 1998 and 1999 and UNOMSIL. After the attack on Freetown in January 1999, Secretary-General Kofi Annan sent a confidential memorandum to the Security Council on February 11. In it he accused the rebels of being responsible for "most of the civilian casualties", but found the pro-government forces just as culpable. He accused them of executing rebel suspects or sympathisers, among them children. In one incident, some 20 patients at Connaught Hospital, who were alleged to be rebels, were executed on January 12. Similar executions occurred at Ferry Junction and again in front of Connaught Hospital at various times, after only "a cursory interrogation". An eight-year-old boy was executed after being caught with a pistol. The report further alleges that the Nigerian forces had bombed civilian targets, shot at "human shields" formed by rebels and mistreated the staff of the ICRC and many other humanitarian bodies. In one bombing raid on January 7, 20 civilians were killed in the centre of Freetown. The report goes on to say that although the human rights violations of Ecomog and *kamajor* forces did not match the scale of rebel atrocities, they were nonetheless totally unacceptable. "Witnesses make clear that, in all cases, the interrogation process was entirely inadequate and that there was no real effort to establish the guilt or innocence of execution victims," the report is quoted as saying.

The Secretary-General then reportedly urged the Sierra Leone government, which was charged with responsibility for these summary executions, and the Nigerian forces, to "ensure that their forces operate in conformity with the letter and spirit of international human rights and humanitarian law".302

Thus, while the rebel forces' observance of human rights was undoubtedly poor, what amazed many people was the equally unrestrained conduct of the government and its forces. Starting with a hit list allegedly prepared while in exile in Conakry, hundreds of civilians, accused of collaborating with the AFRC junta, were killed in the most gruesome manner upon the return of Kabbah's governmen in February 1998. Some were burnt alive after being drenched with petrol and neck-laced with disused car tyres in order to ensure a rapid and spectacular death. Curiously, President Kabbah had stayed behind in Conakry a whole month after liberation, giving plenty of opportunity to his followers to commit atrocities with impunity. No investigation of these unlawful killings has ever been undertaken by his law enforcement agencies.

Similarly, the so-called Radio Democracy, supplied by the British government supposedly to tell the people the truth, needs to be investigated. It gained infamy for spewing scurrilous and malicious falsehoods, inciting party loyalists and fanning the embers of political and ethnic hatred. In some cases, it even named names and directed mobs of loyalist thugs where to go to find alleged junta collaborators. A Sierra Leonean newspaper, *The Point*, tells how invading rebel forces had suddenly changed their minds about laying down their arms after listening to the broadcasts of FM 98.1. Its edition of February 9, 1999 says: "Though one will appreciate the fact that this station [FM 98.1] played a very important part in bringing back our hard-earned democracy, and is still playing a vital role in its sustenance, its personal attack on people at that time and the kind of propaganda mounted during this second coming of the rebels in town has been largely responsible for the destruction of so many lives and property." It goes on to cite examples. It recalls how Julius Spencer, the Minister of Information, had "told the rebels .... that the civilians were leaking information to Ecomog. This gave cause to rampant killing, raping and maiming of civilians in the whole east end of Freetown where the rebels were in complete control till

Monday, 18 January, when Ecomog pushed beyond East End Police .... Anytime Spencer was on the air, it was to cause hell to descend on civilians."

Another example cited was when Septimus Kaikai, Presidential Spokesman, allegedly declared that the government had no intention of releasing Foday Sankoh, a key demand of the rebels. "That," said the paper, "was a dreadful day for civilians in rebel territories. A number of killings and burning of houses was carried out by rebels on that day." These sad stories "have made a lot of people to recall that most of the people whose names were frequently announced as collaborators of the AFRC junta before 5 February 1998 were either killed or jailed on the restoration of democracy."303 Is such propaganda different from a war crime?

President Kabbah too entered the fray. In a national broadcast on February 1, he spoke about "disheartening" and "very disturbing" reports of the "alarming level of collaboration with the rebels by many Sierra Leoneans". Then came the replay of what had become the standard excuse for the sins of his government. "Considering the fact that we have had over two decades of bad governance and rampant corruption," he intoned, "it is perhaps not so surprising that Sierra Leone has bred so many people whose humanity has been reduced to such a level that they could carry out the type of atrocities experienced in Freetown". Again, on February 21, reacting to public complaints about atrocities by pro-government forces, he said: "We should let the rest of the world know that Ecomog, our Civil Defence and other loyal forces are not trying to overthrow this or any other government; that they are not demanding power and destroying, in the process, the lives and property of the very people whom they want to rule. They are not fighting or waging war against the people of Sierra Leone. On the contrary, Ecomog, our Civil Defence and other loyal forces are only acting in self-defence. They are our defenders. Indeed, Ecomog was authorised by Ecowas and the United Nations Security Council to help protect us. On several occasions, the UN Security Council has itself commended, and rightly so, 'Ecomog troops for the courage and determination they have demonstrated in their efforts to maintain security in Sierra Leone'."304 These statements must have dashed all hopes the relatives of victims may have entertained for an official investigation, still less for justice to be done, as demanded by the Security Council in resolution 1231(1999).

Special Criminal Court for Sierra Leone

Making abusers account for their crimes is an objective only few would argue against. After a lot of pressure from human rights activists in and out of Sierra Leone, on June 12, 2000, President Kabbah wrote to Kofi Annan. He asked for help in setting up a special criminal court for Sierra Leone. Stating the purpose of the court as one of bringing to credible justice persons who have committed crimes against the people of Sierra Leone, however, he attempted to retrict the court's jurisdiction only to "members of the RUF and their accomplices".

Few would object to Foday Sankoh being brought to credible justice. As leader of the RUF, he bears vicarious responsibility for the atrocities committed by his forces in the name of his movement. But why did President Kabbah want to limit the personal jurisdiction of the court to the RUF alone? Could one not suspect that he probably wanted to shield certain people from prosecution?[305] Is that also the reason why he had asked for his Attorney-General and Minister of Justice, Solomon Berewa, to be appointed Chief Prosecutor or Co-Chief Prosecutor? In his own words, he wanted "the government of Sierra Leone to play a lead role in the prosecution". Already, even before the idea of a Special Court was conceived, while members of the AFRC junta and their so-called collaborators had been prosecuted for treason and other heinous offences, the government had shown no inclination to prosecute the *kamajors* and other party vigilantes suspected of committing homicide and other serious criminal offences. For these people there is no end to impunity which will inevitably continue to clog the path to national reconciliation. And asking for his Minister of Justice to be appointed prosecutor must obviously mean sealing the impunity of such people.

In the original draft of Security Council resolution 1315 (2000), establishing the Special Court, reputably prepared by the United States, the court's personal jurisdiction was restricted to "senior Sierra Leonean nationals who bear the greatest responsibility for the most systematic and egregious criminal violations of Sierra Leone law and international humanitarian law, in particular those whose actions have posed, since 7 July 1999, serious threats to peace and security in the region". Obviously this would have excluded non-Sierra Leoneans from prosecution. To let such culprits off the hook is to sanctify military intervention, no matter how illegal it might be.

Unsurprisingly, international human rights organisations as well as the Sierra Leone Bar Association objected. The latter, on July 6, 2000, called on the Sierra Leone government to ensure that the prosecution was not restricted to one faction or group. Similarly, Amnesty International, on August 4, protested vehemently that "those most responsible for ...crimes, whether they are members of the RUF, the AFRC, the Sierra Leone Army or the CDF, and regardless of their current political position or allegiance, must be brought to justice." It added: "[C]ontrary to the current draft, the jurisdiction of the court should not be limited to Sierra Leone nationals alone and exclude nationals of other countries who may have committed these crimes. An independent prosecutor, subject to appropriate judicial scrutiny, should decide who should be prosecuted."

Human Rights Watch followed suit. "This court must not stop at prosecuting one man or faction," the Executive Director of its Africa Division said on August 14, adding: "Diplomats keep talking about the 'Sankoh resolution' as if rebel leader Foday Sankoh were the only one responsible for the widespread war crimes in Sierra Leone." HRW also expressed concern that "a possible dominant role in the court by Sierra Leone authorities could lead to political manipulation of the process, leading to biased prosecutions and inadequate protections for persons standing trial before the tribunal. The Sierra Leone judiciary does not have the capacity to play more than a limited role in the court, a fact acknowledged by the Sierra Leone government itself..... The job of bringing the perpetrators of international crimes to justice must reside with the international community...."

These protests, mercifully, did not go unheeded. The final text of resolution 1315 was less restrictive and spoke of prosecuting individuals with "the greatest responsibility for the commission of the crimes". The Secretary-General, following negotiations between Mr Ralph Zacklin, UN Assistant Legal Adviser, and the Kabbah government, recommended to the Security Council the more general term "persons most responsible". He justified this by saying that the term "most responsible" denotes " both a leadership and authority position of the accused, and a sense of the gravity, seriousness or massive scale of the crime".[306] However, Zacklin sought to limit the number of culprits to about 25 or 30. When one considers the large number of armed actors who have taken to the battlefield since the inception of the conflict in March 1991, it is difficult to comprehend this limitation. In any case, it is the responsibility of the prosecutor, based on his assessment of evidence of *prima facie* culpability, to determine who should be prosecuted.

Be that as it may, Article 1 of the proposed Statute of the Special Court gives the Court "power to prosecute persons most responsible for serious violations of international humanitarian law and Sierra Leonean law committed in the territory of Sierra Leone since 30 November 1996."

More controversial was the temporal jurisdiction of the Special Court. In his report the Secretary-General recommended to the Security Council that November 30, 1996, the date of the ill-fated Abidjan Peace Accord, should be the starting date for the Court's temporal jurisdiction. He says that "the government negotiators [had] actively concurred" in that decision. Naturally. What is surprising was that the UN negotiators seemed to have been unwittingly drawn into taking a decision that was pre-eminently political in nature and could easily lead the Court to applying some kind of selective or discriminatory justice.

Why was the government so anxious to limit the Court's temporal jurisdiction? At least two reasons may be advanced. First, it omits from the court's jurisdiction questions relating to the origins of the RUF rebellion and the key accomplices who were behind it. It is widely believed that politicians connected with the SLPP had been behind the RUF whose aim from the start was to topple the APC government. So far as the SLPP was concerned, any action aimed at removing the APC government from power was acceptable since it had always viewed it as "illegitimate". Curiously, the APC government was referred to in the Secretary-General's report as a "one-party military"[307] government, presumably to further underscore this alleged "illegitimacy". One-party, it was; but military, it certainly was not. Second, it excludes from prosecution those criminal elements of the NPRC junta, and their advisers, who massacred 29 people in December 1992 without any form of trial. How more selective can justice get?

It is to be hoped that the Security Council would address these issues creditably and in a manner that would inspire public confidence. If not, it would have failed to give the Special Court the last word on the prosecution of war crimes suspects. In these circumstances, it would be open to a dissatisfied future government to proceed against suspects whom it believes had been exempted from the Special Court because of reasons of discrimination or politics.

That is not all. There is also the all-important question of timing. Before the court begins to function, first things first. First, the peace process should have been restored and UNAMSIL should have been free to deploy throughout the country. This means that the RUF must relinquish armed control of the entire Northern Province and Kono District as they have of other parts of the country. Second, all combatants must be disarmed and demobilised, including in particular the RUF and all civil defence militias, without exception whatsoever. The Constitution of Sierra Leone eschews the establishment of private militias. Third, effective and efficient methods must be found to rebuild confidence among Sierra Leoneans so that they can regain primary responsibility for the peace process, including in particular the convening of a national conference of all key players, political parties and civil society. The conference should be under UN auspices in order to prevent any suspicion that the outcome was rigged by preferential nomination of individuals favourable to the incumbent government. The RUF should be allowed to participate in the process only if it has been fully transformed into a political party, to the satisfaction of the UN, and the same should apply to the AFRC if it still exists. Only when these are in place would it be appropriate for the Special Court to begin its work. In any case, care must be taken to avoid giving rebel commanders the feeling that they have no choice but to fight to the bitter end.

Thus the case for a Special Court for Sierra Leone, though conceived as a treaty-based *sui generis* court of mixed jurisdiction and composition rather than as a subsidiary organ of the UN, such as the International Tribunals for the Former Yugoslavia and for Rwanda, is overwhelming. All the more so since the Rome Statute of 1998, setting up the International Criminal Court, is not due to start functioning until 2002, provided the treaty would have secured the required 60 ratifications. Moreover, it is clear that the suffering people of Sierra Leone want an international judicial process that is genuinely independent and impartial and with an independent international prosecutor. This is of particular importance because, as has been stated, the incumbent government has already shown itself unwilling or unable to investigate, indict, try and punish certain sacred cows alleged to have committed war crimes.

Individual liability for international crimes

(a) *Before international tribunals*

Every accused person, regardless of rank or governmental status, whether belonging to a foreign army, pro-government force, paramilitary or irregular armed unit or rebel force, is personally responsible for such crimes under international law as he or she may have committed. Anyone in a position of command, whatever his rank, from the head of state to the lowest non-commissioned officer, who issues an order to commit such crimes is just as accountable as the subordinate actually committing the offence. They are also liable if, knowing or having received information from which they should have concluded that a subordinate was going to commit such a crime, they failed to prevent it. The defence of military necessity is not available to a person charged with a war crime or crime against humanity. Nor is the defence of carrying out the order of a superior officer available. Soldiers, civil defence forces or rebels are no longer, as in days of old, regarded as unthinking automatons, required only to obey orders, lawful or unlawful. The modern law is that an act done in compliance with an unlawful order, which is obviously, palpably or manifestly unlawful to a reasonable soldier in the circumstances prevailing at the time of the order, is not a defence and cannot be pleaded in mitigation.[308] All these are, however, questions of law.

These principles apply equally to foreign soldiers, whether as interventionists or international peacekeepers. They apply to foreign troops in Sierra Leone, whether as Ecomog or UN peacekeepers. No delinquent Ecomog or UN soldier can be exonerated on that ground alone. Since neither Ecowas nor the UN is a state, and therefore not a party to any treaty relating to the laws of war, their soldiers remain personally bound to comply with the laws of warfare that bind the state whose national they are and under whose command they remain throughout the conflict.

This principle of individual liability is now too firmly established in customary international law to require debate. One needs only to recite the London Charter of the International Military Tribunal appended to the Agreement for the Prosecution and Punishment of the Major War Criminals of the European Axis (the Nuremberg Charter) of August 8, 1945, which gave jurisdiction to try crimes against peace, war crimes and crimes against humanity. Article 7 says that: "The official position of defendants, whether as heads of state or responsible officials in government departments shall not be considered as freeing them from responsibility or mitigating punishment."[309] An identical principle was embodied in Article 6(2) of the proposed Statute of the Special Court for Sierra Leone. The Nuremberg Tribunal declared: "He who violates the laws of war cannot obtain immunity while acting in pursuance of the authority of the state if the state in authorising action moves outside its competence outside international law." Thus, no head of state or other official of government, or leader or member of a rebel force should be in any doubt about their personal liability for international crimes before an international tribunal. They can be charged and no claim of state, head of state or other official or diplomatic immunity would avail.

The Lome Peace Agreement of July 7, 1999 provides for a blanket amnesty for all crimes committed since the beginning of the conflict in 1991. Such amnesties are not uncommon. Indeed, they are recognised by international law as evidenced by Article 6(5) of the 1977 Protocol II Additional to the Geneva Conventions and Relating to the Protection of Non-international Armed Conflicts. It reads: "At the end of hostilities, the authorities in power shall endeavour to grant the broadest possible amnesty to persons who have participated in the armed conflict, or those deprived of their liberty for reasons related to the armed conflict, whether they are interned or detained." So the amnesty under the Lome Accord may be valid as part of the criminal justice system of Sierra Leone. But the United Nations has consistently argued that such amnesties could not be valid *vis-à-vis* the courts of third states or crimes under international law, such as genocide, war crimes, crimes against humanity or other serious violations of international humanitarian law. This was why its Special Representative was instructed to enter a disclaimer during the signing ceremony in Lome. The Security Council recalled this reservation in resolution 1315. Moreover, under Article 10 of the proposed Statute of the Special Court, it is provided that "an amnesty to any person falling within the jurisdiction of the Special Court in respect of the crimes referred to in articles 2 to 4 of the present Statute shall not be a bar to prosecution."

Thus, neither President Kabbah nor any of his ministers is immune from prosecution before the Special Court. In this regard, a precedent has been set when, in 1999, President Milosevic, a serving head of state, was indicted for war crimes before the International Tribunal for the Former Yugoslavia at The Hague. Alternatively, should a serving president or minister, for any reason, escape indictment because he is still in office, he could always be pursued later when he leaves office.

(b) *Before national courts*

Can criminal charges be brought before a national court other than the court of the state of which the accused is a national or in which the crime was committed? Can an accused claim sovereign or diplomatic immunity and can such a claim be a conclusive defence to an international crime?

The traditional law of state or sovereign immunity, expressed in the Latin maxim *par in parem non habet imperium*, was that one sovereign could not be impleaded in the courts of another because he could claim absolute immunity from jurisdiction, whether in criminal or civil proceedings. This was the law, whether he was a serving or former sovereign. Since the worst violations of human rights often occur on account of orders given by heads of state against their own citizens or aliens under their protection, that immunity had serious implications for authorities charged with enforcing international criminal law. The same is true of leaders of revolutionary movements, who, invariably commit, with absolute impunity, the most heinous crimes on their way to the presidency and thereafter, such as killing or maiming their political opponents in order to secure power.

The sacrosanctity of this hallowed maxim came for consideration before the British House of Lords in the celebrated case of *Ex Parte Pinochet Ugarte* in November 1998.310 The first Appellate Committee was asked to interpret the scope of the immunity enjoyed by a former head of state from arrest and extradition proceedings before a foreign national court in respect of acts committed when he was head of state. The question was whether General Pinochet, as a former head of state, could claim immunity from prosecution or extradition proceedings in the United Kingdom in respect of acts alleged to have been committed whilst he was head of state of Chile?

The facts of the case are briefly these. General Pinochet was head of state of Chile from 11 September 1973 to 11 March 1990. Spain charged him with serious crimes committed during that period, including genocide, murder, torture and hostage-taking. When Pinochet came to England for medical treatment in 1998, the Spanish government requested for his extradition to Spain. He claimed state immunity under the relevant British statutes as well as under the common law doctrine of act of state.

Their Lordships, by a majority of 3:2, decided that a serving head of state enjoys absolute immunity from criminal and civil proceedings for all acts whether or not they relate to matters done for the benefit of the state. He enjoys it *ratione personae*. When he leaves office or is deposed, he could be prosecuted because then he enjoys only a limited immunity. This limited immunity relates only to acts that were legitimate or lawful functions of government, not to acts that international law considers unlawful. For example, it is not a legitimate function of state for a head of state to commit or permit to be committed gross violations of human rights. Such acts will be treated as personal, private and unofficial and he can be held accountable because in respect of them he enjoys no immunity. As stated by Lord Nicholls, a member of the majority of the Court:

> "[I]t hardly needs saying that torture of his own subjects, or of aliens, would not be regarded by international law as a function of a head of state. All states disavow the use of torture as abhorrent, although from time to time some still resort to it. Similarly, the taking of

hostages, as much as torture, has been outlawed by the international community as an offence. International law recognises, of course, that the functions of a head of state may include activities which are wrongful, even illegal, by the law of his own state or by the laws of other states. But international law has made plain that certain types of conduct, including torture and hostage-taking, are not acceptable conduct on the part of anyone. This applies as much to heads of state, or even more so, as it does to everyone else; the contrary conclusion would make a mockery of international law."311

Departing fundamentally as it does from the traditional doctrine of absolute immunity for former sovereigns, the decision was hailed as a watershed in the evolving field of human rights law. And coming fortuitously in the fiftieth anniversary of the Universal Declaration of Human Rights, which seminally defined the irreducible minimum standards owed to individuals by their states and state officials under international law, it was celebrated as a great triumph for human rights and for the victims of human rights violations.

So General Pinochet was extraditable to Spain. Only the Home Secretary, in exercise of his political powers under section 12 of the British Extradition Act 1989, could save him. On December 9, 1998, the Home Secretary decided that the extradition proceedings against General Pinochet should proceed. However, on January 15, 1999, a second Appellate Committee set aside the judgment of the first Appellate Committee and ordered Spain's appeal to be heard afresh.312 This was because Lord Hoffman, who had cast the deciding vote in favour of General Pinochet's extradition, had failed to disclose his links with Amnesty International, a party to the appeal. There was nothing of personal benefit; he had only chaired a fund-raising drive for the construction of a new headquarters for Amnesty International in London – merely a potential for judicial bias. It is not sufficient, said the Court, for a judge to be independent and impartial; it is also necessary that he appears to be so, in order to exclude any legitimate doubt on the matter. The Court's ground-breaking decision was that the mere potential for a conflict of interests was sufficient to put a taint on its earlier judgment and to make it unsafe. The rehearing took place before a different appellate panel of seven judges on January 18, 1999. Judgment was delivered on March 24, 1999.

The third Appellate Committee therefore had two key questions before it. The first, which had been subsumed in the first hearing, was whether all the crimes charged against Senator Pinochet were "extradition crimes" within the meaning of the Extradition Act 1989. To constitute an extradition crime, the conduct complained of must be a crime at the date it was committed under the law of both the requesting state and the requested state. This is known as the double criminality rule. The crimes with which Pinochet was charged in Spain included torture. This only became an international crime under the International Convention against Torture and other Cruel, Inhuman or Degrading Treatment or Punishment 1984. Under it, torture was made a crime for which all states parties have universal jurisdiction under the principle *aut dedere aut punire* – either you extradite or you punish. The obligations under the Convention were incorporated into British law by Section 134 of the Criminal Justice Act 1988. That Act came into force on September 29, 1988, making torture a new crime in Britain. Accordingly, torture committed outside Britain before that date was not a crime under British law and therefore not extraditable under the dual criminality rule. Only torture committed after September 29, 1988 can constitute a crime in Britain and therefore extraditable provided it was concurrently a crime under the law of Spain, the requesting state.

If this requirement was satisfied, the next question was whether General Pinochet was entitled to immunity from prosecution. If he is immune, that is the end of the matter and he must be set free. On the other hand, if he is not entitled to state immunity then he is extraditable. The matter then moves from the judicial realm back to the lap of the Home Secretary, who must make a political decision whether to extradite or not, the task of the courts being only to decide matters of law.

Their Lordships confirmed the ruling by the first Appellate Committee, namely that a serving head of state is entitled to complete immunity *ratione personae*, while a former head of state, like a former ambassador, enjoys only limited immunity at common law. He loses immunity *ratione personae* and enjoys only limited immunity *ratione materiae* in respect of acts performed by him as part of his official functions whilst head of state.

The question was whether the commission of an international crime can be said to be an act done in an official capacity on behalf of the state? Torture, said their Lordships, cannot be a legitimate function of the state so as to confer immunity from prosecution on the perpetrator. In other words, as formulated by Lord Phillips:

> "No established rule of international law requires state immunity *ratione materiae* to be accorded in respect of prosecution for an international crime. International crimes and extra-territorial jurisdiction in relation to them are both new arrivals in the field of public international law. I do not believe that state immunity *ratione materiae* can co-exist with them. The existence of extra-territorial jurisdiction overrides the principle that one state will not intervene in the internal affairs of another. It does so because, where international crime is concerned, that principle cannot prevail......Once extra-territorial jurisdiction is established, it makes no sense to exclude from it acts done in an official capacity."

Thus, serving heads of state, who have committed gross violations of human rights against their own citizens, which are in the nature of international crimes, must now be extremely worried about what might happen to them when they leave office. According to the Pinochet decision, they are liable to be prosecuted in foreign courts and to be extradited for that purpose. They are also liable to be proceeded against in civil claims. And, nowadays, the option of sitting tight in the presidency to avoid criminal or civil action is not available, because most modern constitutions limit the tenure of the head of state to one or two terms only. For despotic heads of state contemplating gross human rights abuses against their own citizens, the decision would make them think twice, perhaps more than twice, for there is now no hiding place anywhere. The Pinochet decision has definitely confirmed the principle of personal accountability of heads of state in the courts of foreign states for crimes under international law when they leave office.

In the case of Sierra Leone, nothing stops anyone from bringing members of President Kabbah's government to justice anywhere when they leave office to account for their own human rights abuses. He set the precedent himself when he prosecuted former President Joseph Saidu Momoh for treason in 1998 on the grounds of alleged collaboration with the AFRC junta.

Status mixtus of the armed conflict

To determine what body of international humanitarian law applies to the conflict in Sierra Leone, it is necessary, first of all, to characterise the conflict. Is it an internal or international armed conflict?

There is persuasive evidence that the armed conflict exhibited something of a *status mixtus*.313 At one end of the spectrum lay hostilities between the Nigerian army on the one hand and the combined forces of the Sierra Leone army and the RUF rebels (AFRC), on the other. Arguably, they bear the characteristics of an international armed conflict, and, as such, attract the full panoply of the laws and customs of war. As there was no prior and unequivocal declaration of war, in terms that satisfy the provisions of Article 1 of the Hague Convention 1907, there was technically no state of war between the two armies. However, the United Nations Charter 1945 has so revolutionised the international law of armed conflict that it is nowadays impossible to have a traditional state of war that is compatible with the Charter provisions. Indeed one can list scores of inter-state armed conflicts in none of which war was formally declared. This led Oppenheim's *International Law* to redefine war simply as "a contention between two or more states through their armed forces, for the purpose of overpowering each other and imposing such conditions of peace as the victor pleases". This is also the view adopted by states parties to the Geneva Conventions 1949. Article 2, which is common to all four Conventions, stipulates that "the present Convention shall apply to all cases of declared war or of any other armed conflict which may arise between two or more of the High Contracting Parties, even if the state of war is not recognised by one of them".

Thus, as armies belonging to two contracting states, they were obliged to respect and ensure respect in all circumstances for the laws and customs of war. It is irrelevant that the Nigerian forces in Sierra Leone did not recognise the existence of a state of war or the *de facto* governmental status of the AFRC. They were bound by the fundamental rules that they must at all times distinguish between the civilian population and combatants and between civilian objects and military objectives; accord surrendered rebels prisoner-of-war status; and direct their operations only against legitimate military targets. Accordingly, their indiscriminate aerial and artillery bombardment of civilian residential suburbs or of foreign vessels discharging unprohibited goods at the quay in Freetown or their unlawful blockade of humanitarian assistance, including food and medicines, fall to be evaluated with these rules.314

At the other end of the spectrum lay the military engagements between the RUF/AFRC rebel forces on the one hand and "the civil defence and other loyal forces", on the other.315 These carry the hallmarks of a non-international armed conflict, as did the earlier fighting between the Sierra Leone army and the RUF. In either case, only a limited number of rules apply, including in particular the irreducible minimum standard of humanity reaffirmed in common Article 3 of the Geneva Conventions 1949, supplemented by provisions of the Protocol II 1977, relating to the protection of victims of non-international armed conflicts. In such armed conflicts, the legal status of captured combatants is not affected and the incumbent government may subject them to prosecution for the crime of treason. This was what in fact happened when the Kabbah government prosecuted soldiers for treason in 1998.

At the beginning of the conflict in Sierra Leone, when it was strictly a contest between the RUF rebels and the government forces, its characterisation as a non-international armed conflict was never in dispute even though there were Liberian fighters of the NPFL helping the RUF. At that point, the NPFL was merely a warring faction in Liberia. In January 1999, however, following the rebel attack on Freetown, the Sierra Leone government accused the Liberian government of complicity and insisted that the character of the conflict had thereby changed from being a non-international armed conflict to an international one.316 At the same time, however, it insisted on applying the full weight of its criminal law and refused to accord prisoner-of-war status to captured rebels.

Internal armed conflicts, more often than not, are fuelled by the illicit supply of armaments to the warring parties. As long as such supplies flow and there are assets to pay for them, they dim the prospects of bringing the conflict to an early end. The United Nations tried to stem the flow of arms into Sierra Leone by imposing a mandatory arms embargo under resolution 1132. It failed, because it did not also address the assets available to the rebels to pay for them, namely the illicit mining and sale of the country's diamonds.

In Britain, the arms embargo was translated into British law by the Sierra Leone (United Nations Sanctions) Order 1997 of November 1, 1997. This Order in Council made it an offence for anyone in the United Kingdom, or a British citizen or British company outside the United Kingdom, to supply arms, without a licence, to all parties in or connected with Sierra Leone.317 Sandline International, a private British military company, subsequently supplied 35 tons of Bulgarian weapons to Kabbah's government in breach of this British law and the United Nations resolution. This incident eventually broke into a huge scandal and remained in the public domain for many months. It also generated a lot of controversy in the British Parliament and the British media, and produced three inquiries, the first by Customs and Excise, the second by the Foreign Office and the third by the Parliamentary Select Committee on Foreign Affairs.

According to a letter of April 24, 1998, addressed to the British Foreign Secretary, Sandline's Solicitors advanced two grounds to support their argument that their client had broken no law. First, that while they would admit supplying arms and mercenaries contrary to the embargo, that embargo had applied only to the military usurper, the AFRC, and not to the legitimate government which it was helping. Secondly, that its involvement in Sierra Leone was with the prior knowledge and approval of the British government. Their arguments were put in these terms:

> "At the suggestion of your High Commissioner in Freetown, Mr Peter Penfold, President Kabbah asked our clients to provide assistance. At a meeting held shortly thereafter Mr Penfold confirmed that he had initiated that approach and encouraged Sandline International's

involvement. Thereafter negotiations proceeded with President Kabbah and his representatives and, as those developed, full briefings were given both personally and by telephone to representatives of Her Majesty's Government. At the Foreign and Commonwealth Office those briefed included John Everard, Craig Murray, Linda St Cook and Tim Andrews and our clients were led to believe that clearance was given at Head of Department level. The Ministry of Defence personnel who were briefed included Lieutenant Colonel Peter Hicks in Conakry and Colonel Andrew Gale, the British army military adviser to the UN Special Envoy to Sierra Leone.

Further, Mr Penfold himself called at our clients' office premises on 28 January 1998, just three weeks before the equipment now in issue was delivered, and was given full details of the arrangements including the number of personnel involved and the nature of the military equipment that was to be provided. He was also given a copy of Sandline International's strategic and tactical plan, its concept of operations, for its involvement in the Sierra Leone arena. Our clients were assured throughout that the operation had the full support of Her Majesty's Government.......

Accordingly, it is quite apparent that the involvement of Sandline International in support of President Kabbah had at all times had the approval of Her Majesty's Government and, should it become necessary, we would contend that a licence had been given within the meaning of the Sierra Leone (United Nations Sanctions) Order 1997."318

Sandline's Solicitors also claimed that their client had the support of the United States government:

"At the same time, our clients kept informed the US State Department at the highest level, including John Hirsch, the US Ambassador to Sierra Leone, Charles Snyder, Director, Office of Regional Affairs and Dennis Linskey, Chief, West and Southern Africa Division. Furthermore, following support having been given for the proposed operation by both the US Department of State and the US Department of Defence (represented by Alan

Holmes, Assistant Secretary of Defence for Special Operations), we understand that Michael Thomas, the Country Desk Officer for Sierra Leone at the US Department of State met with Philip Parham, the Africa Watcher at the British Embassy in Washington indicating the US Government's full support for Sandline International's involvement, which was no doubt reported back to your office in London in accordance with the proper procedure."319

This incident also revealed the readiness of President Kabbah's government to use mercenaries just to return to power. Tim Spicer of Sandline, barely recovering from his arrest and deportation from Papua New Guinea in 1997, on account of an abortive mercenary project there, was taking advantage of another desperate government with yet another project reeking of destruction and commercial opportunism.

(a) *British Government's Investigations*

Associating the British government with the activities of persons generally reviled as "dogs of war" was embarrassment enough, though Sandline smartly wears the more glamorous title of "private military company".320 The British government therefore launched two inquiries into the allegations.321 The first was a criminal investigation by the Department of Customs and Excise to ascertain whether the British legislation had been broken. On May 18, Customs and Excise decided not to bring criminal proceedings. The reason given was that: "Even though offences may have been committed, the particular circumstances leading up to the supply affect the fairness of the case to the extent that any prosecution could well fail and would certainly not be in the public interest." 322

Any criminal prosecution of Sandline was likely to collapse, because the defendant could have argued, perhaps successfully, that it believed it had official approval. Not one of the many British officials contacted over several months had even hinted that supplying arms to President Kabbah might be illegal. Moreover, the standard of proof for determining whether a breach of the UN embargo had occurred was not clear.323

That same day the Foreign Office launched its own

administrative inquiry. Chaired by Sir Thomas Legg QC, a retired civil servant of 36 years' standing, and assisted by Sir Robin Ibbs, a management consultant and former Executive Director of ICI, as an assessor, the Foreign Office was keen to deny the allegations that there had been official approval of or collusion in the activities of Sandline, even though they consisted in helping a recognised foreign government against an unrecognised military junta. Its terms of reference were to establish "(a) what was known by government officials (including military personnel) and Ministers about plans to supply arms to Sierra Leone after October 8, 1997; (b) whether any official encouragement or approval was given to such plans or such supply; and (c) if so, on what authority." The Foreign Secretary explained his concerns in these terms:

> "At no point was any ministerial approval given for the activities of Sandline. Nor was there any ministerial discussion of the activities of Sandline, or any meeting between Ministers and Sandline....... No licence was given for the export of any arms; nor is there an allegation that any arms were shipped from Britain. The allegation is that they were shipped from Bulgaria, but that a British company may have arranged the contract. If the allegations are correct ... that gives rise to an offence within Britain under the terms of the UN resolution. That is why we are treating the matter with great gravity, but there has been no suggestion of either arms being shipped from Britain or any licence being approved for such a shipment."[324]

The Opposition had severely criticised him for attempting to hide behind officialdom. They contended that if indeed officials had given approval, it would not be a valid defence to say that ministerial approval had not been given.[325] Unnerved by this argument, the Foreign Secretary uncharacteristically expressed "deep concern" about the conduct of his officials and even went so far as to offer them the services of criminal lawyers to assist them in the inquiry. On May 12, however, he changed dramatically. Taking the cue from his Prime Minister, who the day before had dismissed the whole affair as an "overblown hoo-ha" since, after all, the "good guys" had won, Mr. Cook breathed a sigh of relief. He was now able to defend his Department. From the evidence available to him, he said, he was convinced that no "officials in the Africa Department of the Foreign Office had been involved in any kind of conspiracy with Sandline, or had given any approval to a breach of the arms embargo".326 The fact that this was precisely the matter under inquiry did not apparently deter him from jumping the gun by provisionally clearing his officials of any wrongdoing. Indignant about "wild allegations" against his officials being "recycled as proven fact", Sandline thus stood accused of telling an untruth.327

The Prime Minister's differentiation between good and bad guys seemed to have rekindled the Foreign Secretary's confidence. It was like saying that if there were a foreign regime with which Britain disagreed, it would be right to allow persons in Britain to conspire, for instance, to bomb that country in order to punish its regime. In other words, a conspiracy to kill the bad guys is justified but a conspiracy to kill the good guys is not. Yet, the law says murder is murder, whether the person killed is a rapist or a cleric. To say otherwise is to talk not about law but about anarchy behind a civilised mask.

It is also curious to define who these "good guys" really were that were going to use the arms supplied by Sandline. Presumably, the reference was to the pro-government forces fighting for President Kabbah. With no national army in Sierra Leone loyal to Kabbah at that time, these could only have consisted of Nigerian forces and *kamajor* militias. The Prime Minister could not have meant the Nigerian forces since they were under a binding European Union arms embargo that Britain was duty-bound to respect. It could therefore only have meant the *kamajors*, an ethnic militia known for committing horrendous atrocities against innocent civilians and with child soldiers prominently within their ranks. Thus, the implication of the Prime Minister's statement is that it was justified to arm an ethnic militia or child soldiers with weapons supplied by a British firm to kill the "bad guys" in Sierra Leone, even if those weapons ended up killing innocent civilians. What if those weapons had been turned on other ethnic groups? Would this be consistent with Britain's new ethical foreign policy?

When the 35 tonnes of Bulgarian weapons arrived in Sierra Leone, no time was wasted in handing them over to the *kamajors*, whose sole objective was to fight to preserve their tribal and political hegemony. Even after the restoration of Kabbah's government, they refused to be disarmed or demobilised, and often behaved as if they already had official *imprimatur*. Matters got worse when they were cloaked with some sort of semi-official status. With such awesome fire-power in their hands, coupled with the muzzling of the press, it took little imagination to know what they could do next.

Helping the British government face down its critics, Kabbah's government suggested that it could take refuge behind an admixture of morality and realpolitik by arguing that the end had justified the means. Julius Spencer, Sierra Leone's Minister of Information, contemptuously dismissed the whole incident and became the advocate of a *coup de main*. "If British government officials assisted," he argued, "the British people should be proud of their government. Even if a British law was broken, people in Britain should be happy that it was broken for a good cause."328 On May 16, a rally was organised in Freetown to which several thousands turned out in support of Peter Penfold, the British Envoy in Sierra Leone, who was due to appear before the British inquiry. The demonstrators lavishly praised Penfold, describing him as a "national hero" and crowning him as an honorary chief (Pa Komrabai). There was no love lost for Robin Cook, whom the demonstrators described as the "most hated man in the country". The government-owned *Daily Mail* in Freetown said of him: "How does Cook think we were going to get rid of [Johnny Paul] Koroma? With sticks and stones, bows and arrows? Penfold is a hero for every person in this country and we cannot understand why the British appear to be backing the junta. Does Cook think that these killers should have stayed in power?"329

But an already embarrassed Foreign Secretary did not fall for it. He kept his vision above the fray and spelled out the fundamental principle at stake. As a permanent member of the Security Council, Britain could not afford otherwise than to uphold the supremacy of the rule of international law. "The government have consistently supported the legitimacy of the United Nations. This government abide by the resolutions of the Security Council and are committed to the rule of international law. I assure the House that we have not, and will not, condone any breach of international law," the Foreign Secretary declared.330

(b) *The findings of the Legg inquiry*

The Legg Inquiry found that the failure by the Foreign Office to explain the United Nations arms embargo more effectively to other government departments, to its overseas missions and to the public at large, particularly its applicability to President Kabbah's government, and to consult more widely on the draft Order in Council, had "created a hazard for all affected by the Order."331 The hazard was that British nationals could make an unlicensed supply of arms to President Kabbah's government without knowing it was a breach of the arms embargo and a criminal offence in Britain.

The Inquiry also found that:

"No Minister gave encouragement or approval to Sandline's plan to send a shipment of arms to Sierra Leone, and none had effective knowledge of it. Some officials became aware, or had notice, of the plan. The High Commissioner [Penfold] gave it a degree of approval, which he had no authority to do, but he did not know that such a shipment would be illegal. No other official gave any encouragement or approval. All concerned were working to fulfil government policy, and there was no attempt to hide information from Ministers. However, officials in London should have acted sooner and more decisively than they did on the mounting evidence of an impending breach of the arms embargo, and they should have told Ministers earlier and more effectively. As a result, Ministers were given no, or only inadequate, notice of the matter until the Berwin letter arrived. The failures at official level were caused mainly by management and cultural factors, but partly by human error, largely due to overload."332

On the role of Peter Penfold, British High Commissioner, the Inquiry said:

"He was told of Sandline's plans, in mid-December 1997 by President Kabbah, and later that month by Mr Spicer, and gave them a degree of approval. However, the full effect of the arms embargo had not been properly explained, and Mr Penfold and others were not aware that the unlicensed supply of arms to the elected government of Sierra Leone was illegal. Mr Penfold should have done more to inform himself about the arms embargo, and should have reported his contacts with President Kabbah and Mr Spicer back to the Foreign and Commonwealth office more promptly and effectively."333

Tim Spicer said that in a meeting on December 23, 1997, he had given Penfold a copy of their military plan of operation. Craig Murray, then Deputy Head of the Foreign Office's Africa (Equatorial) Department, later told the Parliamentary Select Committee on Foreign Affairs that he had recommended Penfold's recall from Freetown after learning that he had advised President Kabbah to sign an arms contract with Sandline, contrary to British government policy. Penfold had confessed to him that "he had advised President Kabbah in Conakry to take on Sandline, and that they will be able to train up the *kamajors* as a fighting force and even things up with the junta." Murray said he had passed on his concerns to Ann Grant, Head of the Africa (Equatorial) Department, who then summoned Penfold to a meeting where he was told he had acted contrary to British government policy. "Penfold did not deny this but, on the contrary, replied that he had given such advice in his personal capacity. I have a very clear recollection of this," Murray recalled. Grant later testified before the Select Committee that she and Penfold had had a "heated and lengthy debate" in which she had made it clear that it was not acceptable for him to give advice on a personal basis.334

The Foreign Secretary's response to the mistakes, misjudgements and mismanagement of his officials, as catalogued by the Inquiry, was to say that the report had helped the Foreign Office to close one chapter and open a new one. He announced a programme of sweeping changes to modernise the Foreign Office and address the systemic and cultural deficiencies that had contributed to the problem.

With regard to the incautious contacts with Sandline, the Legg Inquiry recommended that there should be "more explicit guidance on how to manage relations with private military firms". As a result, the Foreign Secretary directed that in future no contact should be made with such firms without prior permission and that where such contacts take place they should be recorded in a full written report.335 The Foreign Affairs Committee supplemented this by drawing attention to the particular difficulties, which could arise when contacts with such firms are with persons who have had previous service with the armed forces or other agencies of central government - the "old boy" network.336 "If people outside government talk the same language and share the same background and social activities as people inside, simple human nature is likely to mean that confidences will be shared and that hand will wash hand," observed the Committee.337

Looking for political scapegoats

At the height of resurgent rebel activities in Freetown, Julius Spencer, Kabbah's Minister of Information, accused Karefa-Smart and I of visiting Monrovia, capital of Liberia, where we supposedly held discussions with rebel leaders.338 This allegation was not only defamatory; it was typical of the way the government was always looking for political scapegoats in order to deflect public attention away from its own foibles. In this instance, it invented such a bareface story that it ceased to be funny. This was not mere mischief-making; on the contrary, it was calculated to incite government supporters, along with the victims of rebel atrocities, into taking the law into their own hands and wreaking revenge on so-called collaborators and their relations. As eloquently observed by a group of independent journalists in Sierra Leone, calling themselves *Ninja*, on December 31, 1998, the reason for this unwarranted outburst might not have been unconnected with the fact that "Smart and Bundu spoke vehemently against military intervention to restore President Kabbah. They stated that the use of military might to resolve the crisis would fail. Now that the use of force has resulted in such wanton physical destruction and horrible atrocities against the people by the RUF, it is thought in some government circles that Bundu and Smart should be demonised by any means at hand so as not to have members of the public thinking that the duo was right. This time, it is not very clear just how successful these propaganda broadcasts will be in unifying the people against peace talks"339

Again, when the arms-to-Africa saga broke into a scandal in Britain, President Kabbah looked for scapegoats. Again he reserved his venom for the democratic opposition. In a spiteful letter to the British Prime Minister on or about May 11, 1998, he blamed me, along with others, for the explosive media and

225

parliamentary interest the affair was generating in Britain. Under pressure, Tony Blair took the unusual course of giving currency to the letter by releasing it to the press for publication. While other newspapers merely quoted excerpts, omitting the defamatory parts, *The Times* published it almost in its entirety on May 13, including the defamatory allegations. These were that I was a supporter of the AFRC/RUF military junta; that I belonged to a group of "unpatriotic, greedy and unprincipled Sierra Leoneans who are determined to destroy" Sierra Leone; that I was a member of a group which was campaigning to "denigrate highly respected British institutions;" that this campaign had started on the day that his wife had died in London; and that the aim of the campaign was "to justify and ensure the return of the illegal AFRC/RUF regime."

These accusations were not only downright libellous, coming from no less a person than the head of state, they amazed a lot of people, who found it hard to fathom why he should find it necessary to vilify his democratic opponents whose only crime had been to criticise his policy of military intervention in Sierra Leone. Indeed his accusations savoured of an elaborate plan to dress up dissenters in rebel garb so as to expose them to public scorn and hatred. So frightened had Kabbah become of dissenters that he even tried to persuade the United Nations to include their names in the travel ban adopted under resolution 1132. It all shows the lengths to which despotic leaders in Africa can go in their desperation to destroy democratic opposition.

Under threat of litigation, *The Times* newspaper published a retraction on May 18, 1998 to "put the record straight." The British government publicly dissociated itself from President Kabbah's libellous remarks when, on May 14, 1998, Baroness Symons told Parliament that: "The Prime Minister's spokesman's briefing....[had] made clear that Her Majesty's Government could not associate with some parts of the letter, including the part to which the noble Lord referred. I can confirm that the Government do not associate themselves with that letter nor with the defamatory comments about the noble Lord or any other persons mentioned in that context."340 I had written a letter of protest to the British Prime Minister on May 13, requesting such dissociation. His Private Secretary, Philip Barton, replied on June 1, to say: "The Government's aim was to use the letter to put the issue in a broader context. The Prime Minister's spokesman did, however, specifically disassociate the Government from parts of the letter. He made clear that there were certain points in the letter which the Government did not share, including President Kabbah's views about other people involved." The BBC, which also became an unsuspecting accomplice, tendered a public apology as part of an out-of-court settlement of a libel suit on June 28, 1999.

Mercenaries in the conflict

Mercenaries played a prominent part in the conflict. Both sides used them. On the government side, they were first introduced by the NPRC, which engaged the services of the Jersey-based Gurkha Security Guards in February 1995. They withdrew after their leader, Colonel Bob McKenzie, was killed, along with Major Abu Tarawallie, aide-de-camp to the NPRC Chairman. They were replaced by the Executive Outcomes in May 1995.[341] Kabbah's government terminated Executive Outcomes' contract only to replace them with a sister company, Sandline International, when it adopted a militaristic policy for resolving the imbroglio. Even as late as September 2000, mercenaries like Neil Ellis were working for Kabbah's government.[342]

On the rebel side, they too have employed foreign mercenaries, mostly from West African countries and Ukraine.[343] In particular, although the Liberian government has denied official complicity, Liberian mercenaries have fought on both sides of the war in Sierra Leone. According to President Charles Taylor: "It is very clear and factual that there are Liberians in Sierra Leone fighting. Liberians have been used as mercenaries in Sierra Leone for a long time by all governments of Sierra Leone. They have always been there, about 3,000 of them. But they are there on their own."[344]

Following the end of its civil war, Liberia became a fertile ground for the recruitment of mercenaries, especially from the ranks of demobilised fighters. Jobless and unskilled, these former combatants, numbering several thousands, apparently fell back on the only skill they can trade in a liberal economy - violence. Unless they are trained in new skills, and the private sector is able to absorb them, this pool of experienced guerrilla fighters is easily recyclable, portending further destabilisation in West Africa in the

227

foreseeable future.

The menace of PMCs

But West African mercenaries are not the only ones stalking Africa's trouble spots. From Russian pilots in the Horn of Africa to Ukrainian trainers in Sierra Leone, foreign mercenaries or so-called private military companies (PMCs) have been most conspicuous. The break-up of the Soviet Union and the contraction of armies in Eastern Europe have brought a glut of potential recruits. Their tools are cheap, robust Eastern bloc arms. Their assets are military skills visibly scarce in a continent where wars are more often armed victimisation of civilians than combat.345 So lucrative has the trade become that PMCs have mushroomed everywhere and are openly trading their mercenary services.346 They say they are filling a vacuum created mainly by the increasing reluctance of Western Powers to commit their troops to United Nations peacekeeping operations outside Europe. In the case of Sierra Leone, for instance, this disinclination was manifested when the United Nations failed to field peace-keepers until the closing months of 1999. It took eight years and tens of thousands of civilian deaths before it was able to field a peacekeeping force at an estimated cost of $260 million every six months.

The known PMCs which have operated in Sierra Leone are the Jersey-based Gurkha Security Guards, the South African Executive Outcomes and the London-based Sandline International and Branch Energy. They each boast of selling highly skilled military services. The Sierra Leonean offshoot of Executive Outcomes, Lifeguard Security (Sierra Leone), has supplied security personnel to mining companies, including diamond-mining firms where Tony Buckingham of Branch Energy allegedly has a close business connection.

These PMCs have deployed mercenaries on many fronts. Foreign private investors, concerned about safeguarding their investments, have also turned to them. They pay them fantastic fees, and they in turn pay their soldiers more than ten times what their counterparts earn in national armies. For example, Executive Outcomes' first contract with Gulf-Chevron and Petrangol was reportedly for $40 million to protect their oilfields in Angola.347

Their contract with the NPRC in Sierra Leone was in excess of $22 million initially, increased to $35.2 million for a period of 20 months. Of this, $15.7 million was paid leaving a balance of $19.5 million, designated as a "sovereign debt".348 Apart from this contract, they also demanded from the Sierra Leone government contracts for fisheries surveillance and for preventing diamond smuggling. These are examples of how easy it is for weak and impoverished governments, with volatile security profiles, to be subdued by arm-twisting PMCs determined to deprive them of their natural and mineral resources.

Kabbah terminated Executive Outcomes' contract in 1996 on the grounds of his government's inability to pay US$1 million, later reduced to $750,000, a month. However, when in 1997 he decided to regain power through a counter-coup against the AFRC junta, he again hired mercenaries, this time Sandline International. Then cash-strapped, he turned to private financiers looking for shady deals. He found Rakesh Saxena, who was then facing extradition proceedings in Canada. He had become something of a *cause célèbre* in Thailand for alleged involvement in a huge loan scam with a bank in Bangkok, an incident that had led to the resignation of both the Prime Minister and the Governor of the Central Bank of Thailand. Saxena agreed to underwrite the deal with Sandline to the tune of $10 million in return for mining concessions worth about $200 million, the so-called Blackstone contract.349 What is again evident here is the usual intertwining of foreign intervention, mercenaries, gun-running and diamond dealing, which, in the past, had contributed in no small measure to the pauperising of the people of Africa.

Self-interest is, of course, at the heart of mercenarism, which also explains why mercenaries are not afraid to serve opposite sides in a conflict. They work for the highest bidder and they are not concerned about changing loyalty at any time. This is at least one factor that distinguishes a mercenary from a regular soldier who is often attracted to soldiering by the desire to serve his country and to do so with honour. Another difference is the control mechanism to which a regular army is subject in a democratic polity in order to ensure that it does not undermine the political process, usurp the authority of government, abuse the rights of citizens or exercise excessive force. This mechanism includes executive control, flowing from the head of state to the cabinet to the minister of defence and to the chief of defence staff. In addition there is parliamentary control over the executive; public control to which parliament in turn is accountable through the electorate; legal control by way of domestic law defining the circumstances and manner in which force may be used and the sanctions which attend its illegal use; international control by way of ensuring respect for the international laws and customs of war; and internal control through education and training programmes designed to inculcate certain values in the soldier. None of these controls apply to mercenaries.350

A mercenary is defined in Article 47(2) of Additional Protocol I of 1977 as any person who (a) is specially recruited locally or abroad in order to fight in an armed conflict; (b) does, in fact, take a direct part in the hostilities; (c) is motivated essentially by the desire for private gain and, in fact, is promised, by or on behalf of a party to the conflict, material compensation substantially in excess of that promised or paid to combatants of similar ranks and functions in the armed forces of that party; (d) is neither a national of a party to the conflict nor a resident of territory controlled by a party to the conflict; (e) is not a member of the armed forces of a party to the conflict; and (f) has not been sent by a state which is not a party to the conflict on official duty as a member of its armed forces.351 These requirements are cumulative and concurrent and must all be satisfied before a person can be determined as a mercenary or not. No single requirement is sufficient, so the definition is easy to evade. However, the moment he is determined as a mercenary, under Article 47(1), he loses the status of "combatant or prisoner-of-war".

In 1989 the United Nations General Assembly adopted the International Convention against the Recruitment, Use, Financing and Training of Mercenaries, making mercenary activity an international crime. Under it, states are prohibited from recruiting, using, financing and training mercenaries, and are obliged to extradite or prosecute them if found in their territory. Though in existence for a decade now, the Convention is yet to receive the minimum 22 ratifications necessary to bring it into force. Some countries regard its definition of "mercenary" as too vague for judicial proceedings, particularly where a conviction must be based upon proof beyond a reasonable doubt. Britain is among them. In fact, only 16 states have so far ratified it. States such as the European Union members (except Italy), the USA, Canada, Australia, New Zealand and Norway are yet to ratify. The British Parliamentary Select Committee on Foreign Affairs has asked the British government to seek an amendment to the Convention or else lead the European Union, Council of Europe or the United Nations in preparing a new international treaty.352

As between African countries, apart from the International Convention, there is also the OAU Convention for the Elimination of Mercenarism of 1977. It came into force in 1985. Its definition of "mercenary" is much the same as that in the Additional Protocol I or the International Convention. Nor is the hire of mercenaries by governments caught by the definition particularly when they are incorporated into the national army. As such they become agents or servants of the government that hires them which is therefore vicariously liable for any human rights abuses they commit. All these emphasise the urgent need for a revision of the Convention.

Thus seen, the absence of an effective international legislative regime to regulate or sanction the activities of PMCs has encouraged them to mushroom and often times to behave with absolute impunity. Worse still, were the maintenance of peace and security to be privatised, as some people have canvassed, it would give space to "neo-colonialism" to become more assertive. As agents of powerful multinational companies seeking to impose their hegemony on small and weak states, PMCs could easily become the forerunners of a new kind of multinational neo-colonialism.

On the vex question of privatisation of international peacekeeping, two schools of thought have emerged. On the one hand, there is the view that state security in delinquent Third World states should be privatised on account of the growing reluctance of Western Powers, induced by the "Somalia allergy", to participate in international security outside Europe. It should be treated like any other commodity or service, subject only to the rules of the market place. Thus, it is open to a state, beset by crisis and unable to cope through its national law-enforcement and security agencies, to buy or hire security from a PMC.

But there are obvious drawbacks. First, all the controls for safeguarding human rights would be thrown to the wind and both hirer and citizen would be at the mercy of the hired. Where mercenaries proliferate, national armies shrink and states weaken. As Machiavelli pointed out in 1513: "Mercenary captains either are or are not skilful soldiers. If they are, you cannot trust them for they will always seek to gain power for themselves, either by oppressing you, their master, or by oppressing others against your wishes. If, on the other hand, they are not skilful soldiers, they will still be your ruin in most cases."353 Secondly, mercenaries never inure in the long term. They withdraw as soon as they deem it strategically not in their interest to stay any longer, invariably leaving the country a lot worse off than before. Barely three months passed, after Executive Outcomes withdrew from Sierra Leone, before the security structure they left behind collapsed and a military *coup* followed in May 1997. This could be viewed either as a damning exposé of their limitations or a clear proof that their presence had somehow induced a false sense of security. The fact that they wanted to prolong their stay should have been sufficient warning that the time was ripe to concentrate upon pacific procedures, not to mention the negative impact their continued presence was having on the autonomy of the government.

The opposing school rests on the hypothesis that the maintenance of public order and national security falls within the reserved domain of the state and should therefore be performed only by its regular military and police forces. It is opposed to privatisation of such functions, because the foundations of state sovereignty and national and international guarantees for the observance of human rights depend on it. Besides, to embrace privatised warfare at this time in history is not only tantamount to a return to an earlier age and a damning portrayal of how little mankind has learnt from the lessons of history but also a most horrific bequest to the new millennium.

The argument here is that although governments are free to privatise many things and many services that lie within their competence, they cannot privatise that which constitutes their very *raison d'etre*. Were they free to hand over security functions to a PMC or to a foreign army, then, in the words of Enrique Ballesteros, United Nations Special Rapporteur on Mercenaries, "it is agreeing to a limitation of state sovereignty, with the further drawback that the substantive legal rights of its inhabitants may be impaired and basic human rights principles and norms of international law violated."354 Ballesteros argues that the consent of the people is necessary before a state can give up such an intrinsic element of sovereignty. To quote him again, it would require "a revision of the very concept of the state as currently employed. It would need to be analysed in depth because it really would affect and change the nature, structure and functions of the state, while at the same time changing the nature of international relations."[355]

Thus stated, in Sierra Leone, the critical question is whether the Kabbah government, while the nation was still in the throes of civil war, had the legal power to disband the national army and transfer responsibility for security to a combined force of foreign soldiers and the *kamajor* militia? Since the foreign forces were concerned only with regime security, the crutucal question is who was responsible for human security?

These questions assume a particular poignancy on account of the fundamental principles of state governance enshrined in Chapter II of the Constitution of Sierra Leone 1991, entitled "Fundamental Principles of State Policy". Section 4 of that Chapter states that "all organs of government and all authorities and persons exercising legislative, executive or judicial powers shall conform to, observe and apply the provisions of this Chapter." Section 5 provides, *inter alia*, that "the security, peace and welfare of the people of Sierra Leone shall be the primary purpose and responsibility of government, and to this end it shall be the duty of the Armed Forces, the Police, Public Officers and all security agents to protect and safeguard the people of Sierra Leone." Though, as stated in the Constitution, these provisions are not justiciable, yet, under Section 14, they are fundamental to the governance of the state and it is the "the duty of Parliament" to apply them in discharging its legislative functions. Additionally, under the Lome Peace Agreement of July 1999, all mercenaries in Sierra Leone, whatever their guise, were to be withdrawn immediately under the supervision of the Joint Monitoring Commission.

These opposing schools of thought notwithstanding, the problem remains that mercenarism is still not illegal in many countries. In Britain, for example, the Foreign Assistance Act 1895 only prohibits the engagement of British citizens in the armed forces of a state at war with a state that is in friendly relations with Britain. It says nothing about the service of British citizens in an internal armed conflict or about their deployment as "military or security consultants" not engaged in combat. In 1998, as a knee-jerk reaction to the horrific bombings in Omagh, Northen Ireland, by the renegade Real IRA in which 28 people died, Britain created a new offence of statutory conspiracy under the Criminal Justice (Terrorism and Conspiracy) Act. This Act makes it criminal for two or more persons in England to agree to commit an illegal act in a foreign state, notwithstanding that the same act, if committed in England, is not an offence at all.

Mercifully, however, the Act does not criminalise incitement. As stated by Lord Williams of Mostyn, Minister of State in the Home Office: "That is deliberate as we did not wish to interfere with a tradition which remains valid, noble and distinctive to our country; that is, that political dissent is important and should be allowed, even when it is disagreeable; in fact, particularly when it is disagreeable."356 Accordingly, it is not an offence in Britain to sympathise with political movements abroad or to support them financially. Nor is it an offence to speak in their favour or encouragingly of them.357

Ironically, despite the fact that mercenary activities were contributing as much as £180 million a year to its economy, South Africa, the home base of Executive Outcomes, is the first country to criminalise such activities. Its Regulation of Foreign Military Assistance Act 1998 has introduced two significant elements. First it contains a broad definition of foreign military assistance as encompassing not only active involvement in combat but also the provision of logistical, intelligence, training, personnel, operational and other forms of military support to a party engaged in armed conflict. Second, it attempts to regulate the activities of South African citizens who wish to render such support. They must first obtain the approval of the Minister of Defence; otherwise their involvement is deemed to be unauthorised and punishable.

Hostage Taking

Hostage-taking is a crime under international law. In the Sierra Leone conflict, it was committed mainly by the RUF. Two staff members of the humanitarian organisation, Médecins sans Frontieres (MSF), were kidnapped in February 1998 as they were driving along the Port Loko-Lunsar highway, and two others were abducted by the RUF in December 1999. Before this, several foreign doctors working at the Catholic hospital in Lunsar were abducted, and by the end of February 1998, no fewer than 25 foreign nationals had been kidnapped.358 In exchange for these hostages, the RUF demanded the release of Foday Sankoh, at that time in detention in Nigeria.359 However, Bishop Giorgio Biguzzi of the Catholic Mission in Makeni mediated and all the hostages were released unharmed.360

During the sacking of Freetown in January 1999, countless numbers of civilians were also taken hostage, including school children. This time the mediation was undertaken by the Inter-Religious Council of Sierra Leone which obtained the release of some of them while the remainder were released after the Lome Accord had come into force. The ICRC was also a prominent mediator. On March 12, 1995, it secured the release of foreign Catholic nuns abducted by the RUF. Again, on April 20, 1995, it combined with International Alert to secure the release of 16 hostages, 10 of whom were expatriates, at the banks of the Moa River at the north-eastern corner of the Guinea-Sierra Leone border. The worst was to come in May 2000, when the RUF abducted more than 500 United Nations peacekeepers. Following mediation by President Taylor of Liberia, all of them were released.

Child soldiers

Children have been the worst hit by the war. Deprived of childhood, thousands of them were recruited – many through abduction and conscription - as front-line combatants. In November 1998, UNICEF estimated that there were at least 4,000 child soldiers, some as young as seven years old. Other estimates have put the figure at over 5,000, divided between pro-government forces and RUF rebels.361 They were used as porters, messengers and spies, but more alarmingly as combatants and sex slaves. Prized by commanders for their fearlessness and bloodlust, the warring parties found them to be more obedient, unquestioning and easier to manipulate than adults. Patrick Zangalaywah, a *kamajor* field commando, for example, admitted that: "In Kailahun District alone, we have 3,000 child *kamajors*. These kids are very brave on the frontline." They were also found to be "unadulterated" and extremely obedient to rules. "We don't trust adults quite as much because many have breached the rules governing our militia and so they get killed by the enemy," he added.362 In other words, child soldiers were cheap, less careful about their own safety and follow orders more readily than adults, and children from poorer homes were by far the most vulnerable.

According to the Third Regional Consultation on the Impact of Armed Conflict on Children in West and Central Africa, held at Abidjan, Cote d'Ivoire, from 7 to 10 November 1995 (the Abidjan Meeting), children become soldiers for a variety of reasons. Among these were "survival, self-esteem, revenge of the death of family members, peer group pressure and coercion by adults and family members."363 To this may be added the motive of acquiring power, freedom and material things. In Sierra Leone, it is not difficult to discover former child soldiers who boast about the number of "enemies" they had killed.

The Abidjan Peace Accord of 1996 was silent on the subject of child combatants, but the parties nonetheless did acknowledge their existence and the need to demobilise them. Following the signing of the Conakry Peace Plan in October 1997, and spearheaded by Major Kula Samba, the first female army officer ever executed in Sierra Leone for treason, the AFRC actually started the process of identifying and registering child soldiers as a first step towards demobilisation. The right of child soldiers to special protection, care and demobilisation was finally recognised in the Lome Peace Agreement of July 1999. Its Article XXX says: "The Government shall accord particular attention to the issue of child soldiers. It shall, accordingly, mobilise resources, both within the country and from the international community, and especially through the Office of the UN Special Representative for Children in Armed Conflict, UNICEF and other agencies, to address the special needs of these children in the existing disarmament, demobilisation and reintegration processes."

Although the government made repeated commitments to end the recruitment and use of child combatants, concern remained about their deployment by government allied forces. Britain made their demobilisation a condition precedent for its assistance in training new, accountable and effective armed forces for Sierra Leone. It also made it a condition that arms supplied to the Sierra

Leone army should be used only in accordance with international human rights standards and international humanitarian law. In particular, that children should not be used by the Sierra Leone armed forces or the civil defence forces. The United Nations Secretary-General's fourth report on UNAMSIL had revealed that up to 25 per cent of combatants in the army and pro-government armed groups were children under 18 years and that some of them had freely admitted that their ages were between seven and fourteen years.

Olara Otunnu, United Nations Special Representative for Children and Armed Conflict, identified five areas requiring urgent action by the international community. These were demobilisation and reintegration of child combatants; resettlement of internally displaced people; tracing the families of unaccompanied children; rehabilitation and support of victims without limbs; and provision and rehabilitation of medical and educational services. He proposed to make the rehabilitation of child soldiers in Sierra Leone a pilot project for post-conflict reconstruction, thus opening the prospects for the special needs of child combatants to be taken into account in the design of national and international programmes of demobilisation and reintegration.

The Abidjan Meeting has vigorously promoted a new concept - the concept of children as a zone of peace. It requires that children be made inviolate and that active measures be taken to ensure this, even in the heat of battle. Moreover, it called on the international community to declare as an international crime the targeting of children as well as their recruitment as combatants.364

International law proscribes the recruitment of children under the age of 15 as an international crime. This is so under the UN Convention on the Rights of the Child, the Additional Protocols to the 1949 Geneva Conventions and the Rome Statute of the International Criminal Court 1998. However, children who have been abducted, drugged or forced under threat of death to commit atrocities are either unlikely to be prosecuted or, if prosecuted, can claim exculpation under the defence of duress.

Restructuring the Sierra Leone defence forces

Driven by vengeance, on September 2, 1998, President Kabbah announced the disbanding of the entire national army. It was like a collective punishment for the misdeeds of the 17 miscreants who toppled him in May 1997. As far as he was concerned, the entire army was guilty.

This decision was unprecedented. It contrasts remarkably with the approach adopted by the two Bintumani conferences of 1995 and 1996 respectively. On those occasions, the NPRC junta was treated as an entity that was separate and distinct from the armed forces as an institution. Kabbah himself had embraced this approach when, on becoming President in 1996, he retired all but two members of the NPRC junta, leaving the rest of the army intact, just as Siaka Stevens had done before him at the end of NRC rule in 1968.

These precedents notwithstanding, the consuming culture of vengeance proved irresistible in the post-restoration period. But this also proved to be Kabbah's own undoing, because the disbanded soldiers replied by attacking the capital on January 6, 1999.

In place of the disbanded army, Kabbah proposed a 5000-strong new defence force. The criteria for its recruitment were stated to be "competence, professional integrity, loyalty to democratic institutions and patriotism" in addition to a favourable character reference from the paramount chief or the local authorities of the area in which the applicant resides. Furthermore, in Kabbah's own words, "ethnic and regional considerations" were also important. All these were unexceptional and perfectly consistent with the traditional criteria the army itself had applied since time immemorial. However, following the attack on Freetown, he changed. Like the desperate man he indeed was, his government broadcast the names of 200 senior and junior officers of the disbanded army whom it said it wanted to re-enlist, and asked radio listeners to register objections if they had any. Ironically, among the names announced were officers who had either been executed or had died in the conflict

Another set of criteria surfaced after the Lome Accord was signed. That agreement speaks of a "new restructured national armed forces" to be created from the ranks of former combatants of the national army, RUF and CDF wishing to be integrated into the new defence forces provided they meet "established criteria". It also speaks of the need to reflect "the geo-political structure of Sierra Leone within the established strength." After much prevarication, it was these criteria that apparently prevailed.

In the reconstruction of the new army, Britain is playing an active role by fielding military trainers to oversee the process. It is also equipping the new army. However, while all these are valuable to the peace process, it is vitally important that Britain also keep a close eye on the recruitment process if only to ensure that it is carried out in accordance with the principles of equal opportunity and non-discrimination. Otherwise, if things go wrong, it cannot escape being tainted particularly if the problems that arise stem from the recruitment or composition of the new armed forces.

CHAPTER 8

The Domestic Fallout of the Rebellion

In the previous chapter we focussed on the extent to which the belligerent parties observed international human rights and humanitarian laws on the battlefield. Here we shall examine the government's own record of respect for human rights obligations, particularly the rule of law, outside of the theatre of combat. This record is important if only because it provides a benchmark against which both democracy and tyranny may be measured.

Government's human rights profile

The government's human rights profile was most unenviable, punctuated by blemishes of all sorts. First, under the guise of an emergency legislation, it arrogated to itself extraordinary powers, derogating substantially from its constitutional obligations.365 Second, it used this emergency power to stifle democratic dissent and detain the democratic opposition without trial. Some of them died in detention, from injuries inflicted by its agents. In no case was a prosecution brought against anyone They were also subjected to perpetual intimidation by primed party thugs and ethnic militias from whom the government seemed powerless to sequester itself.

Prison statistics confirm Pademba Road Prison as Sierra Leone's Gulag under Kabbah's administration. Designed to accommodate not more than 324 inmates,366 it was overstuffed with 3,928 detainees between February and June 1998. By year's end, that figure had risen to 4,685 inmates. The United Nations was forced to describe the conditions there as "overcrowded and unsanitary" and the food and medical care as "inadequate".367

Even the British government, Kabbah's most loyal Western ally, was alarmed. On May 6, Baroness Symons informed the House of Lords: "We understand that some 2,000 are being detained, of whom 59... have been charged with treason, murder or arson. We have taken every opportunity to raise human rights issues with the government of Sierra Leone since President Kabbah's return to Freetown on March 10. Our High

Commissioner has emphasised to him the need to restore full respect for human rights, and the Minister of State, Mr Lloyd, raised this very subject with President Kabbah when he took part in a Commonwealth Ministerial Action Group mission to Freetown on 31 March."368

Chapter 3 of the Constitution of Sierra Leone 1991 protects fundamental human rights and individual freedoms. Section 17 guarantees protection against arbitrary arrest and detention. It demands that a suspect must not be detained for more than 72 hours for ordinary crimes or 10 days for capital offences without being charged to court. Having disobeyed this law and wanting to legitimise its wrongs, the government, on March 16, declared a state of public emergency under Section 29 of the Constitution. It was made retroactive to March 10. It then passed regulations under which President Kabbah assumed sweeping powers to arrest and detain anybody, and to seize any private property.

Like the era of McCarthyism in America or Stalinism in Russia, under Tejan Kabbah, Sierra Leone became a byword for revenge and vindictiveness and also became synonymous with the outlawry of political dissent. Camouflaged as fighting evil, the government grew more and more intolerant of dissent, and all its detractors came to be labbelled as rebel or junta collaborators.

The politics of revenge

Apart from detaining political opponents arbitrarily, the government resorted to other forms of punishment, including unjustified dismissal. Civil servants, whose credo has traditionally been to work for the state without regard to the political complexion of its government, lost their jobs, their only crime being that they had stayed in their jobs during junta rule.

They were condemned as junta collaborators. Among other victims were teachers, journalists, public servants, trade unionists, professors, businessmen, clerics and other distinguished private citizens. Their only crime was that they campaigned for a political rather than a military solution to the crisis. Hit lists, allegedly prepared with official complicity, were seen in the hands of SLPP thugs and some of the people named in them were either slaughtered in the streets or, if lucky, arrested and taken to jail. According to the BBC correspondent, reporting from Freetown on

14 February, "civilians, mostly youths, are actually going out looking for soldiers, RUF rebels and other sympathisers of the AFRC, and in most cases actually killing them on the spot".

Nor were judges immune, particularly those who had stayed in their posts during the interregnum. The Chief Justice, Honourable Samuel Beccles Davies, was the first to fall victim. Swiftly dispatched on leave prior to retirement, his only crime was that he administered the oath of office to the AFRC junta leader on June 17, 1997. Mr. Desmond Luke, an unsuccessful presidential candidate in the 1996 election and a leading supporter of Kabbah's government-in-exile, replaced him.369

Foreign businessmen, suspected of having business dealings with the junta, were bundled out of the country under secret deportation orders. Even naturalised citizens were not spared; they too were expelled after being stripped of their citizenship.370

More than 100 so-called collaborators were charged to court with the capital offence of treason. For these trials, the government tried to get Commonwealth judges, the implication being that it did not have confidence in its own judges. But no Commonwealth judge came. This loss of confidence in the capacity of the judicial system to deliver international fair-trial standards had reached its nadir in 1996. Shortly after taking office, the government went outside the country and appointed Mr Justice L.U. Cross from Trinidad and Tobago to review the findings of the commissions of inquiry that the NPRC junta had established. The climax came in April 1998, at the swearing-in ceremony of the new Chief Justice, when President Kabbah accused the judiciary of impropriety. He said: "Ethics and morality in the judiciary started to decline in the 1960s when some judges became partisan in politics and involved in high-level impropriety."371 The newly appointed Chief Justice replied that he was "prepared to face the daunting task of salvaging the image of the battered judiciary which once ranked among the best in Africa and the Commonwealth about 30 years ago."372 These indictments notwithstanding, the government did not hesitate to haul before the same flawed judiciary its political opponents and charged them with treason and other heinous offences.

In making that accusation, Kabbah must have had in mind the findings of the 1967 Beoku-Betts Commission of Inquiry before which he had been accused of corruption. That Commission had recommended against him as follows: "Mr Tejan Kabbah, one time Permanent Secretary of the then Ministry of Trade and Industry, a highly placed civil servant, lacks integrity and from his showing in this Inquiry we feel he could easily lapse into corrupt practices which in our view disqualifies him from holding high office for which good character and integrity are prerequisites. We are convinced that he was instrumental in making the conspiracy possible. He is very intelligent and according to certain Minutes, which he wrote concerning the affairs of the Sierra Leone Produce Marketing Board, he revealed that at one stage he began to get qualms of conscience. He is not wholly hopeless."

This finding was never challenged in court. Yet, he became the presidential candidate of the SLPP in 1996. Earlier on, in 1992, he had shown himself to be a man, who was not at all antagonistic to military rule, for he was among the first people to accept appointment from the NPRC junta, which had overthrown the constitutional government of President Momoh. He served as Chairman of the NPRC's Advisory Council. His Attorney-General, Solomon Berewa, was also a member of that Council. None of them has ever been accused of being an accessory after the fact. Yet, in 1998, as leaders of the restored SLPP government, they apparently had no scruple in preferring treason charges against people who found themselves in exactly the same situation as they did in 1992. No comment is more apt than that of the respected pamphleteer, Ambrose Ganda. He writes: "Sierra Leone, like other warring nations in West Africa which have been torn apart by civil strife and internal political rivalries, is plagued by endemic revenge fever. Many erstwhile honourable, gentle and morally upright people have suddenly been consumed by an uncharacteristic passion for vendetta. Yet, for most people this new attitude is, rather sadly, in ruthless competition with their own natural instincts which, by tradition and historic acclaim, have been for mildness and tolerance towards adversaries and charitableness towards the unorthodox and deviant behaviour of members in their communities."373

Thus, the post-restoration atmosphere reeked of revenge, intimidation and vindictiveness. People naturally became so cowed that only few mustered the courage to speak out for political dialogue and those who did were immediately branded as rebel collaborators, which carried the instant penalty of mob justice. Even the United Nations Security Council could not disguise its disgust at the new passion for vendetta. It condemned "reprisal killings and related violence in Sierra Leone" and called for "an immediate end to such acts", though it failed to follow this through with the required vigour.374

Although President Kabbah did appear once to denounce the politics of revenge, to this day no prosecution has been brought against any government supporter for reprisal murder. At the signing ceremony of the Abidjan Peace Accord on November 30, 1996, he declared: "Crying for revenge or retribution will surely weaken our country and intensify our pain." He repeated this before the United Nations General Assembly on October 1, 1997, when he said: "I do not believe that any worthwhile national purpose will be served by a policy of reprisals against the misguided elements of the army and others in the junta's camp."

But all this was before he was restored to power. After his restoration, all the fine words quickly turned to empty rhetoric. Why? On one view, he was under pressure from his party hacks who were blood-thirsty for revenge. The fact that they had become a dwindling band whose creed no longer cut favour with the international community, made little impression on them. On another view, the government's rejection of political dialogue was largely the handiwork of ministers who were afraid of losing their coveted positions to the RUF. These garrulous politicians simply could not contemplate political dialogue if it meant sharing the spoils of office with the RUF.

Caught between these acolytes, Kabbah himself became devious. One day he would say this; the next day he would contradict himself. And this went on and on. Before the United Nations General Assembly, he gave the impression of a leader who strongly eschewed vengeance. But, on another occasion, he sounded very much like the representative of the forces of extremism with vengeance in their tongue. A few examples will suffice.

The day after the pro-government forces drove the AFRC from Freetown in February 1998, he spoke like someone who had had foreknowledge of what was about to unfold. Kabbah admonished his supporters that "reprisals should in no way be our pre-occupation." By March 10, he had shifted ground. He excused the "spate of revenge killings and other forms of violence" that accompanied his restoration on the grounds that "the people were hurt and are still being hurt" by the atrocities of the RUF and the remnants of the junta.

Again, in his Address to the Nation on March 10, 1998, he inveighed: "While we unreservedly condemn the junta and its RUF allies, we must not forget to ask ourselves why it happened. Where did we go wrong as a nation?.....We must not ...overlook the atmosphere of greed, corruption, injustice and tribal jealousies in which the rebellion took root and grew to such dreadful proportions.....It encouraged others to deny justice and fair play to the ordinary citizen of this country. If we allow this state of affairs to continue after today, then all our suffering and the death of our close relations and compatriots would have been in vain."375 A week barely passed before he completely forgot his own advice. He gave himself extraordinary powers, under emergency regulations, to detain suspects, restrict freedom of movement and requisition property.

By what name may this be called if not premeditated vengeance? Nor would political or ethnic cleansing be an exaggeration especially when it is recalled that most of the victims were either members of the APC party or from the northern part of the country.376 Recalling the international outrage that had greeted ethnic cleansing in Rwanda, much more subtle devices were put to work by the SLPP, so-called defenders of democracy, to disguise the true character of what they were doing in order not to arouse international opprobrium.

Specially targeted were the democratic opposition and people of northern origin. The President himself had started it all. In 1996 he travelled to the northern city of Makeni, where he advised his audience that they should apologise to the rest of the country because someone with a northern name, Foday Sankoh, was leading the RUF. Northerners, on the other hand, have never even entertained the thought of making an apology of any kind; all the more so after the RUF had literally occupied or destroyed every town or village in the north. This happened after the 1999 Lome Peace Agreement was signed, and the government did nothing to stop them. It was clearly a blatant breach of the cease-fire under that Agreement. Again, in 1997, President Kabbah accused members of the democratic opposition of "inciting the military to seize power" and of "manipulating the soldiers and urging them to stay in power." He condemned these acts as "an affront to all lovers of democracy and smacks of hostility" and threatened "those who are bent on destroying the country would themselves be destroyed.... They will be hunted down even if they hide in rat holes."377

With such unvarnished diatribe falling from the lips of the supreme executive authority of the state, it immediately awoken from slumber that ugly monster called revenge. African Presidents are not like American Presidents, who depend upon Congress. On the contrary, they see their executive powers as akin to imperial powers, especially during emergency; they believe they can do anything without recourse to the legislature or the judiciary. In this case, Kabbah's statement was like giving his followers *carte blanche* to help themselves so far as the opposition was concerned. As a result, they looted and plundered the homes of opposition politicians with relish. In one case, two motor vehicles belonging to this writer ended up in the possession of his Vice-President, Joe Albert Demby, and his Deputy Minister of Defence, Samuel Hinga Norman, respectively. Apart from it being criminal to receive and keep stolen property, it never ceased to amaze the public how such high officials could commit such flagrant abuse of power, especially by a man who was just a heartbeat away from the presidency. For the Vice-President to abuse the rights of a citizen with such impunity, many have rightly questioned the future of human rights in Sierra Leone.

Reprisals were not confined to the capital. In the provinces, the *kamajor* militia became something of a Frankenstein monster, ferreting for so-called collaborators and putting themselves beyond the pale of military command and control. Like the rebels, they committed all sorts of horrendous atrocities against defenceless civilians. So lawless became their frolics in the southern and eastern cities that their local leaders were compelled to ask the Nigerian intervention force "to arrest all roving *kamajors* and send them back to their operational areas."378 Kabbah himself began to have a qualm of conscience, much to the chagrin of the redoubtable Hinga Norman, the *kamajor* chieftain, when he ordered that all *kamajors* be brought within the purview of Nigerian military control in order to contain their criminal activities.379

Treason trials

(a) Changes to the trial rules

The crime of treason in Sierra Leone is codified by Treason and State Offences Act 1963 (Act No. 10 of 1963) and Section 108(8) of the Constitution. The charges against so-called junta collaborators were made under these laws. However, with regard to trial procedure, the Criminal Procedure and Evidence Rules of April 8, 1998, introduced entirely new rules.380 If they were meant to modernise a law hallowed in antiquity, its timing was received with a great deal of scepticism. The subliminal message was that it was an assault on freedom itself.

Contrary to the fundamental prohibition on retroactive criminal legislation, *nullum crimen sine lege*, the new rules were applied retroactively to "acts or omissions done or occurring before 25 May 1997 and having a connection with the offences committed between 25 May 1997 and 13 February 1998 and activities of the members of the AFRC or its collaborators."381 The President justified them on the ground that they were required "to speed up the trials, which would otherwise have lasted for over a year."382 Thus, justice and fairness were sacrificed for speed, making one wonder whether this cynical tampering with trial procedures did not betray a determination by the government to secure a conviction at all cost.

Under the new rules, the absence of an accused does not stop or invalidate a trial so long as he has entered a plea of not guilty and is represented by counsel. This runs counter to the hallowed common law rule requiring the presence of the accused in a criminal trial. The rules also say that jury verdicts need not be unanimous; it is sufficient if they are passed by a two-thirds majority of the original jury. Further, the death or incapacity of a juror does not prevent the case from going to trial provided that the number of jurors on the panel does not drop below nine. This severely curtails the centuries-old fundamental right of an accused person to have his case heard by a jury of 12 of his peers, as stipulated by Magna Carta of 1215. Moreover, according to the new rules, secondary audio, visual or documentary evidence is admissible if the original cannot be traced or produced without undue delay or expense. A photocopy of an accused person's written statement is also made admissible in evidence if made freely and voluntarily and without inducement by way of promise of favour or by menaces or undue terror.

(i) *Legality of new trial rules*

Two questions arise. Are the new rules lawful? Are they compatible with international standards of justice?

An emergency declaration may be warranted but not necessarily the extraordinary powers assumed under it. To be justified there must be a reasonable nexus between the emergency and the extraordinary measures taken to deal with it. The onus is on the government to establish this and for the courts to decide.383 In particular, the court must be satisfied that the measures taken are not aimed at the entrenchment of the rule of a particular political party nor at the elimination of legitimate political dissent in a democratic polity.

The new rules were made pursuant to section 29(5) of the Constitution. This provides that "during a period of public emergency, the President may make such regulations and take such measures as appear to him to be necessary or expedient for the purpose of maintaining and securing peace, order and good government in Sierra Leone or any part thereof." Are the new rules of procedure "regulations" within the meaning of this provision? If not, what are they? They are certainly not "measures" because the Constitution itself makes a clear distinction between "regulations" and "measures" on the one hand and "orders" and "rules" on the other. The latter are subordinate to the former. For example, section 29(9) says: "Regulations made under this section may provide for empowering such authorities or persons as may be specified in the regulations to make orders and rules for any of the purposes for which the regulations are authorised by this Constitution...." Section 29(10)(a) similarly provides: "Every regulation or measure taken under this section and every order or rule made in pursuance of such a regulation shall.......cease to have effect ninety days from the date upon which it comes into operation......." Again sub-section (11) of that section says: ".....every regulation made under this section and every order or rule made in pursuance of such a regulation shall have effect ....." One can go on and on. The argument here is that the new rules of procedure made under section 29(5) of the Constitution are neither "regulations" nor "measures" within the meaning of that provision. They are therefore *ultra vires* the provision.

Even assuming they are not *ultra vires*, the next question is whether they are reasonably justifiable for the purpose of dealing with the emergency situation. A reasonable nexus must exist between the new rules and the emergency situation they are meant to address. Put another way, can the curtailment of the right of fair trial, guaranteed by section 23(1) of the Constitution, be considered necessary or expedient for maintaining peace, order and good government in Sierra Leone?

Section 29(5) of the Constitution gives the President a plenitude of power to make law which is restricted only by the Constitution itself. One such restriction is section 29(18). It provides: "Nothing contained in or done under the authority of any law shall be held to be inconsistent with or in contravention of this section to the extent that the law in question authorises the taking during a period of a state of public emergency of measures that are reasonably justifiable for the purpose of dealing with the situation that exists immediately before or during that period of public emergency."

These two provisions have a common purpose. They are designed to ensure that measures could be taken immediately in a public emergency to deal with the situation, including the arrest and detention of persons, if this is necessary for maintaining and securing the peace, order and good government. However, there is a big difference between them. That difference was made clear by the Privy Council in *Attorney-General of Saint Christopher, Nevis and Anguilla v Reynolds*. As opined by Lord Salmon:

> "The difference between the two laws was that the first law gave an authority absolute discretion, and indeed the power of a dictator, to arrest and detain anyone, whilst [the second law].... allows a law to be enacted conferring power to arrest and detain only if it was reasonably justifiable to exercise such a power......It is inconceivable that a law which gave absolute power to arrest and detain without reasonable justification would be tolerated by a Constitution such as the present, one of the principal

purposes of which is to protect fundamental rights and freedoms. ...As stated in the judgement of their Lordships' Board in *Minister of Home Affairs v Fisher*, a Constitution should be construed with less rigidity and more generosity than other Acts. Their Lordships are of opinion that [the first law] ...should be construed, in the light of section 14 [equivalent to section 29(18) of the Sierra Leone Constitution], as follows: 'The [President] of a state may, during a period of public emergency in that state, make such laws for [maintaining and securing the peace, order and good government] in that state, to the extent that those laws authorise the taking of measures that are reasonably justifiable for dealing with the situation that exists in the state during any such period of public emergency'."384

The Privy Court has thus interpreted the phrase "reasonably justifiable" as a condition limiting the exercise of an otherwise arbitrary power such as that embodied in section 29(5) of the Constitution of Sierra Leone. There is no definition of what constitutes reasonableness and none is attempted here. At best, it is a relative term and, in the nature of things, no hard and fast rule can be laid down as to which matters are relevant or irrelevant for the purpose of determining the reasonableness of an act or restriction. It is up to the courts to decide.

(ii) *Compatibility of the new trial rules with international standards*

Are the new rules compatible with international standards of due process protected by international human rights law?385 In 1995, Sierra Leone acceded to the International Covenant on Civil and Political Rights 1966. It took effect on August 23, 1996. Article 14 of the Covenant protects the right of fair trial. The function of criminal justice being the protection of basic values and norms of society, the United Nations General Assembly adopted resolution 2393 (XXIII) on November 26, 1968, imploring all member states "to ensure the most careful legal procedures and the greatest possible safeguards for the accused in capital cases in countries where the death penalty obtains." It is extremely doubtful whether the new trial rules meet this international standard.

Article 14 of the Covenant does permit a state party to take measures derogating from its obligations under it during a public emergency which threatens the life of the nation. However, the United Nations Human Rights Committee has emphasised that any measures taken under that provision must be of an exceptional and temporary nature and must not last beyond the period that the nation's life is threatened.386

(b) *Number of accused persons*

The treason trials started with 60 so-called junta collaborators in four different courts, including Foday Sankoh, the RUF leader. The first court tried 18 of them. It passed judgment on August 25, 1998. Sixteen were found guilty of treason and sentenced to death by hanging, including a female broadcaster who had given birth in prison, and two were acquitted. The second court handed down its verdict on October 19. Of 20 accused, 16 were convicted of treason, three acquitted and one died in prison. The third court handed down its verdict on November 4. Of 21 accused, 16 were convicted and 5 acquitted. Former President Momoh was among them. He was found not guilty on four counts of treason but guilty on two counts of conspiracy and sentenced to five years imprisonment. The fourth court tried and convicted Foday Sankoh of treason. All convicted prisoners appealed against their convictions and sentences, and their appeals were pending when the rebels struck Freetown on January 6, 1999.

On October 12, a Court Martial handed down its own judgment on 38 soldiers who were prosecuted for treason. It found 34 of them guilty of treason and likewise sentenced them to death by firing squad.387 Unlike their civilian counterparts, the law gave Court Martial convicts no right of appeal. On October 19, of those convicted, 24 were executed while the remaining ten had their sentences commuted to life imprisonment.

As if all this was not enough, on October 27, Solomon Berewa, Minister of Justice and Attorney-General, announced that more charges were contemplated. "We are putting about 50 more people on trial after this, including 16 military officers and soldiers for .... their deeds of complicity with the ousted military junta," he said.388 Of this number, 22 civilians were charged with various offences on December 11, 1998, ranging from treason to aiding and abetting the illegal overthrow of the Kabbah government. This brought the number of civilians prosecuted for collaborating with the junta to 82 which, combined with the court martial trials, made a grand total of 120, the largest treason trial ever in the history of independent Sierra Leone.389 Compared to past administrations, this record took the political offence of treason to epic proportions.

Civilians were thus put on trial for treason the essence of which was that they had "collaborated" with the military junta. But just a few months earlier, the same prosecutor had deposed before the courts in England that although it had been "the clear aim of the junta to coerce the civil population to collaborate with them," they had "failed in this aim." This was the government's deposition in the *Sierratel* case.390 In other words, although it had publicly acknowledged before the courts in England that the civilian population did not collaborate with the military junta, it took a diametrically opposite position before its own courts in Freetown. Small wonder that the treason trials were viewed by many as victor's justice. Others saw them as the clearest example of the SLPP government's obsession with its own brand of rule of law justice. Whichever way one looks at it, the trial of so-called "collaborators" definitely savours of abuse of power. The more the tragedy unfolded the more it became clear that concepts like collaboration and national reconciliation were acquiring strange and extraordinary meanings in Sierra Leone.

(c) The offence of treason

The Treason and State Offences Act 1963 was enacted by the first post-independence SLPP government. The relevant provisions are sections 3, 4 and 17, which create several offences including treason, treason felony and aiding and abetting. Section 3(1) reads: "A person is guilty of treason ... who either in Sierra Leone or elsewhere (a) prepares or endeavours to overthrow the government by unlawful means; (b) prepares or endeavours to carry out by force any enterprise which usurps the executive power of the state in any matter of both a public and general nature." Paragraphs (c) and (d) are not relevant to our present discussion.

Section 4 creates the offence of treason felony in these words: "A person is guilty of treason felony ... who either within Sierra

Leone or elsewhere prepares or endeavours (a) to procure by unlawful means any alteration of the law or the policies of the government; or (b) to carry out by unlawful means any enterprise which usurps the executive power of the state in matters of both a public and general nature." The penalty is ten years' imprisonment.

The offence of aiding and abetting is established by section 17. It reads: "Any person who attempts to commit any offence under this Act or solicits or incites or endeavours to persuade another person to commit an offence or aids or abets or does any act preparatory to the commission of an offence under this Act shall be liable to the same punishment in the same manner and to be proceeded against in the same manner as if he had committed the offence."

The Constitution of Sierra Leone 1991 (Act No. 6 of 1991) also creates, under section 108(8), the offence of treason for any person who suspends, alters or repeals the Constitution in a manner other than by Parliamentary authority.

For the purposes of the events of May 25, 1997, to which the charges relate, only the following four categories of statutory treason appear to be relevant. They are those covered by sections 3(1)(a) and (b) and section 4 of the 1963 Act, summarised as follows:

> (i) Preparing or endeavouring to overthrow the government by unlawful means;

> (ii) Preparing or endeavouring to carry out any enterprise which usurps the executive power of the state by force.

> (iii) Suspending, altering or repealing the Constitution other than on the authority of Parliament.

> (iv) Preparing or endeavouring to procure by unlawful means any alteration of the law or policies of the government. This is treason felony.

Thus seen, there is a substantial difference between preparing to overthrow a government, which is treason if any unlawful means are to be used, and preparing to usurp executive power, which is treason only if force is to be used. It is treason felony if the method to be employed, though unlawful, does not actually involve the use of force. Therefore, it is always important to identify precisely what is the criminal conduct. It is not the act of overthrowing the government or usurping its powers but only the act of "preparing or endeavouring" to overthrow the government or to usurp its powers that the 1963 Act makes criminal. In other words, it is a failed rebellion or a failed *coup* that the Act punishes. Where the rebellion or *coup* succeeds and runs its course, who dare call it treason? Indeed it ceases to be treason and anything done after the overthrow or usurpation cannot, in law, be an act of treason. Unless the person was also involved in the actual process of preparing or endeavouring to overthrow the government by unlawful means or to usurp its powers by force, it is difficult to see how he could be held guilty of treason. So, therefore, in respect of the events of May 1997, the critical questions are: (a) Was Kabbah's government overthrown by the AFRC junta? (b) If so, when did it take place?

The previous Sierra Leone treason cases like *Lansana* (1968), *Mohamed Forna and Others* (1975) and *Kaikai and Others* (1986) all focused on the meaning of the terms "preparing" and "endeavouring" and established the proposition that these are continuing offences, and can continue for years in the course of plotting a *coup*. They do not deal directly with the meaning of the terms "overthrow" and "usurp", as was involved in the AFRC *coup*, and are therefore not relevant authorities in this instance.

(d) *The prosecution's case*

After the *coup*, the AFRC made proclamations by which it suspended all parts of the Constitution that were inconsistent with them, substituted a Supreme Council of State for Parliament, gave decrees the force of law, changed the title of President to that of Chairman of the AFRC, repealed many laws and amended the Constitution. All these were treasonable acts within the meaning of section 108(8) of the Constitution.

However, when it came to so-called junta collaborators, the prosecution sought to widen the treason net. They contended that as from May 25, 1997, the AFRC junta, throughout the eight or nine months it was in power, was only *preparing* or *endeavouring* to overthrow the government of President Kabbah, and that it had never finished the job of *overthrowing* the government or *usurping* its executive powers. Whilst it was still at it, it got kicked out of the capital and Kabbah's government was restored in February 1998. So any person who, prior to that restoration, deliberately assisted the AFRC to remain in power was tainted with the act of "preparing or endeavouring" and therefore guilty of treason, so the argument ran. In other words, the plan to overthrow Kabbah's government did not succeed and there was no break in constitutional legal continuity. The prosecution further argued that, because of the existence of certain factors, the *coup* never succeeded in overthrowing the government. These were, first, that the AFRC junta did not enjoy popular support; second, that it was not in control of the country outside of the capital, Freetown; and, third, that it was not recognised internationally. This was unlike the NPRC putsch in 1992, which the prosecution claimed had succeeded because it was popular. For these propositions, they relied on the decision of Justice Cresswell in the *Sierratel* case. But, with the greatest respect, the *ratio decidendi* in that case is wholly extraneous to the question before the courts in Sierra Leone in the treason trials, i.e. the proper interpretation of a penal statute.

This reliance on the *Sierratel* case confuses two things: the question of recognition of a foreign government on the one hand, and the question of legality of its establishment on the other. These two questions have developed separately though they frequently overlap and are sometimes confused. Recognition (or the lack of it) of the AFRC junta by foreign governments, in this case by the British government, was decided by reference to the relevant principles of international law. This was what the English court did in the *Sierratel* case. On the other hand, the constitutionality of the AFRC is a different question and must be decided in accordance with the constitutional law of Sierra Leone. It is a matter for the courts of Sierra Leone, not for a foreign court. Although Justice Cresswell did raise the question, it was not really before him nor was he required to answer it.

This distinction is crucial because upon the determination of the latter question rests the essential ingredients of the crime of treason as defined by the 1963 Act. Moreover, the guilt of an accused charged with treason must be decided on the basis of fact and law as defined by that Act, which was not before Justice Cresswell for interpretation. It is therefore hard to see the relevance of the decision in the *Sierratel* case to the treason trial, as it had turned simply upon the question of which of two rival governments claiming to represent Sierra Leone, the AFRC or the Kabbah government, was recognised by the British government. The English court answered it by reference to international law and practice as followed by English jurisprudence.

(e) *Was Kabbah's government overthrown?*

The question is whether Kabbah's government was overthrown or whether its powers had been usurped by the AFRC. The prosecution argued that there was no overthrow, basing itself on the three factors mentioned earlier. Therefore, so its argument ran, the overthrow of President Kabbah's government was never consummated or completed as the coupists never got beyond the point of "preparing or endeavouring" to overthrow until Kabbah's government was restored to power again. Civilians who assisted the coupists thus became tainted.

Nothing could be more disingenuous. The question whether Kabbah's government was overthrown or its powers usurped by the AFRC is a question of fact. Neither word – i.e. overthrow or usurp - is a term of art nor do they have a special meaning beyond what is ascribed to them in ordinary parlance. The dictionary meaning of "overthrow" is put variously as "to put an end to," "to take away the power of," "defeat," "overcome," "upset," "overturn" and so on, while that of "usurp" is given as "to seize and hold (power, position or authority) by force or without right," "appropriate," "arrogate," "assume" *et cetera*. These literal meanings must have been the ones on the minds of the members of the United Nations and the British government in particular when they considered the situation in Sierra Leone. The latter communicated its position to the court during the hearing on the *Sierratel* case. Since the prosecution had relied so heavily on that case, it is well to recall what was actually said in that case regarding the crucial question whether President Kabbah's government had been overthrown or not.

On November 28, 1997, the British FCO wrote to Sierratel's solicitors in terms that: "You asked me to set out the British Government's policy towards Sierra Leone....The British Government welcomed the election in Sierra Leone of President Ahmad Tejan Kabbah in February 1996. We have consistently condemned the military *coup* of 25 May 1997 which overthrew the democratically elected government of Sierra Leone. We look forward to the restoration of constitutional order in that country."391

In a letter to the Sierra Leone High Commissioner on January 13, 1998, the FCO again stated: "I attach a copy of my letter to [Sierratel's solicitors] of 28 November 1997. British Government policy on Sierra Leone has not changed since then. I also attach for your information an extract from Hansard showing a written answer to the House of Lords of 12 January 1998. This sets out the British Government's position on Sierra Leone."392 In her written answer to the House of Lords on January 12, 1998, Baroness Symons said: "Where democratic governments have been overthrown by violence we have often worked with them in exile as part of our global support for democracy. Tejan Kabbah is not the 'former' President of Sierra Leone; he remains the legitimate leader of that country."393 In other words, although overthrown by the AFRC junta, in the eyes of the British government, President Kabbah had remained the *de jure* leader of Sierra Leone.

In similar fashion the United Nations also addressed the question of the "overthrow" of President Kabbah's government. On May 27, 1997, two days after the *coup*, the Security Council deplored "this *attempt* to overthrow" the democratically-elected government and called for the immediate "restoration of constitutional order."394 It repeated this on July 11, 1997.395 However, on August 6, 1997, its language changed. In a Presidential Statement, it condemned "the *overthrow* of the democratically elected government of President Ahmad Tejan Kabbah" and called upon the military junta to take immediate steps to bring about the "unconditional restoration of that government."396 Again, on November 14, 1997, the Council repeated "its condemnation of the *overthrow* of the democratically elected government of President Ahmad Tejan Kabbah and its concern about the threat to peace, security and stability in the region which the situation in Sierra Leone continues to present."397

On October 8, the Council adopted resolution 1132. It called upon the military junta to take immediate steps "to relinquish power in Sierra Leone and make way for the restoration of the democratically elected government and a return to constitutional order." What else could this mean if not a plain and simple acknowledgement that the power of the constitutional government had been usurped, overturned or seized by the AFRC which was now being called upon to return it to the rightful owner?

The European Union had the last word on December 8, 1997, when it condemned the *coup* which *"overthrew"* the democratically elected government and called for the "return of the legitimate government to Freetown."

No admission by a government about its own status could be more eloquent than that of its leader. Speaking before the United Nations General Assembly on October 1, 1997, President Kabbah admitted: "Today I appear before you with a heavy heart. As I speak, a great tragedy is unfolding in my country. On 25 May 1997, a combination of elements of the Sierra Leone army and the Revolutionary United Front (RUF) violently *overthrew* my democratically elected government and unleashed on the country a reign of terror, unparalleled in its scope and ferocity." To show it was not a *lapsus lingua*, he repeated this in the same Assembly on July 30, 1998: "My Government was however determined ...that the army would henceforth devote itself entirely to its primary task of defending the nation and its democratic institutions. Our best endeavours notwithstanding, unpatriotic elements of the army, in May 1997, suddenly struck again by brute force, *toppled* the democratically elected government and *confiscated* power. The most bizarre feature of that dastardly act was that the army not only *overthrew* the democratically elected government by force, it entered into an unholy alliance with the RUF rebels who had absolutely no agenda other than to loot, kill and maim innocent citizens."

These statements make plain the unanimous verdict of the international community as well as of President Kabbah himself that the AFRC junta did indeed *overthrow* the constitutional government of Sierra Leone. Nor was this conclusion inhibited by the fact that the junta was facing strong internal resistance or that the overthrown government was trying to function next door in Conakry as a government-in-exile or that it was the only government recognised internationally. To deny this is to make a travesty of the truth merely to be able to secure a conviction. There could hardly be a difference between this overthrow by the AFRC and that of the NPRC in 1992. Both brought about the toppling of the constitutional government and its replacement by a military junta.

(f) *When was the overthrow completed?*

The precise moment when the overthrow was completed is also a question of fact. In this case the circumstances surrounding the *coup* might yield multiple answers. For example, implicit in President Kabbah's statement to the General Assembly is an admission that the overthrow was completed on the day of the *coup*, May 25, 1997. On the other hand, the Security Council took the view that on that day only an *attempt* had been made and that the process of *overthrow* was not completed until on or about August 6, 1997. Whichever view one takes, the fact remains that the AFRC, after driving the constitutional government from the seat of power on May 25, adopted a series of measures aimed at consolidating its hold on power. It suspended parts of the Constitution and usurped legislative and executive powers the result of all of which was the physical displacement of the head of state and a break in constitutional legal continuity. Arguably, therefore, there was technically no crime of treason within the meaning of the 1963 Act.

Judicial authority on timing of overthrow of a constitutional government may be drawn from *Ex parte Pinochet Ugarte* (1998).398 Spain sought the extradition of General Pinochet, the former head of state of Chile, for crimes allegedly committed between September 1973, when he seized power in a *coup d'état*, and March 1990, when he ceased to be President. Regarding the question when General Pinochet became head of state, the House of Lords held, per Lord Steyn, that he "undoubtedly became the head of state at least by 26 June 1974; and I will assume that from the date of the *coup d'état* on 11 September 1973 he was the head of state."399 Lord Nicholls gave a similar opinion: "There is some dispute over whether Senator Pinochet was technically head of state for the whole of the period in respect of which charges are laid. There is no certificate from the Foreign and Commonwealth Office, but the evidence shows he was the ruler of Chile from 11 September 1973, when a military junta of which he was the leader overthrew the previous government of President Allende, until 11

March 1990 when he retired from the office of president. I am prepared to assume he was head of state throughout the period."400

Repatriation by deportation

The case of accused persons brought within the jurisdiction from overseas presents an additional problem. They were returned from Nigeria, Liberia and Guinea. On arrival in Sierra Leone they were arrested, tried and convicted of treason. The procedure by which they were repatriated is unclear, but there is no evidence of any extradition proceedings being undertaken in any of the sending countries. If not by extradition, it could only have been by way of deportation or some other illegal procedure that brought the defendants within the jurisdiction of Sierra Leone. If this was so, then arguably their convictions were unsafe.

In his second progress report on UNOMSIL, the United Nations Secretary-General did allude to this problem. He questioned whether the manner in which a number of defendants had been repatriated to Sierra Leone from neighbouring countries "was in accordance with applicable international standards" and continued to convey this concern to the government "in a timely and forthright manner".401

The case of R v. *Mullen* decided by the English Court of Appeal in 1999 is most apposite.402 The appellant, Nicholas Mullen, had been convicted in England in 1990 of conspiracy to cause explosions likely to endanger life or cause serious injury to property and sentenced to 30 years' imprisonment. Seven years after the trial, he was granted leave to appeal against conviction on the ground of his illegal repatriation and abuse of process by the prosecution prior to his trial. British authorities had apparently initiated and procured the appellant's deportation from Zimbabwe to England in disregard of available extradition procedures. At trial the defence were unaware of material relating to the involvement of the British authorities in the appellant's deportation which should have been disclosed to them.

The Appeal Court quashed the appellant's conviction on the grounds that intelligence officers had broken the law in bringing him to trial through deportation rather than through the correct though cumbersome process of extradition. Lord Justice Rose, with whom Lord Justices Colman and Kay concurred, had this to say:

"This Court recognises the immense degree of public revulsion which has, quite properly, attached to the activities of those who have assisted and furthered the violent operations of the IRA and other terrorist organisations. In the discretionary exercise, great weight must therefore be attached to the nature of the offence involved in this case. Against that, however, the conduct of the security services and police in procuring the unlawful deportation of the appellant in the manner which has been described, represents, in the view of this Court, a blatant and extremely serious failure to adhere to the rule of law with regard to the production of the defendant for prosecution in the English courts. The need to discourage such conduct on the part of those who are responsible for criminal prosecutions is a matter of public policy, to which, as appears from *Bennett* and *Latif*, very considerable weight must be attached."[403]

In another passage, the Court added:

"In these circumstances, the discretion has to be exercised on the basis that, but for the unlawful manner of his deportation, he would not have been in this country to be prosecuted when he was, and there was a real prospect that he would never have been brought to this country at all.

Additionally, the need to encourage the voluntary disclosure before trial of material and information in the hands of the prosecution relevant to the defence is a further matter of public policy to which it is also necessary to give weight. Omission to make such disclosure clearly is a matter to be taken into account, on the exercise of this Court's discretion following a conviction....

In as much as that discretionary exercise now falls to be carried out by this Court, we conclude that, by reason of this abuse of power, the prosecution and therefore the conviction of the appellant were unlawful"[404]

A British intelligence officer had told the Zimbabwean authorities that Britain wanted to avoid "becoming involved in complicated extradition proceedings" but at the same time it did not want to appear to be demanding deportation. The deportation was then stage-managed. The intelligence officer advised the

Zimbabweans that "the ideal would be for Mullen to be arrested shortly before the departure of a direct flight and put aboard it."[405]

Thus, in respect of the Court Martial convictions of the soldiers who were deported to Sierra Leone from neighbouring countries, it is at least arguable that those convictions were unsafe and unlawful, and that their executions were therefore a violation of their right to life. That right is guaranteed by section 16 of the Constitution of Sierra Leone as well as by Article 6 of the International Covenant on Civil and Political Rights 1966.

International reaction to the treason verdicts

News of the convictions and death sentences passed on the accused were greeted around the world with derision and outrage. In Britain, parliamentarians from all parties called on the Prime Minister, Tony Blair, to intervene to save the lives of those convicted. Menzies Campbell, the Liberal Democrat foreign affairs spokesman, in an interview on the BBC Radio 4's programme, *The World at One*, expressed the dismay felt in Parliament about the imposition of the death penalty and added: "It's barely 12 months since President Kabbah was a personal guest in Edinburgh of Tony Blair at the Commonwealth Heads of Government Meeting. That was necessary because he was then deposed....During the period when the handling of this business in Sierra Leone by the Foreign Office was under severe scrutiny, the constant refrain from government ministers was 'okay, things may not have been well handled here, but in essence, the good guys won.' Well, it will take something of the shine off the proposition that the good guys won if one of the actions of the good guys is to execute journalists."[406]

Ann Clwyd, Labour Member of Parliament and Chairperson of the Parliamentary Human Rights Committee, described the death sentences as appalling: "Given that we have considerable clout with this new government in Sierra Leone, I think we should make very strong representations not to carry out the death penalty."[407]

This cross-party appeal forced Tony Lloyd, Minister of State in the FCO, to express concern about the death sentences and to ask President Kabbah to grant a reprieve. He said that he had "expressed, in the strongest possible terms, concern about the imposition of the death penalty on 16 people convicted of treason.

I said that Britain wanted to see peace and prosperity fully restored in Sierra Leone. We believed that the best way to achieve this was through a proper process of reconciliation. Showing clemency in these cases would be an important step in this process. President Kabbah said it could be some months before the appeals process were completed. But he undertook to give our representations serious consideration at the point where individuals could appeal for clemency."[408] He promised to keep the matter in view and then added: "We are urgently contacting our EU partners with a view to encouraging a joint EU response to the sentences. We welcome the UN monitoring of the trials, and continue to make clear to the government of Sierra Leone the need for them to pay due heed to human rights, due process and international norms."[409]

Following the execution of the soldiers on October 19, Tony Lloyd reported that President Kabbah had rejected Britain's plea for clemency. "I regret that 24 executions have been carried out in Sierra Leone following military courts martial. We understand the demand within Sierra Leone for justice to be seen to be done following the appalling and brutal butchery carried out under the junta. But the country needs to embark on a proper process of reconciliation. Britain opposes the death penalty wherever it applies....I hope these executions will be the last in Sierra Leone," he said.[410]

But Tony Lloyd's statement was not strong enough. So Robin Cook decided to step in and remind Kabbah that his restoration had been strongly supported by countries which did not approve of the death penalty. He then urged him "to see that support being returned by … listening to these representations, particularly in the case of the journalists. We would certainly want to make sure that the death penalty was not applied to any of those who have been accused, but I can well understand the very strong reaction particularly at the death sentences against journalists."[411]

Solomon Berewa was not amused, for he gave all these representations short shrift. He categorically stated that while his government appreciated Britain's assistance in restoring Kabbah to power, its appeal for clemency was unwelcome. He claimed that there was "overwhelming popular support" for the convictions but did not disclose how he had arrived at that conclusion.[412] Whatever was meant by "popular support," two things at least were clear. First, unable to speak for fear of intimidation and reprisal, the overwhelming majority of citizens had uncharacteristically remained mute throughout the trials. Secondly, every day through the trial, primed lackeys of the ruling party were seen around the courts, chanting party slogans and vociferously demanding mob justice for the accused. Was it such sloganeering that was being purveyed as representing the true feelings of the "overwhelming majority" of Sierra Leoneans?

On another occasion, on October 13, 1998, following the handing down of convictions against 34 military officers by the Court Martial, Berewa again drew a parallel between the actions of his government and those of the British colonial administration in 1898. He was reported as saying: "Exactly 100 years ago this year, the colonial masters ....executed 96 people for refusing to pay the hut tax of 26 pence....So the capital sentence is not new to Sierra Leone. It is part of our history and a legacy from colonialism."413 This is like saying that because the British colonial administration did it, it is right for the Sierra Leone government to do it again 100 years later, however reprehensible the British conduct might have been.

Although the British protests were the most prominent, apart from them, appeals for clemency had also come from far and near, and from the United Nations Secretary-General, the United Nations High Commissioner for Human Rights, OAU, Ecowas and Human Rights Watch. Amnesty International invited the Sierra Leone government to commute the death sentences, saying that the imposition of the death penalty would not contribute to the process of reconciliation in Sierra Leone. It said: "Amnesty International acknowledges the government's responsibility to bring to justice and punish those responsible for these crimes and also insists that there should be no impunity for human rights violations. It is, however, unconditionally opposed to the death penalty. Nowhere has it been shown that the death penalty has any special power to reduce crime or political violence. Neither has it ever been shown to have any special power to meet any genuine social need. A difficult and daunting task faces Sierra Leone in achieving reconciliation within its society after the atrocities committed by the AFRC and RUF. Amnesty International believes that the use of the death penalty not only gives the false impression that preventative action is being taken, but perpetuates the use of cruel and inhuman punishment, and does nothing to contribute to the process of reconciliation."414

Effects of acts of the military junta

The AFRC ruled the country for nearly nine months. Because its coming into existence was unconstitutional, the question arises whether this also taints all acts performed by it or under its authority. If so, are there any exceptions?

As a general principle, the question of the legal effect of acts of a revolutionary government is dealt with either by the courts or by the legislature, hardly by the executive.415 Siaka Stevens followed this principle after the reign of the NRC was brought to an end in 1968. President Kabbah's first government followed suit when it succeeded the NPRC in 1996.

He dramatically changed course after his restoration in 1998 following his overthrow by the AFRC. In a national broadcast on February 13, 1998, he declared that: "very soon my Government will once again be in full and effective control of the affairs of the country, to exercise its legitimate and constitutional functions." And he added: "It will be doing so with much greater vigour, taking into account the situation which has prevailed in the country since May 25, 1997. Let me at this point say to you that no one had authority to amend any provisions of the Constitution, and the junta and its illegal machinery had no executive or legislative power to do so. Parts of the Constitution can be amended only in accordance with the provisions of section 108 of the Constitution itself, which states in sub-section 8, and I quote: 'Any suspension, alteration, or repeal of this Constitution other than on the authority of Parliament shall be deemed to be an act of treason'. *Therefore, all persons exercising or purporting to exercise governmental authority, and all their actions, including those taken by the junta to award, appoint, promote, dismiss and transfer state functionaries and other personnel, are null and void.* As President, and by the powers vested in me under the Constitution, I now order that the *status quo* on 24th May (that is before the illegal seizure of power) be maintained."

No specificity was given of the constitutional powers he claimed and the declaration was tantamount to an executive blockade on all things done by the AFRC military junta. But the essence of a blockade is to expedite the capitulation of the usurper, and its value decreases inversely with the degree of capitulation. A blockade is therefore hardly valuable where the usurper has already capitulated. Precisely because actions of usurpers have legal consequences, the practice has been to leave such matters to be determined by the judicial or legislative branch of government. It is therefore moot how to construe Kabbah's effusive declaration that "all persons exercising or purporting to exercise governmental authority, and all their acts....are null and void."

Nor is its import easy to comprehend. It is like saying that nature's clock had suddenly ground to a halt on May 25, 1997 and did not start functioning again until February 13, 1998. Yet, in the interval life had to go on. Kabbah himself did make statements, acknowledging that his government was not "in full and effective control of the affairs of the country". If his government was not, who was? If nobody was in control, was there a vacuum? If so, does the law allow this? If not, does the doctrine of necessity or implied mandate apply, recognising as valid governmental acts performed by a usurper who is *de facto sed non de jure*?416

In one sense, Kabbah's attitude was extraordinary. It could be compared to that of the Cambodian Constituent Assembly in 1993 but it contrasts sharply with that of the British government in 1965, following Ian Smith's rebellion in Southern Rhodesia. The Cambodian Constituent Assembly met for the first time on June 14, 1993, and, in an almost surreal first act, declared null and void the March 1970 overthrow of the head of state, Prince Sihanouk. The Assembly thus expunged from the books the act of lese-majesty, which had obsessed Sihanouk for 23 years. Recognising him as the true head of state through all the travails since 1970, it endowed him with unspecified "full and special powers".417

In another sense, the AFRC junta could be likened to the rebel regime set up by Ian Smith after he illegally declared Southern Rhodesia independent from the United Kingdom in 1965. Like the AFRC junta, the Smith regime had received no international recognition. Nevertheless, on March 2, 1970, Michael Stewart, British Foreign Secretary, told Parliament that "in a number of cases, members of the public services, including the court, have joined the rebellion. In other cases, members of the public services still believe that they could continue to function as they did before [the illegal declaration of independence]. But this is not so and can no longer be seen in this light. The former Governor's injunction has lapsed and those who continue to serve a regime which asserts illegally that Southern Rhodesia is a republic – like those appointed by the regime –cannot be regarded as serving the Crown in Southern Rhodesia. This change in their status must, in our view, have consequences for the functions they perform and for the validity of acts done in the performance of those functions; the effects of these matters on individuals will however fall to be considered by the courts in this country."[418] This remains the predominant practice in such cases.

Questionable executions

Of the 34 soldiers found guilty of treason, 24 were executed on October 19, 1998, despite international appeals for clemency or for granting them a right to appeal. The law, as it then stood, did not recognise a right of appeal from a court martial. The only option they had was to petition the United Nations Human Rights Committee (UNHRC) pursuant to the provisions of the Optional Protocol to the International Covenant on Civil and Political Rights 1966 (International Covenant). Although Sierra Leone had ratified the International Covenant, neither it nor the Optional Protocol had been incorporated into Sierra Leonean law through legislation. Ratification, however, constitutes a commitment to observe certain fundamental norms of conduct to be supervised by the UNHRC. And the Optional Protocol gives Sierra Leoneans a right of access to the UNHRC.

When the UNHRC received the petitions of the convicted soldiers, pending their consideration, it immediately asked Kabbah to stay execution. He refused. On November 4, the UNHRC adopted a strongly worded decision, requesting a report from his government pursuant to the provisions of Article 40 of the International Covenant. This decision was communicated to Kabbah on November 16, 1998. As of the time of writing, his government's report is yet to reach the UNHRC.

The question is whether it was lawful for Kabbah to execute the convicted soldiers whilst their petitions were pending before the UNHRC. According to the Privy Council in the recent case of *Thomas and Another v Baptiste and Others* (1999),[419] it was not. The main issue, an appeal from Trinidad and Tobago, was whether a man sentenced to death has a constitutional right to have his petition to the Inter-American Commission on Human Rights considered and determined first before his sentence is carried out.

The background to the case is as follows. The Constitution of Trinidad and Tobago 1976 affirms the right to life, liberty, security of the person and enjoyment of property and the right not to be deprived of them "except by due process of law". The Trinidadian government had ratified the International Covenant in 1978 and had acceded to the Optional Protocol in 1980. It had also ratified the American Convention on Human Rights of 1969, which established the Inter-American Commission on Human Rights and the Inter-American Court of Human Rights. Like the UNHRC, the Inter-American Commission has competence to entertain individual petitions regarding violations of the Convention and to make reports and recommendations in respect thereof. Trinidad had also recognised the compulsory jurisdiction of the Court to give binding rulings on the interpretation and application of the Convention.

By 1997 a significant number of persons sentenced to death in Trinidad and Tobago had petitioned either the UNHRC or the Inter-American Commission and the Court, complaining of violations of their rights under the Conventions. The Court made orders requiring the government to stay execution pending its determination of the petitions. The government nevertheless wanted to carry out the death sentences in defiance of those orders. It is important to note that, like Sierra Leone, Trinidad and Tobago had incorporated neither the International Covenant nor the Optional Protocol into and therefore was not yet part of the domestic law of Trinidad and Tobago. The question was whether, pending the determination of the petitions by the Commission, the government was obliged to stay execution of the prisoners.

By a majority decision of 3:2, the Privy Council opined in the affirmative. First, the Court interpreted the expression "due process of law" in the Trinidadian Constitution, equivalent to section 23(1) of the Sierra Leone Constitution 1991, as excluding "legislative as well as executive interference with the judicial process." Adopting the dictum of Mr Justice Holmes in the American case of *Frank v. Magnum*,420 the Court said that it "embraces the fundamental concept of a fair trial, with opportunity to be heard." It said it had no doubt that "the clause extends to the appellate process as well as the trial itself. In particular, it includes the right of a condemned man to be allowed to complete any appellate or analogous legal process that is capable of resulting in a reduction or commutation of his sentence before the process is rendered nugatory by executive action. The appellants contend that their constitutional right to due process would be infringed if they were to be executed while their current petitions to the Commission were still pending. They seek a stay of execution until the petitions have been determined and the rulings of the Commission and Court have been considered by the authorities in Trinidad and Tobago. To this the Government make several objections. They invoke the fundamental principle that legal rights are neither created nor destroyed by executive action, and contend that the due process clause does not incorporate into domestic law rights created by an unincorporated treaty such as the Convention. They insist that rights granted by the executive may be withdrawn by the executive....They point out that the Commission's only function is to make a Report which the Advisory Committee may but is not obliged to take into account when recommending whether there should be a reprieve. They submit that the appellants cannot have a constitutional right to complete an international appellate or analogous process which merely leads to a Report which the Government of Trinidad and Tobago is not under any legal obligation to take into consideration.

Their Lordships recognise the constitutional importance of the principle that international conventions do not alter domestic law except to the extent that they are incorporated into domestic law by legislation. The making of a treaty, in Trinidad and Tobago as in England, is an act of the executive government, not of the legislature. It follows that the terms of a treaty cannot effect any alteration to domestic law or deprive the subject of existing legal rights unless and until enacted into domestic law by or under authority of the legislature. When so enacted, the Courts give effect to the domestic legislation, not to the terms of the treaty. The many authoritative statements to this effect are too well known to need citation. It is sometimes argued that human rights treaties form an exception to this principle. It is also sometimes argued that a principle which is intended to afford the subject constitutional protection against the exercise of executive power cannot be invoked by the executive itself to escape from obligations which it has entered into for his protection. Their Lordships mention these arguments for completeness. They do not find it necessary to examine them further in the present case.

In their Lordships' view, however, the appellants claim does not infringe the principle which the Government invoke. The right for which they contend is not the particular right to petition the Commission or even to complete the particular process which they initiated when they lodged their petitions. It is the general right accorded to all litigants not to have the outcome of any pending appellate or other legal process pre-empted by executive action. This general right is not created by the Convention; it is accorded by the common law and affirmed by section 4(a) of the Constitution. The appellants are not seeking to enforce the terms of an unincorporated treaty, but a provision of the domestic law of Trinidad and Tobago contained in the Constitution. *By ratifying a treaty which provides for individual access to an international body, the Government made that process for the time being part of the domestic criminal justice system and thereby temporarily at least extended the scope of the due process clause in the Constitution.....*

Their Lordships accept the general proposition that the executive may withdraw rights which it has granted. But this principle is not without exception. Executive action may give rise to a settle practice, and this in turn may found a constitutional right which cannot lawfully be withdrawn by executive action alone. Even when executive action falls short of this, as it does in the present case, it may confer a right for the time being which cannot be withdrawn retrospectively without infringing the due process clause........But the right to be allowed to complete a current appellate or other legal process without having it rendered nugatory by executive action before it is completed is part of the fundamental concept of due process......For the Government to carry out the sentences of death before the petitions have been heard would deny the appellants their constitutional right to due process."

Appeals from Sierra Leonean courts to the Privy Council have been abolished long ago, so its decisions are no longer binding. But its persuasive authority could only be ignored at peril. From the judgment, it is clear that, by their execution while their petitions were pending before the UNHRC, the government had denied the 24 soldiers their right to a fair hearing, contrary to the common law of Sierra Leone and contrary to the Constitutional provision in section 23(1). By ratifying the UN Covenants on Human Rights, Sierra Leone has made individual access to the UNHRC an essential part of its criminal justice system. The convicted soldiers were therefore entitled to have their petitions considered by the UNHRC before their executions were carried out.

The executions were also a blatant violation of the customary international law rule embodied in the Geneva Conventions 1949 Article 3(1)(d) of which prohibits "the carrying out of executions without previous judgment pronounced by a regularly constituted court affording all the judicial guarantees which are recognised as indispensable by civilised peoples." As a rule of customary international law, it is automatically incorporated into the common law of Sierra Leone. Accordingly, it is arguable that by carrying out the executions before the UNHRC had had an opportunity to consider the petitions of the executed soldiers, they were denied the "judicial guarantees" envisaged by that principle.

The role of national reconciliation

Another area, which has excited a great deal of interest, is the role of national reconciliation. On October 1, 1997, President Kabbah assured the United Nations General Assembly that: "If there is anything Sierra Leone needs today more than anything else, it is peace and reconciliation. I have never lost sight of this need and it is the one objective which has influenced every step that I have taken since assuming office in March 1996. The events of 25th May have only further deepened those divisions within our society which my policies had begun to heal. As a result, the adoption of a more vigorous policy of national reconciliation has become an absolute necessity." He claimed he had rejected any idea of a war crimes tribunal because going down that route would "add to our already grave problems and postpone lasting national reconciliation." Later that month in London, he repeated his rejection of a war crimes tribunal in preference to a truth and reconciliation commission as had been the experience of Chile, El Salvador, South Africa and Guatemala, for example.

This commitment, however, evaporated as soon as Kabbah was restored to office. On March 10, 1998, he declared: "Our image as a civilised nation will be greatly enhanced if we are seen to be promoting reconciliation. Let me state, however, that reconciliation should not be construed as letting off the hook those who have brought untold suffering upon our people. Accordingly, these people will be brought to justice as swiftly as possible. It is only then that reconciliation can be meaningful."421

What brought about this change of heart is not clear but he appeared to have been a hostage to the ambitions of vengeful politicians within his party, who, like hounds on a hunting expedition, never tempered their trenchant for a kill. While it was true that many people in Sierra Leone had been hurt - indeed not a single family can boast not to have been – this may be viewed as the inevitable consequence of the long campaign of militarism, which, while it had the upper hand, completely sidelined political dialogue as a veritable option. The choice had always been between treating the rebels as bare-face criminals, subject to the full weight of retributive justice, and pursuing the prudent and pragmatic policy of political dialogue. For a long time, successive governments chose the former.

Not only did this militarism prove counter-productive, it even ran against the grain of historical precedent as exemplified by Bai Bureh's "hut tax" war against British colonialism in 1898. Bai Bureh had fought the British to get them to repeal a house tax they had imposed on the citizens of the then Protectorate of Sierra Leone. The British government despatched Sir David Chalmers, former Chief Justice of the Gold Coast (now Ghana), to Sierra Leone in July 1898 to inquire into the circumstances that had led to the insurrection. He reported in January 1899. Among other things, he recommended that a general amnesty should be proclaimed and that all punitive measures should cease. He also recommended that the Insurgents' Detention Ordinance (equivalent to modern-day emergency regulations) should be repealed immediately and the hut tax discontinued. Although Chamberlain, Secretary of State for the Colonies, rejected the last recommendation, nevertheless in the spirit of reconciliation he instructed in a telegram sent to Freetown in November 1898 that Bai Bureh should be "treated kindly." And, instead of putting him on trial, he was briefly deported to the Cape Coast, Ghana, where he stayed until July 1905.422

A hundred years later, faced with a similar situation, the United Nations Security Council likewise advised reconciliation. In its Presidential Statement of February 26, 1998,423 it called for the adoption of a policy of national reconciliation and political dialogue as envisaged by the Conakry Peace Plan of October 23, 1997424 and the Abidjan Peace Agreement of November 30, 1996.425 It confirmed this policy in resolution 1162 (1998), adopted on April 17, 1998, where it emphasised "the need to promote national reconciliation in Sierra Leone" and encouraged all and sundry to work together towards that objective.

The OAU Council of Ministers reinforced this demand426 as did the British government.427 President Clinton of the United States went even further. He despatched Reverend Jesse Jackson as his Special Envoy to convince the warring parties to end the conflict and seek a peaceful end to the country's civil conflict through dialogue and reconciliation. Speaking at a press conference in Freetown on November 13, 1998, Jackson advised the government to reach out to the rebels and make concessions in order to bring them to the peace table, adding: "They are also Sierra Leoneans, so they are a necessary component to the peace process......Those who demand an eye for an eye and a tooth for a tooth ...could leave all of us blind and disfigured. Someone must break the cycle of pain and violence."428

Even Kabbah's greatest military ally, the Nigerian military junta, lent its weight to this policy after the demise of General Abacha. Britain, which up to that point had had limited influence on the crisis due to its unneutral stance, now crafted a dual-track approach to ending the imbroglio – i.e. maintaining the military pressure on the rebels while at the same time making peace offerings through reconciliation. General Abdulsalami Abubakar, Nigeria's new leader, concurred and persuaded his colleagues in

Ecowas to accept it. He was then planning to withdraw his troops from Sierra Leone to coincide with the transfer of power to an elected government in Nigeria, then scheduled for May 29, 1999.

Ending Sierra Leone's bloodletting through political dialogue and reconciliation resonated the deep but unexpressed passion of the country's silent majority. It also turned out to be in Nigeria's national interest as its own political future was then hanging dangerously on a knife-edge, poised between chaos and reform, and looking every bit as volatile as ever. Getting bogged down in an unending conflict in a foreign land was the last thing that the newly elected government of Nigeria would like to inherit given the mounting human and material costs involved. As the pressure escalated, the triumphalist agenda of the hawks within the SLPP ruling party gave way to political dialogue.

The Lome Peace Agreement 1999

Dialogue was ultimately crowned with the signing of the Lome Peace Agreement on July 7, 1999. With no sanctions for cease-fire violations, the parties agreed to set up a Cease-fire Monitoring Committee (CMC), to be chaired by UNOMSIL and comprising representatives of the government, RUF, the Civil Defence Forces and Ecomog. It is to operate at provincial and district levels and has responsibility for monitoring, verifying and reporting on all cease-fire violations. The CMC reports to the Joint Monitoring Commission (JMC), again chaired by UNOMSIL with membership from the same parties as for the CMC.

Also envisaged is a neutral international peacekeeping force to disarm all combatants and paramilitary groups, to commence within six weeks of the signing of the agreement. To this end, the United Nations was asked to amend UNOMSIL's mandate. This was done in resolution 1270 of October 22, 1999. It is to assist the government of Sierra Leone "in the implementation of the disarmament, demobilisation and reintegration plan" of the Lome peace agreement, a task entrusted to the United Nations Mission in Sierra Leone (UNAMSIL), which succeeded UNOMSIL. However, it did not also give it responsibility for security. This was reserved for Ecomog forces, who would also assist in the creation of a new restructured and ethnically-homogenous national army to include, provided they meet the recruitment criteria, ex-combatants of the disbanded national army, RUF and the civil defence forces. But Ecomog soon disbanded when Mali withdrew its 428 soldiers it had deployed in February 1999 followed by Nigeria.

The Lome agreement also provides for the establishment of "a transitional mechanism to incorporate the RUF into governance within the spirit and letter of the Constitution". It speaks of "a broad-based government of national unity" but, in truth, the edifice created was neither. The existing SLPP government simply incorporated four cabinet and four non-cabinet ministerial nominees of the RUF. In other words, it was a government of inclusion, as indeed the Conakry Peace Plan of October 1997 had envisaged.

The Peace Agreement further provides for the establishment of a ten-member autonomous Board to oversee a Commission for the Management of Strategic Resources, National Reconstruction and Development (CMRRD). The CMRRD was "charged with the responsibility of securing and monitoring the legitimate exploitation of Sierra Leone's gold and diamonds, and other resources that are determined to be of strategic importance for national security and welfare as well as cater for post-war rehabilitation and reconstruction." Accordingly, all previous mineral concessions were to be declared null and void, and all proceeds from gold and diamond transactions "paid into a special treasury account" to be used exclusively for national development, with special emphasis on education, health, infrastructural development, and compensation for incapacitated war victims. Foday Sankoh was appointed Chairman of the Board, a position that carried the protocol rank of Vice-President.

As required under the peace agreement, the RUF transformed itself into a political party. Known as the RUF Party, with the lion as its symbol, it was issued a provisional registration by INEC on November 22, 1999.

Another organ created by the Peace Agreement is the Commission for the Consolidation of Peace (CCP), comprising of two representatives of civil society and one representative each of the government, RUF and parliament. It has overall responsibility for supervising and monitoring the implementation of the provisions relating to the promotion of national reconciliation and consolidation of peace. The CCP makes recommendations to the

President and unresolved disputes are to be referred to a Council of Elders and Religious Leaders. The mandate of the CCP terminates at the end of the next general elections. Johnny Paul Koroma, former leader of the AFRC, was appointed chairman.

A blanket amnesty was given to "all combatants and collaborators in respect of anything done by them in pursuit of their objectives" up to the signing of the agreement. Apart from the fact that in 1999 one was dealing with more than the RUF, there was no real difference between this amnesty and that provided under the Abidjan Peace Accord of 1996. While The UN had raised no objections in 1996, this time under the 1999 accord it entered a disclaimer in terms that the amnesty should not apply to "international crimes of genocide, crimes against humanity, war crimes, and other serious violations of international humanitarian law". Under the principle of universality, any state can bring such offenders to justice provided they have empowered their courts to exercise such jurisdiction under their domestic law.

The United Nations disclaimer has great merit in principle, but moral relativism provides a false kind of understanding. There is always a moral dilemma in reconciling two competing interests: lasting peace versus ending impunity. There is also the all-important problem of timing, already addressed in chapter 7. There is no need to rush, for war crimes never die. The important thing is that the judicial process must not become a source of apprehension whereby rebel suspects might feel that they have no choice but to fight to the bitter end. Moreover, the judicial process must be one that is independent, impartial and credible; meets international fair-trial standards; and is capable of upgrading the dysfunctional judicial system in Sierra Leone.

The Peace Agreement also caters for a Truth and Reconciliation Commission (TRC) as well as an autonomous quasi-judicial National Human Rights Commission. Knowing and telling the truth is not only fundamental; it is an essential ingredient of peace and reconciliation. Without it peace is empty and reconciliation is everything but genuine. Such instrumentalities are valuable in situations where the country is emerging from a protracted war; where there is only a negotiated agreement, not an imposed peace; only a government of inclusion, not a change of government; in short, where there is no victor and no vanquished.

The TRC will help to establish an historical record, address violations of human rights and questions of impunity, provide a forum for both victims and perpetrators to tell their story, respond to the needs of victims as well as promote healing and reconciliation. This requires an atmosphere that is conducive to encouraging ordinary folks, victims and witnesses alike, to confidently come forward and tell their story. Therefore it is important to select as commissioners persons of outstanding national and international repute and integrity who would serve in their individual capacities, totally independent of any organisation to which they might belong. And to ensure independence and impartiality, the majority of the TRC should be non-citizens. As enacted, however, the TRC consists of seven members, of whom four are Sierra Leoneans and the rest non-citizens, possibly including the Chairman. Imperfect as this mechanism might be, its creation would go a long way towards facilitating the otherwise tortuous process of genuine national reconciliation.

Whether the prospects of success are greater for the Lome Accord than they had been for the Abidjan Peace Accord before it, is a question that waxes eloquence especially from the fact that, in many respects, they are not very different one from the other. However, three main determinants underpin success. First, the signatories must remain faithful to their commitments, including in particular their obligation to disarm voluntarily. Second, though UNAMSIL has a robust mandate to defend itself and the defenceless civilian population against violent attacks, this only puts it on the "edge of the Mogadishu Line". Giving UNAMSIL adequate operational capability is the measure that could make or break it, a wholly exogenous factor. Third, there is a somewhat surreal conception about resolution 1270 in that it gives UNAMSIL, essentially a peacekeeping force, a robust defensive mandate simultaneously as it gives a parallel peace enforcement mandate to Ecomog forces, making no provision for coordination between the two. It looked doomed from the start, for peace and war simply cannot co-exist. In the end, Nigeria withdrew its forces from Sierra Leone and those that remained were absorbed into UNAMSIL.

This potential conflict nevertheless made little impression on President Kabbah, who, as late as May 2000, continued to believe that UNAMSIL, a peacekeeping force, could conveniently co-exist with a parallel, rival Ecomog force with a more robust mandate of its own and under a separate command. His apparent distraction was the independence of UNAMSIL and his penchant for playing commander-in-chief. This made him to prefer Ecomog even as the Nigerians, who constituted the bulk of the Ecomog force, were making it pellucidly clear that any additional forces they provided were to be part of UNAMSIL.429

The next general elections

Parliamentary elections are due not later than April 2001. Under Section 85 of the Constitution, if they are not held before the expiration of the parliamentary five-year term, Parliament "shall stand dissolved" unless there is a state of emergency and the President says it is not practicable to hold elections. In such a case, Parliament may extend its five-year term for a period of six months at a time.

Similarly, under Section 49 of the Constitution, President Kabbah would cease to be President unless he is re-elected for a second and final term. However, he is not required to resign or retire from office at the expiration of his term if a parliamentary election is pending within the ensuing three months or there is "a state of emergency" in existence.

This probably explains why Kabbah has refused to lift the emergency, despite pleas by the democratic opposition for him to do so. He has even appointed an Election Commission without consulting "with the leaders of all registered political parties" as he is required to do by the Constitution before submitting nominations to Parliament for approval. He believes that merely by writing about his decision to appoint the Commission and sending the letters to the registered offices of each party is sufficient to constitute "consultation" within the meaning of the Constitution. He ignored totally those political leaders who happened to be out of Sierra Leone even though he and his

278

government knew their whereabouts. Of course, he is not required to act in accordance with their advice, a matter the courts are barred from inquiring into, but to ignore entirely the injunction to consult them is to render the constitutional provision completely otiose. Obviously this raises implications. Imagine, for example, that Kabbah refuses to lift the emergency until nearer the poll, denying opposition parties a level playing field. Elections are then held under the supervision of his Election Commission but only in areas outside rebel control and he is declared winner. Would such an election be accepted as free and fair? Would denial of the right to vote to nearly one-half of the country under rebel control be conducive to national peace and security?

In order to avoid dangers such as these, the following proposals may be posited. First, that President Kabbah serve out the remainder of his term. Second, that the elections take place only if there is complete disarmament, to be verified by UNAMSIL. Third, that a Bintumani-type national conference be convened, under UN auspices, but only after the emergency has been lifted. The conference would seek to reach agreement on the establishment of a broad-based transitional government of national unity to take over the administration of the country at the end of Kabbah's term. It would govern for such period as is stipulated by the conference during which it would ensure that, aside from the new national army, all other combatants are properly disarmed and constituency-based democratic elections are held in keeping with the Constitution. Fourth, that elections be organised and supervised by an independent and impartial international body.

These proposals avoid the use of emergency powers to prolong the life of the presidency and parliament. That procedure, although part of the Constitution, should always be seen as extraordinary and therefore not quite in keeping with democratic precepts. Quite apart from this, no election would be valid under the Constitution if not based on a new electoral register compiled for each constituency. There are other conditions precedent to a general election that also need to be fulfilled. None of them is likely to be fulfilled before the due date in 2001. In these circumstances, were the incumbent government to force the issue nevertheless, it could hardly escape the criticism of exploiting the war situation and the misery of ordinary people to perpetuate itself in power contrary to their wishes.

CHAPTER 9

The Way Forward

In the previous chapters we have shown how, despite almost four decades of self-government, Sierra Leone's peace and security have remained dangerously fragile. In particular, the institutions that guarantee individual liberty and freedom are still intermeshed with pernicious executive interference from which they are yet to extricate themselves. As a result, public confidence remains persistently flat. The situation grew worse after 1991, following the RUF rebellion, which has ruined the country and put its development on hold. So grotesque have the consequences been that today the country is little more than a shadow of its former self. And so widespread is the panoply of tragically disconnected consequences that many see no bright prospects on the immediate horizon.

The questions this begs are, first, how can the country extricate itself from its self-imposed trauma? What lessons can the rest of Africa and the developing world at large learn from this tragedy? Indeed what lessons are there for the international community as a whole, and the United Nations in particular?

Since 1991, politics and principles have atrophied in the face of widespread violence. The restoration of peace and security therefore remains topmost on the nation's agenda, and, until this is achieved, its democratic reconstruction will inevitably stay in abeyance. The incumbent government has all too often demonstrated that without intervention by the international community, its capacity is limited, a symptom of diminished self-esteem. This dependency has to be broken to enable the nation as a whole regain its self-respect and accept responsibility for its own crisis; otherwise the future will continue to look bleak. This is the first ingredient of permanent peace.

The second ingredient is that the international media have to stay deliberately focused. Indeed, such are the ways of the new international order that unless an African crisis is sufficiently media-driven - the so-called CNN effect - its relegation to the bottom of the heap of international concerns is almost certain. Not only the military, sensational, headline-grabbing horrific stories of the rebel war deserve publicity; peace-building efforts, embracing the essential ingredients of democratic reconstruction, equally deserve international attention.

The third condition is the need to keep the management and implementation of the Lome Peace Agreement of 1999 under constant national and international scrutiny. This is fundamental if the peace process is to be free of corruption and nepotism. Equally important, just like the Abidjan Peace Accord of 1996 before it, the Lome Agreement is not immune from the vagaries of mistrust between the signatories. They need to be told in no uncertain terms by both the citizens of Sierra Leone and the international community that the retreat from the path of peace towards another Armageddon of bloodstained anarchy will no longer be tolerated. For this message to impress, however, the international community must demonstrate an unbiased adherence to the principles of the United Nations Charter, an unstinting support for genuine democratic reconstruction and unflagging respect for the constitution and sovereignty of the people of Sierra Leone.

Sierra Leone is thus at the crossroads. In the short-term, it is necessary that the incumbent government be allowed to complete its five-year constitutional term, after which it should be replaced by a transitional government of national unity fashioned out by all the stakeholders meeting in a national conference convened under the auspices of the United Nations. No favouritism and no fix-it or tilting mentality towards anybody must be shown either by the international community or by those assisting the country to return to permanent peace and security. Certainly not for the RUF, whose atrocities against defenceless civilians have been so horrendous that they have thoroughly disarticulated the political content of its violence. Nor for the so-called democratically-elected government either, whose governance of the country has been so driven by a combination of militarism and greed, hate and revenge, and duplicity and deviousness, that it has long ceased to be comprehensible.

Yet, there can be no denying that it is the political content of the conflict, democracy in short, more than any other, which is at the core. And democracy's most fundamental right, the right to vote without intimidation, is still in mortal danger in Sierra Leone despite 40 years of independence, as already exemplified by the scandalous rigging of the vote in 1967 and again in 1996, both of which precipitated military *coups*. Nor is Sierra Leone unique in this regard. Many other examples, particularly from the Third World, may be cited. This is why, in this twenty-first century, international action is needed to protect the vote from executive intrusion and corruption of any kind. Perhaps the best way is for the international community to step into potentially explosive situations and supervise elections and referenda, as the case may be, to ensure that they are unquestionably free and fair.

Such international invigilation would avert disputes which often arise from the conduct of elections and which can easily degenerate into crisis. If the bedrock of democracy is the right to vote, then that right must be protected at all cost. To this end, not only should international supervision of elections become the *raison d'etre* of the future role of the international community in this area; it should be recognised as a veritable buffer against internal insurgency. And it is not just the fairness of the poll that matters; the surrounding conditions are just as important, for elections are only as good as the conditions in which they are held. Therefore international monitors must be empowered to pass judgment on both aspects; otherwise they cannot and should not escape blame if there is trouble.

This recommendation is particularly vital for countries emerging from the throes of civil conflict. The Balkans, Yugoslavia, Cote d'Ivoire, Liberia and Sierra Leone are examples which fall into that category. For these countries, post-conflict reconstruction would mean very little if not underpinned by a system of justice that is wholly independent, impartial, credible, effective and commensurate with international standards. This means not only that serious violations of international human rights must be punished but political governance too must be determined solely by way of genuinely democratic processes if they are to be prevented from degenerating into violence. In other words, there is no substitute for a culture of respect for human rights and genuine democracy.

This culture has been long in entrenching itself in most developing countries for understandable reasons. Unlike the American colonies of the eighteenth century, which had had prolonged experience in the complex and hazardous business of self-government, these nations emerged into independence rather precariously with hardly any prolonged period of previous apprenticeship in self-government to speak of. So the democratic political culture has been relatively slow in domesticating itself. Yet it need hardly be stressed that in Africa it is not what others want that matters; it is what African leaders do with their peole that really matters in the end. To be sure, however long it takes, democracy will prevaiil. Caribbean countries and parts of Asia are already shining examples of how democracy can be domesticated. South Africa offers a precious example of how a notoriously oppressive and undemocratic system can be reshaped and transformed into a democratic national mould. The momentous fall of apartheid as well as the collapse of commuunism in Eastern Europe teach at least one clear lesson, namely that a people with diverse ethnic origins, subscribing to no common unifying culture, can hardly be held together in perpetuity, not even by force of arms.

These historical events took a great deal of time, courage and sacrifice. And so it shall be for a large number of African countries where the creation of an enabling environment for domesticating democracy remains the biggest challenge. Yet it is by far the best pressure valve against internal convulsion and for fostering peace and development.

A functioning democracy – in terms of a freely and fairly elected legislature, an independent and impartial judiciary, an incorruptible civil service, accountable police and military, a government subject to the rule of law and a free press – is basic to the enjoyment of human rights. Its enthronement, as much as its violation everywhere, is a matter of legitimate concern to the international community. This is affirmed by the International Covenant on Civil and Political Rights 1996, Article 22 of which recognises the right of every person to freely associate with others. Article 25 stipulates the right of every citizen to take part, without unreasonable restrictions, in the conduct of public affairs, directly or through freely chosen representatives. It also recognises the right of the citizen to vote and be voted for at genuine periodic elections. Thus democracy is recognised not only as a fundamental human right but also as a veritable forum for settling political contests rather than through violence.

My submission, therefore, is that in plural societies no culture glues better than the collective will of the people, freely expressed and symbolised by representative institutions rooted in the principles of consent and the rule of law. Where these values prevail, society is better able "to react on itself, to identify changed circumstances or new needs and begin to address them".430 Mutual tolerance and mutual respect provide additional reinforcements, as does the principle that ensures that political differences are resolved in a peaceful and thoughtful manner, without recourse to violence.

Democratisation, however, works better when the electoral machinery is truly independent and impartial, for example, where the United Nations is itself the electoral supervisor. Within the last decade or so, it has performed this vital task, on an *ad hoc* basis, in Namibia, Angola, Mozambique, El Salvador, Haiti, Cambodia and East Timor, to name a few.

Moving on from *ad hoc* arrangements to more permanent structures for such tasks is perhaps an idea whose time has come. As a crisis prevention mechanism, it is worth investing in. Western Powers have tried to help African countries enhance their peacekeeping capability in many ways. For example, in 1996, the United States launched its African Crisis Response Initiative (ACRI). The message is clear: fewer and fewer peacekeepers from Western nations would in future take part in African conflicts. Dubbed, somewhat cynically but not without truth, as the "Somalia allergy", this reluctance on the part of the Western Powers stems from the tragic fiasco of the American raid on Mohammed Farah Aidid's stronghold in south Mogadishu in October 1993, where it lost 18 soldiers.

Hard on the heels of ACRI came President Clinton's "Africa Initiative" and his state visit to a number of African countries in 1998 followed by his Secretary of State, Madeleine Albright, in October 1999. Both encouraged African governments to stay the course of economic and political reforms in order to stimulate American trade and investment for the continent and make the American market accessible to African products as never before. Clinton translated the initiative into law – the Africa Growth and Opportunity Act - and added one more on debt relief – the reformed Heavily Indebted Poor Countries (HIPC). Well-intentioned as these initiatives may have been, they were up against stiff resistance from the American legislature, which took many years to pass them.

The problem has to do with something more than partisan politics in the West. The truth is that not enough is being done to educate and inform people in the West that Africa matters, and matters in ways that affect their daily lives. Nor is there a strong, organised and sustained constituency in the West, ready and willing to fight for Africa and her interests. This is why their response has been relatively poor, and is likely to remain poor. Thanks to the international media, Western populations, of different generations for that matter, still perceive Africa as the "Dark Continent", as remote as ever from the modern highways and byways of the globalised economy, just as it had been during colonial times.

Recent studies confirm this. Declining generosity has become a world-wide phenomenon and overall international assistance has dropped precipitously since the end of the Cold War by at least 21 per cent in inflation-adjusted terms between 1992 and 1997. Nowhere is this decline more evident than in Africa. As observed by Karen DeYoung of *The Washington Post* on November 25, 1999: "The principal loser in this equation has been Africa, where the impact of declining funds and shifting priorities is felt in increasingly scarce resources to combat hunger, homelessness and disease." Even with regard to private venture capital, "Africa has been largely bypassed by the mushrooming flows of private investment funds that have offset the decline in foreign aid in other regions, such as East Asia and Latin America, where investors have seen better potential returns," she adds.431

Quite apart from this, there is also the troubling tendency of shifting priorities of Western nations and of their threatening retreat into a fortress mentality. Small wonder that even as late as 1999 the American Congress did not hesitate to cut the Administration's foreign affairs budget to below 40 per cent of its 1985 level, despite its growing engagement in the Third World. This stifling by Congress even forced President Clinton to beat a retreat from internationalism. He declared that the "United States simply cannot become engaged in every one of the world's conflicts", and his National Security Adviser confirmed that America cannot do everything or be everywhere. The differential treatment Western nations have given to conflicts in Europe and Africa is also too stark to be mistaken, and African diplomats at the United Nations have wondered whether it might not be connected with a recrudescence of racial overtones in the West.

What does all this mean? On one view, Africa must wait until public opinion in the West takes a more enlightened perception of her problems and rejects the so-called Darwinian theory of development, whereby the unfit are discarded by the wayside as unworthy. But this may take generations. On another view – one preferred by this writer – present attitudes in the West send a wake-up call to Africa as a whole. In particular, its marginalisation in the global marketplace will not end until it is able to create its own enabling environment for sustainable peace and for long-term recovery and development. Democracy is fundamentally that enabling environment. By embracing it fully, future crises would be avoided and forward defences constructed for both African and global interests.

The poor response to ACRI is not accidental. The problem is that it is predicated upon peace being broken. To wait until peace is broken before helping might prove to be too late and too costly for both helper and victim. And there is no guarantee that the helper would stay the course if costs escalate. Witness the crises in Liberia and Sierra Leone where, for a long time, save for insubstantial contributions from outside West Africa, that region was made to bear the brunt. Nigeria alone reportedly spent $8 billion in Liberia and $1.6 million a day in Sierra Leone before UNAMSIL stepped in. Perhaps the time has come for Africa as a whole, and West Africa in particular, to develop its own capacity to attack conflict at source and prevent them from escalating into violence in ways that threaten national as well as regional peace and stability. The best preventive strategy is for the states concerned to take the lead in redoubling their own capacity to entrench democracy and fundamental human rights as unifying and civilising elements for, and as critical links between, sustainable peace and sustainable development. This should be at the top of their national agendas. Later on, the rest of Africa and the world can follow. I agree with Boutros Boutros Ghali when he says: "there [is] a critical linkage between peace, development and democracy. Without peace there could be no development. Without both peace and development, democracy could not take root. But democracy [is] the key in the chain: without democracy neither peace nor development could be expected to last long. A people deprived of democratic expression would eventually turn to confrontation and conflict. And development that did not benefit from the freedoms of thought, assembly and expression that democracy provides would slowly fall behind those societies and economies that benefited from democratic creativity."432

To that end, I submit that a permanent international, continental or regional mechanism is needed for electoral supervision at state level. Genuinely democratic periodic elections are not only critical to the democratisation process and to the strengthening of national institutions. They are the leitmotif for the survival of democracy and human rights for that matter in Africa and elsewhere.

The international community could help in three ways. First, it could help in strengthening the democratisation process at the national level via governmental and non-governmental institutions working to enlarge and deepen democracy and human rights. Today there is no dearth of evidence of the desire of the Western Powers, under United States leadership, to claim kudos for the propagation of democratic principles and values throughout the countries of the world. This is unobjectionable. However, what is sometimes difficult to comprehend is their desire to shirk the correlative responsibility that this carries. These Powers must know from their historical experience that propagating their fundamental beliefs and values inevitably carries correlative benefits and burdens. Accepting the benefit while rejecting the burden of democracy and freedom is not only self-defeating but is capable of undermining international security as a whole. The Western Powers cannot therefore afford to abdicate responsibility in this regard; they must be fully engaged if the world is to become a safer and better place for everybody.

Second, it could help in establishing and funding a permanent international, continental or regional electoral supervision mechanism.

Third, with carnage and wanton destruction characterising most recent insurgencies in Africa, it could help in entrenching in public institutions a culture of respect for democracy and fundamental human rights. This is necessary if change in mentality is to be effected in the judiciary, election commissions, police, army, public service, schools and colleges, adult educational programmes, religious institutions, the media and in the body politic as a whole.

I submit all these as necessary and urgent. Unless and until the crisis of public confidence in the independence and impartiality of national electoral and judicial systems is halted and reversed, responsibility for electoral supervision, not mere monitoring, should be vested in an impartial international agency, be it at continental or regional level. It would ensure that the elections are not only fair but are seen to be fair, in order to elicit unqualified public acceptance of their verdict. For countries emerging from the throes of civil war, this strategy could be made an essential part of any integrated conflict prevention or post-conflict peace-building support structures.

National electoral commissions work better where the embedding of democratic values and fundamental human rights has taken deeper root on national soil. That stage has not yet been reached in many developing countries, despite more than four decades of independence. It will come but naturally it will take time. For the present, an external electoral supervisory mechanism seems more ideal to their particular circumstance. Only politicians who see nothing wrong in defrauding the electorate would object to impartial international electoral supervision. If they have defrauded a first time, they have no right to expect to be trusted a second time, because they could easily do worse.

Imagine a government that is genuinely democratically elected, adheres to a national democratic constitution, respects fundamental human and constitutional rights of its people, including in particular the rights of the democratic opposition, and avoids doing things that shock and outrage the public conscience. Which army chieftain would have a reasonable excuse to want to overthrow it? In plain truth, this is where the line of demarcation runs between the politics of the First and Third Worlds. It also accounts for the rarity of *coups* in the former and their surfeit in the latter.

Some might object to the proposal on the grounds that it might introduce a new form of neo-colonialism and militate against the hallowed doctrine of national sovereignty. With regard to neo-colonialsm, it is not a new thing. The phenomenon has been creeping into the developing world in a variety of ways. For example, since the 1980s, aid-dependence has brought a new form of monitoring by the International Monetary Fund. Countries implementing economic reform programmes often require the IMF's seal of approval to qualify them for more aid or debt relief from donors such as the Paris Club or the European Union. The United States issues annual certificates, signifying how well or badly a country is doing in combating drug trafficking in order to qualify for further United States aid.[433]

With regard to the dilution of national sovereignty, it may be argued international electoral supervision dilutes a country's sovereignty no more than that country's membership of economic integration organisations. The bulwark against creeping neo-colonialism is for countries themselves to practice good governance and self-reliance, including in particular the conduct of genuinely democratic elections, respect for fundamental human rights and upholding the rule of law. In any event, the phenomenon of globalisation is nowadays slowly neutralising the concept of the nation-state. Kofi Annan is right when he says that: "State sovereignty, in its most basic sense, is being redefined – not least by the forces of globalisation and international co-operation. States are now widely understood to be instruments at the service of their peoples, and not *vice versa*. At the same time individual sovereignty - by which I mean the fundamental freedom of each individual, enshrined in the Charter of the UN and subsequent international treaties - has been enhanced by a renewed and spreading consciousness of individual rights. When we read the Charter today, we are more than ever conscious that its aim is to protect individual human beings, not to protect those who abuse them."[434] Chief Emeka Anyaoku, former Commonwealth Secretary-General, reinforces this thinking. "The nation state in many respects is under siege," he says. "In some cases, it is too large to provide a means of identity or a channel of participation for the individual, but also in an increasing number of cases, it is too small to be able to confront the new challenges of a globalised world."[435]

As long as developing countries continue to be weighed down by the albatrosses of mass illiteracy, excruciating poverty and ethnic divisiveness, the contest for state political power will continue to run along regional, ideological or ethnic lines. If the contest is not conducted fairly, or is perceived as being conducted unfairly, it would create resentment and foster an environment for violent response. To avoid this, new mechanisms are required in such countries, particularly in plural societies, that could inspire public confidence in the independence, impartiality and fairness of the national institutions that dispense justice and conduct elections. Without such public confidence, no amount of foreign aid and no degree of pious hope would make the difference between peace and conflict. And without reform, guided by enlightened self-interest and liberal principles, the prospects for future crises, particularly in plural and divided societies, will remain unlimited.

When democracy will have taken firm root throughout the developing world, and because of the great values it seeks to protect, it could evolve as a peremptory norm or a *jus cogens* rule of international law. That is to say, it will become a norm that enjoys a higher rank in the international hierarchy than treaties or rules of customary international law. One obvious consequence would be to deny any derogation that is not universally recognised, and every state would have more than a common interest, in a peaceful manner, to protect it with all its might.

---

[1] Larry Siedentop, *Democracy in Europe* p. 22

[2] *New African*, November 1999, No. 379, p. 45.

[3] For example, on July 20, 1998, General Abdulsalam Abubakar, the Nigerian Head of State who succeeded General Sani Abacha, stated that "Nigerians want nothing less than true democracy in a united and peaceful country.... where fairness, justice and equality are not mere slogans." To clear the slate of late General Abacha's malignant influence, General Abubakar dissolved all political parties, seized their assets, cancelled the results of all elections and sacked the national electoral commission. As *The Times* editorial of July 22 commented: "These political institutions were not merely defective; they were deliberately created in order to perpetuate the Abacha regime. This was a system rigged by and for the military.....The genuine independence of this commission will thus be a key test of whether Nigeria's highly politicised military really intends to keep its hand off the tiller...That is something that international observers, whose involvement General Abubakar has requested, should immediately make their concern.....He has asked his countrymen to take a great deal on trust; and trust, among people thrust into the ninth circle of hell, is quite properly in short supply."

[4] The other contesting political parties were the United Progressive Party (UPP), the National Council, the Labour Party, the Sierra Leone Independence Movement and the Kono Progressive Movement.

[5] According to Foray, "the 1962 elections have so far been the freest and fairest elections held in Sierra Leone". C.P. Foray, *The Road to the One Party State: The Sierra Leone Experience* (1988), p. 5.

[6] Siaka Stevens, *What Life Has Taught Me* (1984), p. 203.

[7] As reaffirmed by President Momoh in a Speech to the Extraordinary National Delegates Conference of the APC on 4 October 1991: "From its founding the APC Party has been dedicated to the common people – a populist party based on the belief that the ultimate goal of government is the well-being of the people. This party was founded out of concern for the downtrodden. It was to be their protector against physical abuse, tribalism, élitism and cronyism. Unfortunately, and probably as a result of the lethargy created by non-competitive politics, the party lost sight of some of these concerns. As of today, we must therefore reaffirm our faith in these values of equality, freedom and justice, which motivated the founders of the party three decades ago. As such, our focus must be on the people of Sierra Leone, their needs and aspirations." See also Siaka Stevens, *What Life Has Taught Me*, An Autobiography, (1984).

[8] Sierra Leone became a British Crown Colony on January 1, 1808.

[9] Adam Hochschild, *King Leopold's Ghost* (Macmillan, 1999)

[10] Roger Tangri, *Politics in Sub-Saharan Africa* (1985), p. 29.

[11] William J. Foltz, "Political Opposition in Single-Party States of Tropical Africa," in Robert A. Dahl (ed.), *Regimes and Oppositions* (1973), p. 148.

[12] Siaka Stevens, op. cit., p. 163.

[13] Ruth First, *The Barrel of a Gun, Political Power in Africa and the Coup d'Etat (1970)*, p. 102.

[14] Roger Cohen, "Marble Mogul Caters to the Nigerian Capital's Elite," in *The New York Times*, 30 July 1998, p. A4.

[15] Quoted in Richard Jefferies, *Class, Power and Ideology in Ghana: the Railwaymen of Sekondi-Takoradi* (1978), p. 125.

[16] Michael Cohen, *Urban Policy and Political Conflict in Africa: A Study of the Ivory Coast* (1974), p. 62.

[17] Siaka Stevens, *What Life Has Taught Me* (1984), p. 234.

[18] John Cartwright, "The Limits to Leadership: Sierra Leone Under the Margais," in *Politics in Africa: Dependence and Development* (ed. by Shaw & Heard), pp. 147-148.

[19] Act No. 46 of 1965.

[20] Cartwright, ibid. p. 145. See also Christopher Allen, "Sierra Leone," in (ed. by John Dunn), *West African States: Failure and Promise – A Study in Comparative Politics* (1978), pp. 190-192; Fred Hayward, "Sierra Leone: state consolidation, fragmentation and decay" in (ed. by Donal Cruise O'Brien, John Dunn and Richard Rathbone*), Contemporary West African States* (!989), pp. 165-180; Martin Kilson, *Political Change in a West African State* (1966).

[21] The validity of this Act as against the Constitution of 1991 now needs to be tested in the courts particularly s. 26 thereof.

[22] Foray asserts that: "The issues, apprehended or actual, were the change from a monarchical to a republican constitution, with its corollary, the one-party state". Op. cit., p. 19.

[23] The arrested officers were Col. John Bangura, Major M.S. Tarawalli, Captain Jawara, Captain Abu Noah, Captain Francis Johnson, Captain Seray-Wurie, Lt. George Caulker, and Lt Josaiah.

[24] Christopher Allen, op. cit. p. 191. The Dove-Edwin Commission of Inquiry Report on the conduct of the 1967 General Elections stated, in part: "There can be little doubt that Sir Albert Margai was prevented from staging a wholly falsified election by the fear of opposition from those areas where his personal influence carried little or no weight....... Just as all cash crop producers had been threatened with bankruptcy by the political patronage exercised over the SLPMB so the lower echelons of the civil service and the army became increasingly worried by the politicisation of those in authority."

[25] The SLPP won only one seat in the North (A.H. Kandeh in Koinadugu) and vice versa for the APC in the South (Mr Valesius Neale-Caulker in Moyamba). In the Western Region, including Freetown, the SLPP did not win a single seat.

[26] Roger Tangri, *Politics in Sub-Saharan Africa* (1985), p. 38.

[27] *Lansana v R* (1970-71) ALR-SL 186, 196.

[28] Thomas S. Cox, *Civil-Military Relations in Sierra Leone: A Case Study of African Soldiers in Politics* (1976), p. 74.

[29] Ibid., p. 134-5

[30] John R. Cartwright, *Politics in Sierra Leone 1947-67* (Univ. of Toronto Press, 1970), p. 251

[31] Foray, op. cit. p. 20

[32] Cox. Op. cit., pp. 136-7

[33] Siaka Stevens, op. cit., p. 270.

[34] Joe A.D. Alie, *A New history of Sierra Leone* (1990), p. 248.

[35] His Deputy, Brigadier Julius Maada Bio, ousted Captain Strasser in a bloodless palace *coup* on 16 January 1996.

[36] Robert D. Kaplan, "The coming anarchy: how scarcity, crime, overpopulation and disease are rapidly destroying the social fabric of our planet," in *Atlantic Monthly*, February 1994, pp. 44-76. See also, Kaplan, *To the Ends of the Earth* (1997).

[37] But see the RUF publication, *Footpaths to Democracy: Toward a New Sierra Leone*, vol. 1 (1995).

[38] *Sierra Leone Web*, Documents.

[39] Paul Richards, Fighting for the Rain Forest: War Youth & Resources in Sierra Leone (1996), p. xvii.

[40] See Arthur Abraham, "War and Transition to Peace: A Study of State Conspiracy in Perpetuating Armed Conflict," in (1997) 22 Africa Development 101, at p. 103.

[41] *New African*, November 1999, No 379, p. 45

[42] The Nigerian High Commissioner to Sierra Leone alleged that "Sankoh was held in Nigeria by security forces for entering into the country with a pistol and ammunition." *Sierra Leone Web*, 12 March 1997. Sankoh denied this: "I came here to see General Abacha, the Chairman of Ecowas, for his contribution to the peace accord. There is a delay and I have not yet seen him. I think the government in Sierra Leone has a hand in the delay.....we can call it psychological warfare." Regarding allegations that he had breached Nigerian laws, prohibiting the illegal importation of firearms, he said: "Four bullets were found in the suitcase of my bodyguard". Ibid., 22 May 1997. In any case, Sankoh was never charged to court.

[43] Palmer was later reported as blaming their troubles on President Kabbah whom he accused of playing "a double role by promising us

political and financial support if we are to overthrow Sankoh and sign an agreement of co-operation with his administration." Ibid. 29 December 1997.

[44] Quoted in a State House Press Release of 18 February 1997.

[45] *The Economist*, 21 February 1998, p. 72.

[46] Major-General Victor Malu, Field Commander of Ecomog was reported as saying that "there is no need for panic over the non-evacuation of Nigerians in Sierra Leone.---He promised the safety of both Nigerians and other nationals in Sierra Leone." *BBC Summary of World Broadcasts*, 6 June 1997.

[47] Police raided the offices of three newspapers in Freetown on July 2, 1998, arresting the editors of two of them, Joseph Mboka of *The Democrat* and Jonathan Leigh of the *Independent Observer*. Police also went to the offices of the *New Storm* newspaper, but found no one there. The officers, carrying warrants signed by the Attorney-General and Minister of Justice, Solomon Berewa, also searched the newspapers' offices before leaving. The arrests followed a warning by the Minister of Information, Communication, Tourism and Culture, Dr Julius Spencer, the week before, that the government was prepared to crack down on editors who published "disturbing reports likely to cause alarm or despondency to public safety, public tranquility and the maintenance of public order". See ibid, 2 July 1998. It is a bit ironic that Spencer should be seeking to punish journalists considering that he himself had resisted a similar law in 1995 for which he was prosecuted by the NPRC.

[48] *We Yone* Newspaper (Sierra Leone), 25 October 2000.

[49] *Sierra Leone Web*, 26 December 1998.

[50] Ibid. 31 December 1998.

[51] Ibid. 27 December 1998.

[52] Ibid. 4 January 1999.

[53] Ibid. 25 January 1999.

[54] BBC Online Network, 18 January 1999.

[55] *The Times* (editorial), 15 January 1999.

[56] Ibid., 25 May 1997

[57] INEC, Report on the Work of INEC 1994-1996, p. 64.

[58] Id. p.71.

[59] Id. p.73.

[60] *The Vision*, 27 May 1999.

[61] *Sierra Leone Web*, 4 July 1997 (emphasis added).

[62] Sierra Leone Web, 31 May 1997

[63] *The New York Times*, 6 June 1997.

[64] *The Times*, London, 3 June 1997.

[65] HC Debates, 2 March 1999, col. 931(Italics added).

[66] *Sierra Leone Web*, 27 October 1997

[67] The AFRC's casualty figures were 80 dead and over 100 injured, mostly women and children. Hospital sources confirmed at least 62 dead. "Most of the civilians were killed when shells directed at the AFRC's military headquarters at Cockerill Barracks fell instead on residential areas," as reported in the *Sierra Leone Web*, 3 June 1997.

[68] Ibid. 12 June 1997. The AFRC claimed it captured 300 Nigerian soldiers, including 13 officers. Ibid. 3 June 1997.

[69] Ecowas Authority Decision A/DEC.1/8/90 of 7 August 1990.

[70] The initial five were The Gambia, Ghana, Guinea, Nigeria and Sierra Leone.

[71] In addition to the five above, Benin, Burkina Faso, Cote d'Ivoire, Senegal, Mali and Niger later contributed contingents.

[72] Compare Ecomog for Guinea-Bissau in 1998, which had 725 peacekeeping troops from five Ecowas states (Benin, Gambia, Mali, Niger and Togo).

[73] Mali did not send its 428 soldiers until 20 February 1999. According to the Malian government, its troops were to do only peacekeeping duties, not combat duties, in Sierra Leone though the Nigerian Chief of Staff, who welcomed them at Lungi, said: "We are happy that you have come to Sierra Leone as our main constraints have been *fighting* men and logistics" (emphasis added). It is clear that these were entirely two different roles. *Sierra Leone Web*, 20 February 1999.

[74] See reports by Francois-Xavier Harispe in Agence France Presse (AFP), December 17, 1997.

[75] Press Briefing by Ambassador James O.C. Jonah, New York, February 17, 1998 in the *Sierra Leone Web*. Moreover, a senior Nigerian officer was reported as saying on March 17, after the Nigerian army had pushed the junta into the countryside, that contributions of troops from other Ecowas countries were needed to reinforce its final push to dislodge remnants of the junta holding out in eastern Sierra Leone, ibid. 17 March and 30 September 1998.

[76] See UN Doc. S/1999/1003, 8th Report of the Secretary-General on UNOMSIL, 23 September 1999.

[77] President Kabbah is reported to have stated: "For now, Khobe will be in overall charge of ECOMOG operations in Sierra Leone as well as the security system of the country", see *Sierra Leone Web*, 16 April 1998.

[78] *Sierra Leone Web*, 31 August 1997.

[79] Ibid. 1 September 1997.

[80] Ibid. 22 October 1997; *House of Lords Debates*, 27 November 1997.

[81] *Sierra Leone Web.*, 21 October 1997

[82] See Carey W. English, "Sierra Leone: A coup plotter is tripped up," in *U.S. News & World Report*, 9 February 1998, p. 48; *The Globe and Mail* (Toronto), 1 August 1997.

[83] *Sierra Leone Web,* 8 July 1997 in which the AFRC spokesman was reported as alleging that "the *kamajors* are being supplied arms and ammunition by Nigeria." See also ibid. 20 June and 26 November 1997; *New Africa Magazine* for December 1997; and Howard French, A West Africa Border and Back-to-Back Wars, *New York Times,* 25 January 1998, p. 3 for independent reports.

[84] *Sierra Leone Web,* 25 January 1998. The *kamajor* leader, Chief Hinga Norman, reportedly told the BBC on January 19 that "Tongo [a major diamond mining area} is going to be a tug of war. I can tell you that all civil defence fighters throughout the country will be summoned to retake Tongo." Ibid. 19 January 1998.

[85] *Sierra Leone Web,* 18 June 1998

[86] Ibid., 27 June 1997

[87] Ibid. 20 July 1997. Again on July 28, the radio confirmed that the Nigerian forces were already enforcing an air, sea and land embargo against Sierra Leone, citing Khobe's warning to "all ship owners, shipping agents, airlines, and travel agents that any violation of the sanction and embargo by them will be at their own risk."

[88] Ibid., 31 July 1997

[89] *New Nigerian,* 4 August 1997

[90] *Sierra Leone Web,* 3 August 1997

[91] Ibid. 6 August 1997. He repeated this warning on 5 September, saying: "This final warning has become necessary in view of the continuous attempt by some unscrupulous shippers to violate the Ecowas embargo in total disregard for the Heads of State of the sub-region. Henceforth, any ship or aircraft seen violating the Ecowas economic embargo shall be doing so at their own risk as they will be attacked by the ECOMOG force," ibid. 5 September 1997.

[92] Ibid., 8 August 1997

[93] Ibid., 31 July 1997

[94] Ibid. quoting from *The Expo Times.*

[95] *Sierra Leone Web,* 28 September 1997.

[96] Ibid. 11 September 1997. Similarly, on 23 September, the Nigerian army threatened to bomb the *MV Sky* if she attempted to berth in Freetown. The ship was reportedly carrying dozens of containers of provisions and other consumer goods, including sugar, which had been ordered by merchants in Freetown.

[97] UN Office of Humanitarian Affairs Internal Report, February 1998.

[98] *Sierra Leone Web,* 12 September 1997.

[99] Ibid. 16 November 1997.

[100] Ibid. 10 December 1997.

[101] *Sierra Leone Web,* 3 June 1997.

[102] *House of Lords Debates,* col. 99-100, 10 March 1998.

[103] *House of Commons*, 12 March 1998, col. 842.

[104] OAU CM/DEC.373 (LXVII); OAU CM/Dec.356 (LXVI) Sierra Leone – Doc. CM/2004 (LXVI) –c.

[105] Before this, President Laurent-Desire Kabila had installed himself as Head of State of the Democratic Republic of the Congo (Kinshasa) in May 1997 after a multi-national insurgency which resulted in the capitulation of the established and internationally recognised government of President Mobutu Sese Seko. Again the OAU was most eloquent by its silence as was also the case with the *coup* in Niger in 1999 in which President Manassira was assassinated.

[106] S/1997/499

[107] The four members of the Committee were Nigeria (chair), Cote d'Ivoire, Ghana and Guinea. Later, after the Liberian elections of July 1997, Liberia was added as a fifth member and the Committee was renamed the Committee of Five.

[108] Emphasis added. The ECOMOG Force Commander, Major-General Victor Malu stated on July 1 that: "If after two weeks of consultation they report to the Chairman that these people are still adamant in reversing the situation as it is supposed to be, then all the measures can be applied at the same time." Sierra Leone Web, 1 July 1997.

[109] *Sierra Leone Web*, 18 August 1997

[110] Consensus Statement by the Alliance for Peace and Democracy in Sierra Leone on the Situation in Sierra Leone – Call for an Ecowas Peace Plan for Sierra Leone," issued on 25 August 1997 and published in the *Sierra Leone Web*, paras. 7 and 9. See also the Resolution of the Standing Conference on Sierra Leone adopted on 22 September 1997.

[111] ICG Sierra Leone Project, Sierra Leone Situation Analysis, February 1998.

[112] S/PRST/1997/36, 11 July 1997.

[113] Sierra Leone Web, 11 July 1997

[114] The dialogue that Chief Ikimi had denied to the AFRC delegation, he claimed for himself when he presented Nigeria's case to the 54th session of the UN Commission on Human Rights in Geneva on 15 April 1998. "A few powerful countries should not be allowed to use their subjective criteria as yardsticks to judge, condemn and malign others. They should not use the human rights issues at the UN merely as tools to project their narrow foreign policy interests and objectives. Efforts should be made at all levels to recognise the importance of consultations and dialogue among member states as these offer immense potentials to influence political leaders not only in the promotion of human rights but also in enhancing international relations as a whole," he said.

[115] Ibid., 2 July 1997

[116] Ibid.

[117] Ibid., 30 July 1997

[118] Ibid., 31 July 1997

[119] Letter of 31 July 1997 from the Chairman of the AFRC to the Foreign Secretary of the AFRC published in the *Sierra Leone Web*.

[120] S/PRST/1997/42, 6 August 1997.

[121] For the text of the Ecowas Peace Plan for Sierra Leone, see Security Council Document S/1997/824.

[122] See the observations of the Standing Conference on Sierra Leone on the Ecowas Peace Plan for Sierra Leone signed in Conakry on 23 October 1997.

[123] BBC despatches from Elizabeth Blunt in Freetown, 12 November 1997.

[124] Sierra Leone Web, 12 November 1997.

[125] Ibid. 18 December 1997.

[126] *Sierra Leone Web*, 21 December 1997.

[127] *Sierra Leone Web*, 5 and 6 February 1998.

[128] Agence France Presse, 10 February 1998.

[129] *Sierra Leone Web*, 11 February 1998.

[130] Press Briefing by Ambassador James Jonah, New York, 17 February 1998.

[131] Id., 20 October 1997.

[132] S/1997/886

[133] *Sierra Leone Web*, 12 November 1997.

[134] Article 5 of the Decision stipulated that: "Member States shall abstain from shipping and delivering humanitarian goods to the illegal regime, except with the approval of the Authority of Heads of State and Government of Ecowas."

[135] For the text, see S/1998/1232.

[136] President Kabbah's Address to the Nation, 21 February 1999 (S/1999/186).

[137] President Kabbah's Address to the Nation, 1 February 1999. At the same time, his Chief of Defence Staff, Major-General Maxwell Khobe, in a press conference in Lagos on 3 February, accused Angola, Burkina Faso, Cote d'Ivoire and Ukraine. *Pana News Agency*, 3 February 1999.

[138] Ibid. 29 January 1999.

[139] The Malian troops arrived on 19 and 20 February 1999.

[140] Ibid. 21 January 1999.

[141] Sam Kiley, "Send in the mercenaries, Mr Cook," *The Times*, 22 January 1999, p. 20.

[142] HC Debates, 2 March 1999, col. 899.

[143] Okelo was reported as saying that Sankoh was "100 percent committed to peace....He is willing to order a ceasefire and recognise the legitimacy of President Kabbah." Amara Essy and Koffigoh reported that

Sankoh had expressed "his willingness for peace" and for a "political, not a military solution" to the crisis. *Sierra Leone Web*, 12 January 1999.

[144] *Sierra Leone Web*, 15 January 1999.

[145] *Sierra Leone Web*, 17 January 1999.

[146] AFP, 3 March 1999.

[147] So say the British Foreign Secretary, see HC Debates, 19 January 1999, col. 710.

[148] Ibid. 28 January 1999; *Pana News Agency*, 28 January 1999; *Africa Confidential*, Vol. 40, No. 3, 5 February 1999, p. 3; James Walker, "Problems loom for Nigerian economy," in BBC News website, 17 February 1999.

[149] In reaction to President Kabbah's national broadcast of 1 February, the *Standard Times*, 5 February 1999, wrote the following leader: "Notwithstanding the rebels' unreliability, Sierra Leoneans would have loved to hear in President Kabbah's speech attempts by the government to lure the rebels to a negotiating table. Since that did not happen, many thought President Kabbah is not serious about bringing the eight-year-old rebellion to a close. And since peace is not on President Kabbah's agenda, many are wondering how and where his government will start off from after the dust shall have settled following the month long upheaval. Indeed, to many Sierra Leoneans, the speech was nothing but a disappointment."

[150] On 2 February 1999, a spokesman for the Nigerian leader, General Abdulsalami Abubakar, told a news conference in Abuja that Nigeria was urging President Kabbah to negotiate with the RUF. "Nigeria has been talking to Tejan Kabbah about negotiating with the rebel leader if that will be s step to a solution," the spokesman said, adding that Nigeria hopes to pull out the troops before handing over to a civilian administration. *Sierra Leone Web*, 2 February 1999.

[151] President Kabbah's Address to the Nation, 1 February 1999.

[152] *Sierra Leone Web*, 2 February 1999.

[153] Ibid. 11 February 1999.

[154] Ibid.

[155] *Sierra Leone Web*, 7 February 1999.

[156] Ibid. 8 February 1999.

[157] Resolution 1220 (1999) of 12 January 1999.

[158] See President Kabbah's Address to the Nation, 28 February 1999; Fifth Report of the UN Secretary-General on UNOMSIL, S/1999/237 of 4 March 1999.

[159] *Sierra Leone Web*, 15 March 1999.

[160] See S/1999/20, paras. 14 and 15.

[161] HC Debates, 19 January 1999, col. 710.

[162] Press Statement by M. Lee McClenny, Acting Spokesman, US Department of State, 28 December 1998; *Sierra Leone Web*, 7 January 1999.

[163] Policy Statement by the Government of Liberia on Allegations by the Government of Sierra Leone and the ECOMOG High Command at the Extraordinary Meeting of the Committee of Five on Sierra Leone of the Involvement of the Government of Liberia in the Civil Crisis in Sierra Leone, Monrovia, Liberia, 29 December 1998. See also S/1999/193.

[164] *Sierra Leone Web*, 31 December 1998.

[165] S/1999/213.

[166] S/1999/193.

[167] See a Press Statement by the Liberian Minister of Justice and Attorney-General, 24 February 1999.

[168] HC Debates, 1997, col. 625.

[169] *House of Commons Debates*, 6 May 1998, vol. 311, col. 727.

[170] Italics added.

[171] Sir Thomas Legg and Sir Robin Ibbs, *Report of the Sierra Leone Arms Investigation* (House of Commons Paper 1016, 27 July 1998), p. 15.

[172] Legg and Ibbs, op. cit., p. 15

[173] Even after President Kabbah had been restored, the British Government was still reluctant to allow arms to reach Ecomog. In answer to a parliamentary question on the matter, the British Foreign Secretary said: "[W]e shall consider any such request. However, ...there is an embargo against Nigeria. Progress in meeting such a request must be balanced against progress within Nigeria on the democratic track, which, at some future time, we are ready to reward with a winding down of the embargo that was placed on the previous military junta." HC Debates, 19 January 1999, col. 711.

[174] H.C. Debates, 12 March 1998, col 841 (emphasis added). See also the Second Report of the House of Commons Select Committee on Foreign Affairs, Vol. 1, 3 February 1999, paras. 16-19 for similar interpretations of the resolution. However, the Sierra Leone Sanctions Order in Council made it clear that the arms embargo applied to all parties in the Sierra Leone conflict.

[175] Ibid. para. 19

[176] Article 7 of Resolution 1132 (1997).

[177] S/RES/788 (1992) of 19 Nov. 1992.

[178] S/RES/917 (1994) of 6 May 1994.

[179] See S/RES/1127 (1997) of 28 August 1997, and UN Press Release SC/6479 of 23 February 1998; for Iraq see S/RES/1137 (1997) of 12 November 1997.

[180] SC/6472

[181] *New African*, "American justice: Sierra Leonean diplomat rots in New York jail without trial," No. 385, May 2000, p. 36.

[182] Letter dated 20 September 1999 from Peter Hain, Minister of State in the FCO to Lord Avebury. This apology was repeated again in another letter from the Minister to Lord Avebury on November 9 as follows: "I would like to take this opportunity to repeat my apologies for the failure of communication between the FCO and the Immigration Service which inconvenienced Dr Bundu in June. We will do our utmost to prevent such mistakes from recurring."

[183] *The Times* (leader), 8 May 1998. See also Berthan Macauley, op. cit.

[184] A British Foreign office official was reported as saying: "It is clear that it [the resolution] applied to the good guys as well as the bad guys. That was clearly understood when the resolution was transcribed into British law. That is the way it was written. You may think that was stupid, but the only way to put yourself on the right side of the argument is to get the law changed." Contrast Mark Weller, "London was right to provide support," in *The Times*, 12 May 1998, p. 13.

[185] Select Committee Report, op. cit., para. 13. But the UN Legal Adviser seems to have overlooked the practice of the organisation whereby preventive and enforcement measures are only taken against "states", not against non-state entities. This is why, usually, in drafting UN sanctions decisions within the context of internal armed conflicts, the imposition is directed at the state and then exemptions are made for those who are not intended to be affected. Accordingly the UK was correct when its law imposed the embargo against Sierra Leone as a state (see Article 2 of the UN Charter).

[186] *The Times*, 21 May 1998

[187] *Sierra Leone Web*, 11 February 1999.

[188] *Commonwealth Press Release*, No. 99/08, 2 February 1999.

[189] See S/1999/237 of 4 March 1999. See also Chapter 9.

[190] *The Economist*, May 16-22, 1998, pp. 29-30

[191] *House of Commons Debates*, 18 May 1998, col. 648

[192] HC Debates, 19 February 1999, col. 710.

[193] See *House of Lord Debates*, 27 November 1997 (emphasis added).

[194] See (1990) 13 ILM 1323-36, 1561-56.

[195] See L.C. Green, *The contemporary law of armed conflict* (1993), p. 322

[196] HC Debates, 19 January 1999, cols. 707-711; Letter dated 19 February 1999 from robin Cook to Lord Avebury.

[197] Tony Lloyd's letter of 3 March 1998 to Lord Avebury stated, in part: "You ask whether we had any prior knowledge of the Nigerian military intervention in Sierra Leone. The answer is that we did not. We were not therefore in a position to dissuade ECOMOG from such a course of

action. We agree that the action was not covered by a Security Council mandate; we have said so."

[198] S/1997/958, para. 21 (emphasis added).

[199] S/1998/103, 5 February 1998, Third Report of the UN Secretary-General on the Situation in Sierra Leone, para. 26.

[200] S/1998/103, para. 28.

[201] Paragraph 14 of Resolution 1132 (1997)

[202] *Sierra Leone Web*, 6 October 1997

[203] Ibid., 9 September 1997

[204] Sierra Leone Humanitarian Situation Report, 16-30 September 1997, prepared by the UN Department of Humanitarian Affairs, para. 8.

[205] There was some attempt to talk as if there were two separate and distinct sets of sanctions, one imposed by the Security Council and the other by Ecowas. For instance, President Kabbah in his 1997 Christmas Message to the Nation of 25 December said: "At Christmas time last year, there were no United Nations and Ecowas sanctions". The Third Report of the Secretary-General (S/1998/103, para. 16) referred to the "enforcement of both Ecowas and United Nations sanctions by Ecomog forces". Legally speaking there was only one set of lawful and binding sanctions and embargo, and that is the one imposed by Security Council resolution 1132 on 8 October 1997. The embargo, however called, was an enforcement action and, as such, no regional agency can impose it without the specific authorisation of the Security Council under Article 53(1) of the UN Charter.

[206] UN Department of Humanitarian Affairs, Sierra Leone Humanitarian Situation Report 3-19 December 1997, para. 9. In his Third Report (S/1998/103), the Secretary-General stated that:

> "The requirement that ECOMOG inspect humanitarian shipments at the border of Sierra Leone and Guinea has now been entrusted by Ecowas to the Guinean army. However, the Government of Guinea has also requested that Ecowas provide inspectors to supervise the task of the Guinean troops. Ecowas has requested United Nations assistance in financing this deployment of inspectors, and United Nations agencies have indicated that they will do this on a cost-sharing basis."

[207] Sierra Leone Web, 14 February 1998.

[208] *House of Lords Debates*, 21 January 1998.

[209] The British Minister of State in the Foreign and Commonwealth Office, Tony Lloyd, stated in the House of Commons that: "The most immediate requirement is for a humanitarian relief effort, to which we are ready to make a major contribution. The Department for International Development (DFID) has sent an expert to the region to liaise with the UN and NGOs over the quickest and most effective way to achieve this."

302

House of Commons Debates, 2 March 1998. *The Times*, 5 March 1998 reported that a British naval frigate, HMS Cornwall, had supplied emergency food and medical aid to vulnerable families in Freetown. The ship's captain said that the scenes in Freetown were "harrowing" and that his medical team had found large numbers of people whose injuries from the fighting had been untreated. Children were also suffering from malnutrition.

[210] S/1998/155.

[211] UN Press Release SC/6481, 26 February 1998.

[212] S/PRST/1998/5 of 26 February 1998.

[213] The Alliance for Peace and Democracy in Sierra Leone wrote to the British Prime Minister on January 7, 1998 to appeal to his government to take a firm stand against the illegal Nigerian blockade of Sierra Leone, contrary to resolution 1132. This was preventing humanitarian supplies from coming in, resulting in the further deterioration of the situation, which by then was spiralling into a crisis. The letter stated in part: "We would be most grateful for any action you might take to ensure that the people of Sierra Leone get the humanitarian assistance they need. To the extent that your government had played a lead role in the search for a peaceful solution to the crisis within the framework of the United Nations Security Council, so we plead that it now takes a lead in ensuring that the Council's resolution is not misapplied by anyone. This plea, we might add, is born not only of the historical ties between the peoples of the United Kingdom and Sierra Leone but also of the international obligation of the United Kingdom as a permanent member of the Security Council".

[214] *House of commons Debates*, 3 June 1998, col. 355.

[215] See the Security Presidential Statements of 27 May (S/PRST/1997/29), 11 July 1997 (S/PRST/1997/36) and 6 August 1997 (S/PRST/1997/42).

[216] Nigeria has seen some 15 attempted and successful *coups* and has been ruled by military juntas for 29 out of its 39 years of independence. Washington regards the Nigerian military regime headed by General Sani Abacha as "politically illegitimate and undemocratic---," reported Thomas Lippman, "US Ready to Train African Peace-Keepers," *Washington Post*, 4 July 1997.

[217] *The Economist*, 17-23 January 1998, p. 61.

[218] Press Statement on the Situation in Sierra Leone by the United States Department of State, 13 February 1998.

[219] S/PRST/1998/5, 26 February 1998.

[220] *Sierra Leone Web*, 2 March 1999.

[221] John L. Hirsch, "Saving Sierra Leone," in *The Washington Post*, 4 March 1999, p. A21.

[222] ARTICLE 19 Press Release, 2 March 1999.

[223] See generally L.T. Galloway, *Recognising Foreign Governments: the Practice of the United States* (1978).

[224] Press Briefing, 1 May 1978, pp. 12-13. See also (1978) 72 A.J.I.L. 879.

[225] Press Statement by John Dinger, Acting Spokesman of the U.S. Department of State, 26 May 1997.

[226] *Sierra Leone Web*, 5 December 1997. On December 4, 1997, it was reported that lawyers representing the exile government had succeeded in obtaining an injunction from the English courts to restrain the currency printing firm, Thomas de la Rue, from printing billions of the Sierra Leone national currency for the AFRC under a contract. The new notes were intended for circulation in Sierra Leone at the end of that month.

[227] See (1974) XX *Annuaire Francais du Droit International*, pp. 1031-1033.

[228] P. Jessup, The Estrada Doctrine, (1931) 25 A.J.I.L. 719.

[229] House of Commons Debates, vol. 485, cols. 2410-2411 (emphasis added), quoted in D.J. Harris, *Cases and Materials on International Law* (second ed., 1979) pp. 145-146; Colin Warbrick, "The New British Policy on Recognition of Governments," (1981) 30 I.C.L.Q. 568-592; C. R. Symmons, "United Kingdom Abolition of the Doctrine of Recognition of Governments: A Rose by Another Name?" (1981) Public Law 249-262. The British practice in the fifties was heavily influenced by the writings of Sir Hersch Lauterpacht, *Recognition in International Law* (1947) at pp. 61-66, 88 where he argued that there was a duty to recognise once the conditions for recognition had been fulfilled.

[230] See generally A. C. Bundu, "Recognition of Revolutionary Authorities: Law and Practice of States," (1978) 27 I.C.L.Q. 18. An important instance in which the British policy was not applied was in respect of East Germany before 1973 which has been explained by reference to the legal responsibility the Soviet Union then had for the territory under the post-war accords, see F.A. Mann, "Germany's Present Legal Status Revisited," (1967) 16 I. C. L.Q. 273.

[231] *House of Lords Debates*, vol. 408,cols. 1121-1122.

[232] Ibid., vol. 409 cols. 1097-1098 (emphasis added).

[233] See Crawford, "Decisions of British Courts during 1985-86 involving Questions of Public or Private International Law," (1986) 57 BYIL 405; Ian Brownlie, "Recognition in Theory and Practice," (1982), pp. 53, 197.

[234] Per Hobhouse J in *Republic of Somalia v. Woodhouse Drake & Carey (Suisse) SA and Others (The Mary)* [1993] 1 All ER 371, 380; Mann, *Foreign Affairs in English Courts* (1986).

[235] See Warbrick, op. cit. p. 575, note 35.

[236] Id., p. 576, note 36; *The Times*, 17 September 1980, p.5.

[237] S/PRST/1997/31 of 29 May 1997.

[238] HL Debates, 30 October 1997, col. 262, Written Answers.

[239] HL Debates, 8 April 1998, Written Answers.

[240] S/PRST/1997/47 of 16 October 1997. The EU issued a similar statement in November which the UK supported; S/1997/8 14 of 21 October 1997.

[241] The United States representative in the Security Council, Mr Burleigh, pointed out that the Foreign Minister of Angola had made a public commitment that his country's forces would be withdrawn by 15 November, adding that "we expect this commitment to be honoured". Yet, according to the Portuguese newspaper *Diario de Noticias* of 27 December 1997, the Angolan military forces continued to remain in Brazzaville with no prospects of an early return home. The report continues as follows: "During his recent visit to Paris, Nguesso said that the Angolan troops, estimated to number 1,500, would stay 'for as long as possible'. The presence of the Angolan soldiers in the Congolese capital is discreet but strategically significant. Law and order are being maintained by the Angolans, especially in and around the airport but also in Pointe Noire and in the southern region of Dolisie, former President Pascal Lissouba's home territory......The Angolan troops guarding Brazzaville airport are quartered in the top floor of the air traffic control tower. Those in the streets of the capital are seen in small numbers and keep a low profile."

[242] The rivalry between Britain and France, often reflected in Anglophone and Francophone dichotomy in Africa, was made a relic of nineteenth-century colonial history in March 1999, when, in keeping with a decision of the Anglo-French summit in Saint-Malo in December 1998, a joint visit was undertaken by the two countries' Foreign Ministers to Ghana and Cote d'Ivoire. According to press reports, Robin Cook and Hubert Védrine plan to co-chair the first ever joint meeting of British and French envoys in Africa where they would proclaim a new era of Franco-British co-operation in order, as put by the French Ambassador in London "to contribute to the stability of the African continent as a whole". *The Times*, 9 March 1999, pp. 13 and 23; 11 March 1999, p. 14.

[243] This non-recognition of the political status of a revolutionary regime does not necessarily mean that its *de facto* acts cannot be valid *vis-à-vis* non-recognising states especially if this would lead to injustice, for example, the validity of certificates relating to births, deaths and marriages. See the *Advisory Opinion on Namibia* (1971) I.C.J. Reports 16, 56. In English law, see *Luther v. Sagor* [1921] 1 K. B. 456; per Lord Wilberforce in *Carl Zeiss Stiftung v. Rayner and Keeler, Ltd. (No. 2)* [1966] 2 All E.R. 536, 577; per Lord Simon, P., in *Adams v. Adams*

[1970] 3 All E.R. 572, 587; per Lord Denning in *Re James* [1977] 1 All E.R. 364, 370 and per Scarman, L.J. at p. 377; per Lord Denning in *Hesperides Hotels Ltd. v. Aegean Turkish Holidays Ltd.* [1978] 1 All E.R. 277, 283; D.W. Greig, "The Carl Zeiss Case and the Position of an Unrecognised Government in English Law," (1967) 87 L.Q.R. 96.

[244] Ibid. p.6

[245] See HL Debates, 3 September 1998, col. 123.

[246] [1939] 1 All ER 719, 722; [1939] A.C. 256, 264-265.

[247] *House of Commons Debates*, 19 June 1997, cols 251-252. See also the FCO Bulletin of 28 May 1997.

[248] *House of Lords Debates*, 12 January 1998

[249] On 22 December 1997, Baroness Symons, in reply to another question, stated in the House of Lords that "Where democratic governments have been overthrown by violence we have often worked with them in exile as part of our global support for democracy." See *House of Lords Debates*, 22 December 1997. This contradicts another statement by an Foreign Office spokesman, in relation to Iraqi exiles, that: "Although we obviously have a similar interest in wanting to see a change of government in Iraq, as a policy we don't recognise governments-in-exile." *The Sunday Times*, 15 February 1998, p. 17.

[250] Ibid.

[251] When Britain withdrew its recognition of Pol Pot in December 1979 as the government of Kampuchea on the grounds of loss of effectiveness, it did not exceptionally accord recognition to the Heng Samrin which it viewed as an entity with no authority independent of its Vietnamese backers. In a sense, therefore, in the eyes of the British Government, Kampuchea was a state without a recognised government. Similarly, on 17 June 1997, the British Minister of State for Foreign and Commonwealth Affairs stated in relation to Sierra Leone after the coup of 25 May, that "it is unclear who, if anyone, is now governing Sierra Leone."

[252] *The Times Law Report*, 25 February 1998; [1998] 2 All ER 821.

[253] [1993] QB 54

[254] See *Buck v. Attorney-General* [1965] Ch. 475, 770 per Diplock L.J; *Underhill v. Hernandez* (1897) 168 U.S. 456, 457 per Fuller C.J.

[255] Quoted in [1998] 2 All ER 821, 829-830

[256] Ibid., p. 830

[257] Ibid

[258] Ibid., pp. 830-831.

[259] [1993] 1 All ER 371; [1993] QB 54.

[260] [1993] 1 All ER 371, 383

[261] Ibid., at p. 383

[262] Ibid., p. 381

[263] Ibid., at pp. 381-2 (emphasis added).

[264] Ibid., at p. 380.

[265] Ibid., at p. 383.

[266] HC Debates, 3 June 1998, col. 354.

[267] See Louise Doswald-Beck, "The Legal Validity of Military Intervention by Invitation of the Government," 56 Brit. Y.B.I.L. 189, 227 (1985); Ved P. Nanda, "The United States Action in the 1965 Dominican Crisis: Impact in World Order – Part II," 44 Denv, L.J. 225 (1967).

[268] See Brad R. Roth, "Governmental Illegitimacy Revisited: 'Pro-Democratic Armed Intervention in the Post-Bipolar World," 3 Transnat'l L. & Contemp. Prob. 481, 488 (1993); Robert J. Beck, "International Law and the Decision to Invade Grenada: A Ten-Year Retrospective," 33 Va. J. Int'l L. 765; Christopher C. Joyner, "The U.S. Action in Grenada: Reflections on the Lawfulness of the Invasion," 78 AJIL 131.

[269] See David J. Scheffer, "Use of Force After the Cold War: Panama, Iraq and the New World Order," in *Right v. Might – International Law and the Use of Force* (Louis Henkin et al. 2nd. Ed., 1991), 109, 118.

[270] Karsten Nowrot & Emily W. Schabacker, "The Use of Force to Restore Democracy: International Legal Implications of the ECOWAS Intervention in Sierra Leone," 13 Am. U. Int'l L. Rev. 321, 385-6

[271] SC Res. 940 (1994) of 31 July 1994.

[272] The only other contingent from an Ecowas member state was the one from Guinea. However, they never participated in any Nigerian military action in Sierra Leone. In any case, according to a Press Release dated 13 Jan. 1998 by the Sierra Leone Embassy in Washington, DC, Guinea had only "100 troops …. in Sierra Leone." See *Sierra Leone Web*.

[273] See *The Times* (Editorial) of 29 May 1997; also of 3 June 1997; *The Financial Times*, 4 June 1997; *The New York Times*, 6 June 1997; *The Guardian*, 9 September 1997; 1997 Report of the Commonwealth Secretary-General to the Commonwealth Heads of Government Meeting in Edinburgh; Final Communiqué of the Commonwealth Heads of Government Meeting in Edinburgh, 24-27 October 1997. It all looked as if the tragedy of Sierra Leone was being used by Nigeria to earn kudos as the champion of democracy in West Africa, deserving of the forgiveness of a grateful international community. See also *New African*, July/August 1997, pp. 16-18; *The News*, 23 June 1997, pp. 12-17.

[274] *Sierra Leone Web*, 25 July 1997.

[275] S/1997/776.

[276] *West Africa*, No. 4175, 24-30 November 1997, p. 1852 (emphasis added).

[277] S/1997/814.

[278] Id.

[279] S/PRST/1997/47 of 16 October 1997.

[280] S/PRST/1997/36 of 11 July and S/PRST/1997/42 of 6 August 1997. The Secretary-General described it as "illegal" in his letter of 7 October 1997 to the President of the Security Council (S/1997/776).

[281] S/1999/976, 14 September 1999, Annex, para. 6.

[282] Simon Jenkins, "A faraway island," *The Times*, 8 September 1999.

[283] H.C. Debates, 24 March 1999, col. 483

[284] Ibid, cols. 485-6

[285] Ibid, col. 484

[286] *The Sunday Times*, 28 March 1999, p. 1.

[287] Quoted in *The Times*, 26 March 1999, p. 6.

[288] *The Times*, 26 March 1999, p. 6.

[289] Quoted in ibid.

[290] Foreign Affairs Committee's Fourth Report on Kosovo, Vol. I, HC 28 – I, 23 May 2000, para. 132.

[291] Cm 4825, pp. 7-8.

[292] See General Assembly Res. 2625 (XXV), 1970, containing the Declaration on Principles of International Law concerning Friendly Relations and Co-operation among states in accordance with the Charter of the United Nations.

[293] 1949 I.C.J. Reports 4, 35. See also *Military and Paramilitary Activities in and against Nicaragua, Merits, (Nicaragua v. U.S.)* 1986 I.C.J. Reports 14, 119.

[294] *House of Commons Debates* June 1997. Also, in reply to another question on 17 June, regarding the time-table for the release of funds for aid projects in Sierra Leone through NGOs, Ms Short said: "The time scale for resumption of normal aid to Sierra Leone, provided through non-governmental agencies, will depend on progress in establishing peace and the return of the democratically elected government of President Kabbah. The Office of the UN Humanitarian Co-ordinator for Sierra Leone has established principles and guidelines for the provision of humanitarian aid. Funding is being provided through EU Humanitarian Office and my Department is also considering bilateral support through the ICRC." Ibid. Col. 615.

Humanitarian considerations seemed also to have informed the British Home Department's classification of Sierra Leone as a country in upheaval. On November 28, 1997, the Minister of State, Mr Mike O'Brien, stated:

> "In view of the situation in Sierra Leone, following the overthrow of the democratically elected government by rebel soldiers, we decided to declare that the country had undergone such a fundamental change of circumstances that we would not normally order the return of a person to that country for the time being. The declaration was made on I July 1997.-----No-one will

be returned to Sierra Leone unless we are satisfied that it is safe to do so.

"The effect of making such a declaration is that a Sierra Leone national who was stranded in the UK and applied for asylum within three months of the declaration being made also became eligible to make a claim for social security benefits while his application was being considered by the Home Office, providing that claim for benefits was lodged within the three-month time scale. All applicants who claim asylum at the port or airport of arrival are eligible to claim social security benefits in a similar way."

Similarly, the United States Attorney-General, Janet Reno, on 28 October 1997, designated Sierra Leone under the Temporary Protected Status pursuant to sections 244(b)(1)(A) and (C) of the Immigration and Nationality Act, as amended (8 U.S.C.A. 1254 (West Supp. 1997) for one year from 4 November 1997. It was renewed for another year in November 1998. About 4,000 Sierra Leoneans in the United States were eligible for TPS. The Attorney-General justified the granting of TPS to Sierra Leoneans on the basis of the ongoing armed conflict in Sierra Leone and that their return to the country would pose a "serious threat to their personal safety as a result of the armed conflict in that nation." See *Federal Register,* 4 November 1997 (Volume 62, No. 213, pp.59736-37).

[295] Authority for this proposition can be found in the Israeli case of *Attorney-General of Israel v. Eichmann* (1962) 36 ILR 5; the American case of *Demjanjuk v. Petrovsky* (1985) 603 F. Supp. 1468, affirmed in 776 F. 2d. 571; and the judgement of the international tribunal for the territory of the former Yugoslavia in *Prosecutor v. Anto Furundzija* of 10 December 1998.

[296] *The Economist,* 18 September 1999.

[297] *West Africa,* No. 4221, 10-16 April 2000.

[298] *Sierra Leone Web,* 30 May 1998

[299] Human Rights Watch, Vol. 10, No. 3(A), July 1998, pp. 4, 23-26.

[300] Amnesty International, Sierra Leone 1998 – *A year of atrocities against civilians* (Nov. 1998), AI Index: AFR 51/22/98.

[301] AI Index: AFR 51/03/99 of 22 January 1999, News Service 015/99.

[302] See BBC News, 13 February 1999; Anne Penketh, "UN accuses Nigerian-led peacekeepers of summary executions," Agence France-Presse (AFP), 12 February 1999; and Judith Miller, "UN monitors accuse Sierra Leone peacekeepers of killings," *The New York Times,* 12 February 1999. See also *Sierra Leone Web,* 12 February 1999, for an account of the summary execution of Abdulai Jumah Jalloh, news editor

of the *African Champion* newspaper by Nigerian soldiers in Freetown on 3 February. See also S/1999/237, 4 March 1999, paras. 20-30.

[303] *The Point*, 9 February 1999, under the caption "98.1 is a killer" on pp. 1 and 2. In another account by Labor Fofana, "Lying Spencer, the people are angry with you," published in *For di People*, 1 February 1999, he wrote: "Julius Spencer...you lied to the people of this city...When Calaba Town and its environs were under heavy firing, you reported that everything was under control and the people need not panic....How unprofessional of you to have said...that government forces were able to rout the rebels because civilians gave you and Ecomog information as to their locations and hide outs....Whether...a shortfall or not, you wilfully exposed the unprotected people of the East and the mid-West to unnecessary horror and terror. Equally so, you deliberately or inadvertently put journalists on the chopping board....Spencer, you must realise that when you talk on the radio...you are doing so as a minister, not as an individual...You could have saved lots of lives if you had pinned your lips."

[304] President Kabbah's Address to the Nation, 21 February 1999 (italics added).

[305] See Simon Bureh Kamara, "Who is afraid of war crimes tribunal?" *New African*, October 2000.

[306] S/2000/915, 4 October 2000, p. 7.

[307] Ibid, p. 5.

[308] See the South African case of *R v. Smith* (1900) 17 SC 561; the German case of *The Llandovery Castle* HMSO, Cmnd. 1422 (1921); the *Nuremberg Judgement*, where the Tribunal stated: "Superior orders, even to a soldier, cannot be considered in mitigation where crimes have been committed consciously, ruthlessly and without military excuse or justification.....Participation in such crimes as these has never been required of any soldier and [they] cannot now shield [themselves] behind a mythical requirement of soldierly obedience at all costs as excuse for commission of these crimes."

[309] 82 UNTS 279. See also the Charter of the International Military Tribunal for the Far East; the Statute of the International Tribunal for the Prosecution of Persons Responsible foe Serious Violations of International Humanitarian Law Committed in the Territory of the Former Yugoslavia since 1991 in Security Council Res. 827 (1993); Article 6(2) of the Statute of the Tribunal for Rwanda 1994 in Security Council Res. 955 (1994); and Art. 27 of the Statute of the International Criminal Court 1998.

[310] [1998] 4 All E.R. 897.

[311] Ibid, at pp. 939-940; [1998] 3 W.L.R. 1456, 1500.

[312] See [1999] 2 W.L.R. 272.

[313] President Kabbah in his Address to the Nation of 21 February 1999 spoke about "the joint internal and external aggression". In another passage, he said: "[W]e must let the rest of the world understand the real nature of this conflict; that this [is] not just another internal conflict in some small and distant developing country, but an externally-inspired and maintained armed rebellion against the people of Sierra Leone and their democratically-elected government."

[314] See Arts. 48, 54 and 86(5) of the Additional Protocol I of 1977 to the 1949 Geneva Conventions (Nigeria and Sierra Leone ratified the Protocol on 10 October 1988 and 21 October 1986 respectively.

[315] President Kabbah described the pro-government forces as "Ecomog, Civil Defence and *other* loyal forces" in his Address to the Nation of 7 February 1999 (italics added).

[316] See *Sierra Leone Web*, 29 January 1999 for James Jonah's allegations; President Kabbah's Address to the Nations of 1 February 1999.

[317] Statutory Instrument No. 2592 which came into force on November 1, 1997. See also S.I. No. 2593 (for the Dependent Territories), S.I. No. 2599 (for the Channel Islands) and S.I. No. 2600 (for the Isle of Man).

[318] For the text of the letter, see *The Times*, 9 May 1998, p.2

[319] Ibid.

[320] In an article entitled "Why we can help where governments fear to tread" published in *The Sunday Times* News Review, 24 May 1998, p. 5, Tim Spicer of Sandline International wrote: "Unlike the 'dogs of war' to whom people like to compare us, once contracted and deployed PMCs (private military companies) operate as a military hierarchy with associated discipline, observance of the laws and customs of the host nation and finally, adhering to the principles of the Geneva Convention and the international law of armed conflict". He said PMCs have sprung up in France, Israel, USA, South Africa and UK. He acknowledged that PMCs have a "real problem" when they are contracted by insurgents who are "in the right", and said he would welcome international regulation, similar to the one adopted by South Africa, to prevent the less scrupulous companies working for the "bad guys".

[321] The Minister of State, Tony Lloyd, told the House of Commons that private military companies which supply, or offer to supply, mercenaries or related military services "could have – and in some cases clearly would have – an adverse impact on the implementation of the Government's foreign policy objectives" quoted in the Select Committee's Second Report, para. 88.

[322] *House of Commons Debates*, 18 May 1998, col. 616.

[323] On 25 May 1998, the EU Foreign Ministers reached agreement on establishing common standards to govern the sale of arms to non-EU

countries. Under them, exports should not be allowed to states that might use them for external aggression, internal repression or supporting terrorism. France, however, insisted that a verdict on human rights violations that would prevent arms sales had first to be delivered by a "competent body", such as the EU, the Council of Europe or the UN. The French proposal may be difficult to implement as such formal verdicts might be long in coming even amid media reports of such violations. *The Guardian*, 26 May 1998.

[324] *HC Debates*, 6 May 1998, cols.722, 723-4

[325] *The Sunday Times, The Observer, The Sunday Telegraph*, all of 3 May 1998; *The Times, The Guardian, The Telegraph, The Independent*, all of 4 May 1998. A leader in *The Times* of 5 May said: "For Mr Cook [the Foreign Secretary], this is embarrassing whatever the inquiry reveals. Ministers either knew about this operation, or did not, which sounds incompetent; if their Africa desk knew, then arms controls are not working as intended. A deliberate British breach of UN sanctions would be a serious matter. And yet common sense suggests that such sanctions should not penalise the lawful government of a country." For the view of William Hague, Leader of the Opposition, see *The Times*, 11 May 1998, p. 10.

[326] *House of Commons Debates*, 12 May 1998, col. 154

[327] Ibid.

[328] *The Times*, 7 May 1998, p.2; *The Independent*, 7 May 1998, p.4.

[329] Quoted in *The Times*, 11 May 1998

[330] *House of Commons Debates*, 6 May 1998, col. 722. See also ibid. 12 May 1998, cols. 153-4.

[331] Legg, op. cit., p. 105

[332] Ibid., p. 3.

[333] Ibid.

[334] Select Committee Hearings, 10 November 1998. See also Select Committee's Second Report, 3 February 1999, paras. 53-55

[335] *House of Commons Debates*, 27 July 1998, col. 21.

[336] Select Committee, op. cit. para. 89.

[337] Ibid.

[338] *Agence France Presse* (AFP), 31 December 1998.

[339] Ninja Website, 31 December 1998.

[340] *House of Lords Debates*, 14 May 1998, cols. 1175-1176, reproduced in *The Times* leader, 18 May 1998.

[341] See Millius Palayiwa, "Mercenaries, Big Business and Arms Proliferation," a paper delivered at a Conference on Mercenaries and Instability in Africa organised by the Africa Research and Information Bureau, London, 1997.

[342] *The Times*, 9 September 2000, p. 18; *Punch*, 4-17 October 2000, pp. 20-21; *New African*, November 2000, p. 15.

[343] In his letter to *The Times* of 23 February 1999, the Ukrainian Ambassador in London demanded proof of the participation of Ukrainian nationals in the Sierra Leone conflict. He said: "The Government of Ukraine shares the concern repeatedly expressed by the UN Security Council at the escalating armed conflict in Sierra Leone and upholds the strong condemnation of all those who have afforded support, including the supply of arms and mercenaries, to the rebels in that country. As far back as 1990 Ukraine signed and later ratified the international convention against the recruitment, use, financing and training of mercenaries, and, in accordance with the criminal code of Ukraine, all these practices, as well as the participation in armed conflicts without authorisation of relevant government bodies, are considered to be criminal offences punishable by imprisonment of up to 12 years. The Ukrainian authorities have received no evidence of the presence which you report; neither was such a presence confirmed in the latest special report of the Secretary-General on the United Nations observer mission in Sierra Leone. I would be grateful for any information on the participation of Ukrainian nationals in the conflicts in Sierra Leone and Ethiopia."

[344] Ibid. 31 December 1998.

[345] *The Times* (leader), 20 February 1999.

[346] Private military companies include Executive Outcomes, and its holding company, Strategic Resources Corporation; Military Professional Resources Inc. (MPRI) based in Alexandria, Virginia, USA; Keeni Mine Services; British Defence Systems; and Air Scan based in Titusville, Florida.

[347] *New African*, Dangerous Dogs of War, Nov. 1995, p. 11

[348] Those who see nothing wrong with the "privatisation of state security" argue that this deal was good value for money as a UN observer force, earmarked for Sierra Leone in early 1997 but never deployed, was budgeted at $47 million for 720 men for eight months. See Jeffrey Lee, "Peace is worth Sandline's price," in *The Observer*, 17 May 1998. Lord David Steel, former Leader of the British Liberal Party, wrote in a letter to *The Times*, 18 May 1998, that "we should not be so mealy-mouthed about privatised organisations which succeed where others fail but which (surprise, surprise) exist to make money." If the *Sunday Times Magazine* of July 2, 2000 is to be believed, Lord Steel has been on Tony Buckingham's Heritage Oil and Gas Board of Directors and has travelled to Africa for him.

[349] *The Times*, 15 May 1998, p. 16. See Carey W. English, "Sierra Leone: A coup plotter is tripped up," in *U.S. News & World Report*, 9 February

1998, p. 48; *The Times*, 5 May 1998 p. 2; *Africa Confidential*, 6 March 1998; *The Guardian*, 5 May 1998 and the *Toronto Globe and Mail*, 1 August 1997 which was the first to allege the existence of a conspiracy to use mercenaries to overthrow the military junta in Sierra Leone involving Kabbah's government, Rakesh Saxena, head of Vancouver-based Tidewater Management Corporation and Tim Spicer of Sandline International. Sandline International's chairman, Tony Buckingham, was a major shareholder in Diamond Works Ltd., a Vancouver company which held six diamond-mining properties in Sierra Leone.

[350] See Laurie Nathan, "Trust Me I'm a Mercenary: The Lethal Danger of Mercenaries in Africa," a paper delivered at a Seminar on the "Privatisation of Peacekeeping" at the Institute for Security Studies in South Africa, 20 February 1997; and "The Dogs of War: Mercenaries and the Foreign Military Assistance Bill of South Africa.

[351] Article 47(2) of Protocol I of 1977

[352] Select Committee, op. cit. para. 93

[353] Quoted in G.S. Thomas, *Mercenary Troops in Modern Africa* (Westview Press, Boulder, 1981), p. 116

[354] Report on the question of the use of mercenaries as a means of violating human rights and impeding the exercise of the right of peoples to self-determination, submitted by Mr Enrique Bernales Ballesteros, Special Rapporteur, pursuant to resolution 1995/5 and decision 1997/120 on the UN Commission on Human Rights, E/CN.4/1998/31, 27 January 1998, para. 74.

[355] Ibid, para. 88.

[356] HL Debates, op cit. col. 14.

[357] Ibid. col. 124.

[358] Ibid, 24 February 1998.

[359] Sierra Leone Web, 20 February 1998.

[360] Sierra Leone Web, 28 February 1998.

[361] Ibid. 11 November 1998.

[362] Ibid., 20 June 1998.

[363] General Assembly Doc.A/51/306/Add.1, 9 September 1996, Part III, p. 32.

[364] Doc.A/51/306/Add.1, 9 September 1996, pp. 29, 30.

[365] See Public Notice No. 1 of 1998 published in the Supplement to the Sierra Leone Gazette, vol. CXXIX, No. 13, 12 March 1998; Public Emergency Regulations, 1998, Public Notice No. 2 of 1998.

[366] Ibid, 21 May 1997. The largest number of inmates recorded before the *coup* was 579, which was 60% more than its capacity, according to the Chief Superintendent of Prisons. The majority of these, 328, were on remand, outnumbering convicted prisoners.

[367] S/1998/750, 12 August 1998, para. 42.

[368] *House of Lords Debates*, 6 May 1998, Written Answers.

[369] *Sierra Leone Web*, 30 March and 29 April 1998.

[370] Twenty-two persons, mostly Lebanese, were expelled from Sierra Leone on April 2, 1998. Of this figure, ten were naturalised Sierra Leoneans. Sierra Leone law forbids dual citizenship and a naturalised person is required to have renounced his other citizenship before naturalisation. By this deprivation, they were *prima facie* rendered stateless.

[371] Ibid. 29 April 1998.

[372] Ibid.

[373] Ambrose Ganda, *Focus On Sierra Leone*, Vol. 3, No. 1, December 1998, p. 9

[374] S/PRST/1998/5 of 26 February 1998

[375] Italics added.

[376] As observed by *Africa Confidential*, "Politically, Kabbah has to resurrect the old Sierra Leone People's Party government (April 1996-May 1997) without fuelling ethnic hostilities. Kamajor militias are wreaking revenge on what they see as the enemy, particularly Limbas and those from Makeni, Binkolo and other northern areas. Koroma's regime was seen as Temne-Limba based, with much support from the north." Vol. 39, No. 4, 20 February 1998.

[377] *Sierra Leone Web*, 1 August 1997.

[378] Ibid., 29 April 1998.

[379] Ibid. 28 April 1998.

[380] Public Notice No. 4 of 1998.

[381] Section 11 of the Criminal Procedure and Evidence Rules, 1998

[382] Statement by President Kabbah at the Special UN Conference on Sierra Leone on 30 July 1998, p. 6.

[383] See John Hatchard, *Individual Freedoms and State Security: The African Context* (1993).

[384] [1979] 3 All E.R. 129, at p. 136 (italics added).

[385] David Harris, "The Right to a Fair Trial in Criminal Proceedings as a Human Right," (1967) 16 ICLQ 352.

[386] A similar provision is contained in Article 15 of the European Convention on Human Rights of 1950 whose interpretation is dealt with by the European court of Human Rights in *Re Lawless* 1 EHRR 15.

[387] Three were acquitted while one died during the trial, see *Sierra Leone Web*, 12 October 1998.

[388] Ibid. 27 October 1998.

[389] Before this, the biggest trial had involved 22 people in 1974, and this had included Brigadier Bangura, Dr M.S. Forna and Mr Ibrahim Taqi.

[390] *Sierra Leone Telecommunications Co. Ltd v. Barclays Bank plc*, [1998] 2 All E.R. 821, at pp. 830-831.

[391] Ibid. (italics added).

[392] Ibid.

[393] Ibid. (italics added).

[394] S/PRST/1997/29.

[395] S/PRST/1997/36.

[396] S/PRST/1997/42.

[397] S/PRST/1997/52.

[398] [1998] 4 ALL E.R. 897.

[399] Ibid. at p. 942.

[400] Ibid. at p. 936.

[401] S/1998/960, para. 26.

[402] [1999] 2 Cr. App. R 143

[403] Ibid, pp. 156-7.

[404] Ibid, at p.157.

[405] Ibid, at pp 147, 148. See also *R. v. Horseferry Road Magistrates' Court, ex p. Bennett* (1998) 98 Cr. App. R 114, [1994] 1 A.C. 42.

[406] *The Times* and *The Daily Telegraph*, 27 August 1998.

[407] *The Times*, 27 August 1998, p. 2.

[408] *Sierra Leone Web*, 27 August 1998. This statement was repeated in a reply that the British Government sent to the London-based Alliance for Peace and Democracy in Sierra Leone on 12 October 1998.

[409] Th*e Daily Telegraph*, 27 August 1998; *The Times*, 28 August; *The Sunday Times*, 30 August 1998. The European Union issued a statement on 4 September 1998 expressing similar concern.

[410] *Sierra Leone Web*, 27 August 1998.

[411] Ibid.

[412] Ibid. 28 August 1998.

[413] Ibid. 13 October 1998.

[414] Ibid.

[415] See the Southern Rhodesia Act 1965. The Southern Rhodesia Constitution Order 1965 was promulgated in pursuance of this Act, section 6 of which declared for the avoidance of doubt that "any law made, business transacted, step taken or function exercised in contravention of any prohibition or restriction imposed by or under this Order is void and of no effect."

[416] An interested reader may find the following English authority useful: *Adams v. Adams* [1970] 3 All E R 572.

[417] William Shawcross, *Deliver Us from Evil: Warlords, Peacekeepers and a World of Endless Conflict* (Bloomsbury, 2000), pp. 88-89.

[418] H.C. Debates, 2 March 1970, col. 13 (emphasis added)

[419] [1999] 3 WLR 249 (Italics added). See also *Higgs v Minister of National Security* (Privy Council, December 1999); *The Times*, 23 December 1999, p. 30.

[420] (1915) 237 U.S. 309, 347

[421] President Kabbah's Address to the Nation, at the Siaka Stevens Stadium, on 10 March 1998.

[422] A. B. C. Sibthorpe, The History of Sierra Leone (4th Ed. 1970), pp 131-132.

[423] S/PRST/1998/5

[424] S/1997/824, Annexes I and II

[425] S/1996/1034

[426] OAU Res. CM/Dec.373 (LXVII).

[427] *H.C. Debates*, 12 March 1998, col. 845.

[428] *Sierra Leone Web*, 13 November 1998, AFP, 13 November 1998.

[429] Ibid. 28 May 2000.

[430] Larry Siedentop, *Democracy in Europe* (2000), p. 80.

[431] Karen DeYoung, "Generosity Shrinks in an Age of Prosperity," *The Washington Post*, 25 November 1999, pp. A1 and A31.

[432] Boutros Boutros-Ghali, *Unvanquished, A UN-US Saga* (1999), p. 319

[433] Guy Arnold, "Monitoring the new colonialism," *West Africa*, 20-26 November 2000.

[434] Kofi Annan, "Two concepts of sovereignty," *The Economist*, 18 September 1999.

[435] *West Africa*, No. 4221, 10-16 April 2000.

Printed in the United States
955600001B